THE PSYCHOLOGY OF LEARNING APPLIED TO TEACHING

The Great Didactic

Setting forth

The whole Art of Teaching
all Things to all Men

or

A certain Inducement to found such Schools in all
the Parishes, Towns, and Villages of every
Christian Kingdom, that the entire
Youth of both Sexes, none
being excepted, shall

Quickly, Pleasantly, & Thoroughly

Become learned in the Sciences, pure in Morals,
trained to Piety, and in this manner
instructed in all things necessary
for the present and for
the future life,

in which, with respect to everything that is suggested,

ITS FUNDAMENTAL PRINCIPLES are set forth from the essential
nature of the matter,
ITS TRUTH is proved by examples from the several
mechanical arts,
ITS ORDER is clearly set forth in years, months, days, and
hours, and, finally,
AN EASY AND SURE METHOD is shown, by which it can
be pleasantly brought into existence.

B. R. Bugelski

The Psychology of Learning Applied to Teaching

Second Edition

The Bobbs-Merrill Company, Inc.
Indianapolis · New York

FRONTISPIECE: John Amos Comenius, *The Great Didactic,* the Great Didactic of John
Amos Comenius now for the first time Englished, M. W. Keatinge, ed. and trans. (London,
Adam and Charles Black, 1896, title page and verso, pp. 155, 156, 188–90, 204–8. First
published 1628–32.)

to OLIVE PECKHAM LESTER

Introduction

This text is designed to familiarize the classroom teacher with those findings of psychology that pertain to the process of instruction. I recognize that teachers play complex roles in the process of "education," but I think that some useful and meaningful distinctions can be made between education and instruction. Actual instruction may occupy only a fraction of a teacher's daily activity. It is with this fraction that this book is concerned. This fraction, however, has occupied many psychologists during the last hundred years, and a large and complicated body of knowledge about it has been accumulated. This book is an effort to distill those parts of this knowledge that have some practical applications to the classroom. Many changes have occurred in the views of learning psychologists in recent decades. Teachers who learned their "psychology" some years ago may find themselves surprised by some of the newer conclusions from laboratory studies. Teachers in training should find these conclusions challenging.

In the present world situation teachers have come under attack from many fronts. Many teachers feel ignorant, confused, and defenseless in the face of various kinds of cures or innovations in methods and techniques fostered by politicians, businessmen, and parents, all of whom sometimes act as if education were too important to be left to educators. These teachers are not confident about their reactions to television teaching, teaching machines, teachers' "aides," and other dynamically promoted panaceas. My hope is that a review of the pertinent fundamentals of learning, as presented here, will help all such teachers develop defenses against unwarranted pressures and recognize worth where worth exists.

This book is relatively short for two reasons. First, teachers generally are more concerned, and justly so, with practical information and are not greatly occupied with the theoretical speculations of psychologists. Therefore, I have presented only a minimum amount of theoretical material to make more meaningful the practical suggestions that are developed. Second, at the present time there is little to offer by way of practical advice to harassed teachers. Some psychologists would even argue that really there is nothing to say, and these will question the propriety of such a text as this. Obviously, I think that at least some words of advice can be offered. Even if it were true that nothing of value can be stated about teaching, it would be worthwhile for teachers to learn that psychologists who have studied learning intensively do not really know much about the process. The teacher who feels inferior about his work can, at least, find that he has considerable company among learning psychologists. It may be comforting to know that the "experts" are not much wiser than he is.

In developing this text I tried to avoid vague generalities and to offer as specific advice as possible. I make no pretense of having actually included all the useful hints and suggestions that might make a teacher's work better and more effective. Undoubtedly, there are words of wisdom that never have occurred to me and might never occur to me. In every instance I tried to avoid rules of thumb or unsupported opinion. If readers can offer supplements, I will be grateful. Many of the suggestions that are developed are negatively toned. They tell the teacher what not to do. I consider such negative suggestions to be equally as valuable as the more positive sounding ones. Many potential students can be nipped in the bud by incorrect handling. As the future of learning psychology unfolds, we can look forward to more effective application of research findings. At present this work can only be considered a start.

In preparing this volume, I have had the benefit of considerable "feedback," of occasional "reinforcement" as well as "nonreinforcement" from professional working teachers. These teachers, coming to class from a trying day in their own classrooms, were in no mood for nonsense and vague generalizations. They wanted practical advice, and I tried to supply it. These teachers were the working critics of this text.

A word of appreciation goes to my wife for her confidence in my ability to do something about helping teachers and, indirectly, students. The academic adventures of our two daughters provided an unending series of dinner-table challenges all beginning with: Why can't something be done about . . . ? This book is an attempt to do something about. . . .

Preface

The favorable reception of the first edition of this text has encouraged me to prepare this revised and expanded version. Toward this end I have added some sections and expanded others without dropping much from the first edition. The original chapters have been updated to take account of some new contributions from research. The new sections include more material on the topic of attention and on learning through imitation, areas that received inadequate treatment in the original version of this text, and a summarizing chapter, which includes a theory of instruction. This theory, as well as the rest of the text, is tested in a final chapter on the psychology of reading. This chapter is included as an example of the application of the propositions detailed in the text. It is not suggested that the problem of teaching reading is solved in this chapter; rather, the ways are outlined in which a teacher might handle the problems that arise in teaching any subject. Reading was chosen because of the broad and intrinsic interest in the problem.

I am grateful to the many users of the first edition who took the trouble to write to me about their problems. I can only hope the present volume arouses equal interest.

In preparing this revision I had the dedicated assistance of Mrs. Bettye Berman, to whom I am more than grateful for her careful preparation of the manuscript.

B. R. B.

Buffalo, N. Y.
January 2, 1971

Contents

Figures

Chapter One

The
Psychology
of
Learning
and
Educational
Practice

In the past decade the technological advances in space research, the continued hot and cold wars, the emerging nations, the population explosion, the ecological catastrophes, the struggle for civil and sexual rights, the rising crime rate, and the growing crisis in drug abuse have converged upon the consciousness of the world's peoples in the form of increased demands upon our schools for better educated leaders and trained personnel or for answers to the world's problems. Automation has progressed to the point where formerly adequate levels of training are no longer of any social or economic value. Students are becoming disenchanted with the prospects that might face them upon completion of normal educational programs. Schools themselves are subjects of attack, both physical on the part of disgruntled students who see no relevance to their needs and verbal on the part of the citizens who blame the schools for failing to solve the problems of our complex society.

In recent years a torrent of abuse has been hurled at our educational system by champions of opposing armies of our citizenry. On the one hand our schools are described as inadequate, staffed by incompetently trained teachers,[1] and on the other hand they are blamed for failing to solve social and personal problems. The products of our schools are seen by some as illiterate, physically unfit, morally corrupt, and maladjusted. Never before has education come under such severe criticism and abuse. Along with the attacks come proposals for remedies: centralized schools, integrated classes, teacher's aides, team teaching, teaching by television, and in the modern spirit of automation—teaching by machine. In most instances the proposed remedies are perceived as panaceas promising solution to all manner of problems, but unfortunately, in most cases the proposals have not been tested or analyzed or otherwise evaluated in terms of the problems they

[1] An example of such an attack of teacher-training is *The Miseducation of American Teachers* by James D. Koerner (1963). Complete references will be found in the bibliography that begins on page 329.

3

are designed to solve. Except in the case of teaching machines, little trouble has been taken to consider the functions and operations of a classroom teacher, and virtually no attention has been paid to the nature of learning or the psychology of teaching.

The possibility of teaching by machine was introduced and enthusiastically fostered by some psychologists who had become convinced that not only was the educational system in need of help from psychologists but also that psychologists were indeed able to provide at least some help for the solution of educational problems on the basis of what they had learned in their laboratories about the learning process.

Foremost among the psychologists who felt that the time had come to apply laboratory findings to education was B. F. Skinner, Professor of Psychology at Harvard University. Professor Skinner had long concerned himself with problems of behavior control, and he perceived education as only one aspect of such control. His extensive experience in effectively controlling the behavior of rats and pigeons culminated in a bold leap to proposals for the control of human behavior that he described in a provocative Utopian novel, *Walden II*. In this novel Skinner (1948a) shows how an entire society could be reared (properly educated) to become productive, adjusted, and happy. The novel was not too well received by the general public at the time of its publication; perhaps it challenged too many vested interests and comfortable ideas, or, perhaps, it was too large a program, too general. The critics castigated Skinner for trying to engineer society, for treating people as if they were automatons. Whatever the reason, Skinner turned his attention to a more detailed and specific program of developing procedures and techniques for more effective teaching. Out of his work came the teaching machine and the concepts of programmed learning. On several later occasions this book will return to Skinner's work and thought, but for the present, we can leave him with the observation that he would probably endorse with enthusiasm the oft-quoted but unfulfilled boast of John B. Watson (1930), the founder of Behaviorism:

> Give me a dozen healthy infants, well-formed, and my own special world to bring them up in and I'll guarantee to take anyone at random and train him to become any type of specialist I might select—doctor, lawyer, artist, merchant-chief and, yes, even beggarman and thief, regardless of his talents, penchants, tendencies, abilities, vocations, and race of his ancestors.

The enthusiastic offer of Watson might be tempered and reduced in scope by a somewhat different proposal. American psychologists, especially those of a Skinnerian persuasion, might put the matter thus: anyone can learn anything if the proper conditions are met. It might be that some require more time than others (i.e., more care, more experience, more background), but sooner or later anyone can be brought to the same level of achievement. The hypothetical situation is described in Figure 1 for three individuals at some learning task.

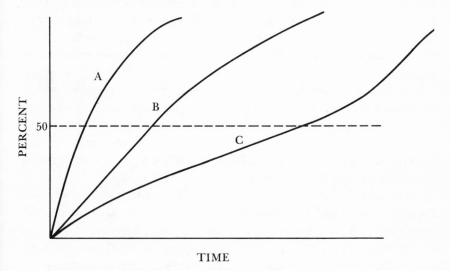

TIME

FIGURE 1. *Learning Curves for Three Hypothetical Learners*

A (fast), *B* (moderate), and *C* (slow) all reach the same level at different times. The Continuity Hypothesis (see p. 73) assumes all normal individuals can learn, given enough training time. While the curves all start at zero, the learning psychologist is inclined to assume that the zero point really varies for every learning task with individual backgrounds. Some backgrounds favor rapid learning and some hinder. A "true" zero might be at the level shown by the dash line. *A* begins with the task half-learned.

Individual A may come to the task with some background, have all the necessary sensory and motor skills and motivation. He learns quickly. Individual B might be less well favored in some aspect (s) , but he also learns. He takes longer. C appears hopeless for a long time (maybe years), but eventually he, too, can attain mastery if the teacher does not surrender first. C might need special aids. Watson proposed making piano keys narrower for students with a small finger span. In more practical terms, if the subject is calculus and C has had problems with arithmetic, he needs to master that basic skill first, and calculus will suffer accordingly.

Although some teachers may be less than taken with this proposal, it does contain some very important educational considerations. First, it means that there are no permanently failing students, and teachers should stop thinking in terms of failure. The student who does not "pass" a certain exam should be regarded as not having passed *yet*. A lady in England passed her driver's test on the 39th attempt after some 39 registrations at a driver school. Second, there should be no onus attached to repeating courses. Students should be given the privilege of repeating as often as necessary to attain a standard. Failing to meet a desirable standard dooms them to successive failures later on when their backgrounds prove inadequate.

The practical issues involved do present problems. There probably is not enough time for every student to learn everything to 100 percent efficiency. Here some freedom of choice in curriculum might help. At the college level, with a free selection of courses, anyone who can get in can graduate and even earn honors. With a fixed curriculum in grammar schools, extra time must be found for those who need it.

Some psychologists who have been working in education, industry, and the armed forces have also thought that their work was applicable to the solution of educational and behavioral problems. These men think of themselves as "applied experimental psychologists"[2] and consider their work as concerned with "human factors." In their attempts to apply psychological findings to industrial and military problems, they have enjoyed many successes during and since World War II. And, while much of their work has involved such matters as equipment design, effectiveness of displays, and control devices, man–machine systems, and human capacities and limitations, they have been most effective in the area of training.

The work of Fred Keller (1953) and of Omar K. Moore[3] provides two appropriate illustrations of the application of psychology to learning problems. Keller is closely allied with Skinner in his approach to psychology. Moore is a sociologist who, in the account below, will be seen to work like a psychologist.

During World War II, when the army needed well-trained telegraphers, Keller undertook to improve the army method of teaching telegraphy. The problem of teaching Morse Code (at least 36 symbols) to beginners seemed formidable enough, but that humans can learn this had been amply demonstrated. Keller wanted to make the training more efficient, and he applied what he knew about learning to the task, with the most satisfactory results. During the course of his work he analyzed the task, finding out where troubles arose—where errors of omission and of com-

2 See A. Chapanis, W. R. Garner, and C. T. Morgan (1949).
3 See M. Pinas (1963).

mission were most likely to occur. For these items he devised special, additional practice. In teaching code-receiving, he introduced the practice of immediate knowledge of results, a major departure from the traditional method. A learner would hear a series of dots and/or dashes representing one symbol. Immediately he would write down his translation. In three seconds the instructor would announce the correct symbol. The student now could and would correct his error, if any. The final answer to any signal would always be correct. By this simple expedient Keller was able to improve the progress strikingly. For sending code, Keller would similarly provide knowledge of results by immediate comparison of the pattern of key pressures with those of an expert (the expert providing this knowledge of results).[4] Such immediate knowledge of results is considered to be the equivalent of an immediate reward. Immediate rewards are believed by some theorists to be essential to learning, as we shall see later. Keller added some other controls and changes in the learning situation with generally satisfactory results. The net effect of the introduction of "psychology" was to cut training time by about 25 percent and the failure rate by two thirds. The war ended before Keller was able to add further improvements based on an error analysis. Had he devoted himself to the problem for a longer time, there appears to be no reason to doubt further improvements.

A rather more remarkable instance of what can be done by way of teaching if one really gets busy with some problem is the result of the efforts of Omar K. Moore, who has been able to teach three-year-old children to read, spell, and type by the touch method. Moore starts out with a special typewriter—the keys are painted different colors. The child's fingernails are painted with similar colors, each nail being painted to match the color of the keys that are to be struck by that finger. Starting off with only a few keys, the child is allowed to press a specific key, say, *d*, when the teacher says *d*. Other letters, for example, *o* and *g*, are then introduced and the child instructed to tap the three keys in sequence. Next the letters are shown on cards and vocalized at the same time until the child is able to type *d-o-g* while merely looking at a cue card. Then the teacher can pronounce the word while the child types it out, and eventually the child can type the word itself from the sound of the word.[5] He has learned to type,

[4] Modern "language laboratories" follow this same principle. The student tries to mimic the native speaker who repeatedly pronounces words and phrases on a tape recording. The student pronounces what he hears, and a moment later he hears the instructor's "correct" pronunciation.

[5] In a later development the whole process has been automated and involves a rather elaborate apparatus with tape recorders, electric typewriters, and other equipment so that no human teacher is present. Note that, as in the case of Keller, this training also calls for immediate "feedback" or knowledge of results.

spell, and read at the same time. New words can be introduced as the first ones are mastered and Moore claims effective results in such operations.

Assuming these claims are based on adequate evidence, educators have here an important lesson that might have quite general application: some things are difficult to learn because we do not know how to teach them. With improvements in technique we can expect to increase the efficiency of learning more and more. An important implication of Moore's investigation is that if three-year-olds can learn to read with his methods, then our current classroom methods that work with five- or six-year-olds must be useful *only at that age level;* they are not good enough below that level. Instead of recognizing this, however, we resort to such concepts as "readiness" and blame the child's lack of progress on his lack of readiness, instead of lack of an efficient method. It may be a lack of readiness on the part of the teacher, and not of the learner. As a logical extension of Moore's findings, we should be able to teach two-year-olds to read if we could devise the right methods.[6] We leave open the question of why two- or three-year-olds should be taught to read. There might be better ways for such tots to spend their time. It becomes a question of values.

HUMAN ENGINEERING

These brief accounts of what two psychologists have been able to accomplish suggest that education may need a new orientation, an orientation that can best be described under the heading of "human engineering." This approach, sometimes labeled "engineering psychology," is one of which every teacher should be thoroughly cognizant even though he or she may not wish to or be able to be guided by it.

Human engineering had its origins in the work of Franklyn W. Taylor,[7] an "efficiency expert," who in the late nineteenth century began to suggest improvements in industrial practices. In one of his most effective efforts, Taylor succeeded in improving the job of loading pig iron onto

6 Actually, mothers have taught two-year-olds to "read" by the procedure of repeatedly showing them cards with letters, then words, then short sentences printed in bold sizes. After a few showings accompanied by the mother's announcement of *A* or *boy, nose,* or whatever is printed on the card, the mother asks: "What is this?" In this way a child can eventually build up a sizeable recognition vocabulary. The developers of a method and materials for such training—G. Doman, G. L. Stevens, and R. C. Orem (1963)—claim, in fact, that the *younger* the child, the easier it is for him to learn to read. They urge that all preschool children be taught to read on the grounds that not only can they do so, but also they want to read at this age and will not be so eager when they attain school age. By then, apparently, they are too old to be taught effectively!

7 The story of Taylor's work is nicely described in M. S. Viteles *Industrial Psychology* (1932).

flatcars by almost 400 percent. To achieve this phenomenal success, he selected specific workers who appeared strong enough for the work program he had in mind. Later it turned out that only one man in eight could do the work to his specifications.

Taylor's methods differed in one important respect from those of modern human engineers. His approach involved the selection of men to *fit the job*. This procedure, of course, resulted in the immediate unemployment of all the "unfit." Taylor argued that such misfits were really doing themselves a disservice by working at jobs for which they were unsuited; they should look for more fitting employment. The procedure of selecting specially qualified personnel for specific jobs might work (if we ignore social implications) when there are enough skilled people seeking employment. When the demand for workers is greater than the supply (as in wartime) or when there are not enough workers with suitable skills (as in the current teacher shortage), then the modern human engineer argues that the job must be modified and *fitted to the man*.

The redesign of a job can sometimes be so successful that almost anyone can be trained to do it. Occasionally we hear suggestions that chimpanzees could be trained to do some of the work on modern mass-production lines. Frequently enough the effort to redesign a job results in its complete elimination or automation. The modern teaching machine, for example, has been viewed with alarm by some educators who see teacher status dropping to that of clerks and machine tenders. Such fears are far from justified, as will be seen later, but they are common enough.

"The Better Way"

Aside from personnel selections, however, the other principles that Taylor described are currently being followed in practical applications of psychology to work analysis. These principles can be summed up in the slogan: "There is a better way." Taylor assumed that any job can be done better than it is being done, an assumption that seems justified when we think of the improvements in almost every kind of device employed by man since its first appearance. We have come to expect annual improvements in automobiles, refrigerators, television sets, and all manner of implements. Even the modern beer can has been "improved"; it no longer requires a can opener. On the human abilities side, the annual falling of athletic records points up our steady improvement in athletic contests. The 17-foot pole vault and the 4-minute mile are already historical events, and no one now doubts the eventual achievement of the 9-second 100-yard

dash. The records fall because of improvements in equipment and training methods.

The assumption of "the better way" requires that one face any current
human operation with the attitude that, while it may be reasonably satisfactory now, sooner or later the task will change, there will be improvements, and the improvements might as well be attempted deliberately (as
they are in industry through Research and Development departments)
than left to chance.

Professor Skinner (1956), in a biographical sketch, illustrates the attitude involved in "the better way" in his description of how he came to
devise the famous Skinner box, or as he modestly describes it, the "lever-
press box." In such a box a small animal is provided the opportunity to
obtain food as a result of its own activities. In the lever-press situation, a
small bar is inserted into the box. If a rat moves this bar downward a
fraction of an inch, a piece of food will drop into a food cup located under
the bar.

When Skinner first started working with rats, he built a small runway
along which a rat ran from start to goal where it was rewarded with food.
Skinner found that the process of walking down the runway to the goal to
pick up the rat for another trial was a tedious chore. He then introduced
a turn in the runway so that the rat would go around and come back to a
point near the start. This saved Skinner the walking effort and the time
between trials. But he still had to feed the rats and saw no reason for doing this by personal exertion. He therefore constructed a mechanical device that discharged a food morsel automatically when the rat arrived at
the goal. The running time in the alley was serving no purpose as far as
Skinner was concerned and he eliminated this by, in effect, placing the rat
in the goal situation and providing the means for the rat to perform the
necessary response to activate the mechanical feeder, and the Skinner box
was born. Skinner attributes the whole process of invention to sheer laziness; others recognize, of course, that it was really insistence on "the better
way."

"The Better Way" and Educational Practices

Before it can act on the basic assumption of "the better way," human engineering as currently developed seeks the answers to questions pertaining
to four aspects of the work to be improved: Goals, Criteria, Job Analysis,
and Determination of Variables. It is this human-engineering approach, or
methodology, that can be applied to education.

1. Goals. What are the desired objectives? How well do current procedures attain these? In terms of an academic situation involving arithmetic, for example, the question could be: How much arithmetic do you
want this student (or this class) to know and how much is being learned
by present methods of instruction? All the goals must be spelled out. It is
not enough to indicate that the students must learn arithmetic. If you
also desire that they learn good manners, geography, and cooking, you
must state such requirements. It may turn out that contradictory goals
are involved, and such contradictions must be appreciated and compro-
mises determined. It is also important for you to spell out what is *not*
wanted or what can be dispensed with. Otherwise, a solution to one problem may merely create others.

In the United States the problem of educational goals is a very complex
one. There is little agreement on even what should be taught, far less on
how well it should be learned. Almost anything can be found in one curriculum or another—as Martin Mayer (1961) has pointed out. Perhaps
this is as it should be in a free, mobile society. About all that is agreed to
is that we want our educational system to produce good citizens—but we
do not define even these. What we expect from our schools is a matter of
social and moral values. The psychologist cannot help much in decisions
concerning values. He can only help when the goals are stated and when
they are stated precisely, hopefully with objective standards.

2. Criteria. As just indicated, goals must be specified with precision
in the same way that a buyer specifies the characteristics he wants in a
refrigerator, automobile tire, or television set. When the U. S. government buys an airplane from a manufacturer, it details its specifications
down to the smallest part, even to the number of threads on a screw. In
education we might not care to be so specific, but it is not enough for us
to say, for example, that we want someone to be a "good speller." *Good*
must be defined. One possible working definition of *good* might be "95
percent perfect," and by a "good speller" we would mean: The student
who is able to spell correctly 95 (or some other specified) percent of all
the words in *this* dictionary. The specification of the goal is not enough.
There must also be agreement on how the goal is to be measured, the
kinds of tests to be used or the standards to be met at various stages during
and after the training. There must be some allowance for failure and an
acceptable failure rate must be defined. In industry this is referred to as
"tolerance."

The specifications or criteria should include an evaluation of present

successes and the costs involved in attaining the desired level of difference. A small improvement in education might call for great costs in personnel, extensions of time in school, various kinds of devices and aides as
well as aids.

3. Job Analysis. What is the current method of operation? How can
the work involved be described? Just exactly what is being done now at
each step in the activity? When the answers to the questions are found,
such a job analysis might reveal that some step (s) are quite unnecessary.
In industry, it might be found that a highly paid worker is doing parts
of a job that could be done by a lower paid worker. In our earlier arithmetic example, students may be required to perform twenty exercises
where ten might be adequate or forty might be required to attain certain
objectives. In another classroom, the teacher might be found spending
time on activities that could be done better in homework or self-study
assignments. The practices of the most effective teachers and the least
effective might be scrutinized to isolate the significant as well as the useless
activities. In general, job analysis calls for a highly specific determination
of the essential steps in any task with the purpose of eliminating anything
that is wasteful or harmful to the final goal.

4. Determination of Variables. What are the variables (the environmental or stimulus factors) that determine or regulate the behavior
(movements and/or responses) of the subjects involved? In other words,
what are the relationships between the stimuli and the responses? Are
these relationships describable as "laws"? If so, are these laws being violated by any unnecessary or undesirable extraneous factors? What tools
and methods are being used, and are these the most effective tools and
methods for attaining the goals? Are the steps being followed arranged
in the most effective sequence? In terms of some human skill, writing, for
example, is this skill most effectively taught by supplying ballpoint pens,
typewriters, steel nib pens, pencils, crayons, or what? Is the skill being
taught at the appropriate point in the curriculum? Is reading, to take another example, being taught in relationship to an appreciation of the
variables involved in reading or is some "method" being followed either
in terms of blind tradition or rebellion? The question of *how* reading
should be taught is, of course, not to be answered by opinion—violent, expert, or other. It is an experimental question as Roger Brown (1958) so
nicely stated, a question involving an appreciation of the stimulus and

response variables and the laws relating these. Similar questions arise in connection with teaching a foreign language.[8]

Thus far we have spoken of variables as if only environmental and task factors were important. We have ignored any organismic or "personality" variables, such as intelligence, talent, aspirations or motivation level, and the thousands of ways in which individuals differ. Human engineers do tend to ignore such differences. Their general aim is to arrange jobs or tasks so that virtually anyone can perform successfully. We will have occasion from time to time to question such interchangeability of people either as students or teachers. Such personality variables are indeed important. The human engineer, however, might argue that they are secondary problems, that they should be taken into account after the job itself has been arranged as nearly as possible into the most efficient operation for the greatest number. The approach is, of course, one-sided. The human engineer can counter with the suggestion that "the better way" is found by taking one thing at a time.

Human Engineering and Education

What was described above as human engineering and the search for "the better way" is not a panacea for industry, the armed forces, or for education, although each of these enterprises can and has benefited from it. Essentially, human engineering is an approach, a way of thinking about problems. Thinking about educational problems in terms of goals, criteria, job analysis, and variables does not automatically provide answers; it only raises, and, perhaps, illuminates these problems. Once the problems are raised a methodology is provided by which answers might be obtained.

In the area of education it is rather obvious that there are no hard and fast, objective and factual, determinations of the goals of education. Criteria are certainly vague; no job analysis has ever been performed on the operation of teaching—we do not know the difference between a good teacher and a poor one—and the variables in education have never been spelled out with precision. Such a statement need not imply dismay or surrender. It must be recognized that education is the biggest business in the world and probably the most complex; it involves more people than

---

8 The reader might test himself by reviewing the situation in foreign-language teaching in terms of the questions raised by the human engineer's goals, criteria, job analysis, and determination of variables. What position can we adopt with justification in connection with the controversy between the advocates of the aural-oral method and the traditional grammarians?

any other single kind of activity, and it would be more than surprising if it had somehow stumbled upon the best ways of conducting its activities. The situation in manufacturing and merchandising is only relatively easier, but even in these areas human engineers have no magic answers; they have only their approach. The approach involves recognizing problems and applying solutions either from available knowledge acquired in the past or from the necessary information acquired by research and experimentation.

When human engineers approach the problems of education, the amount of useful information readily available for application appears rather inadequate for the task. Much of the information is not in suitable form; frequently it is sketchy in amount and obscured by theoretical verbiage and equivocation. In subsequent sections of this chapter I will try to explain why this is so. For the present you must also recognize that in the field of education the amount of research required appears staggering if not overwhelming. Hardly a single educational practice has an adequate foundation in scientific observations. In his small volume describing the Woods Hole conference on education, Jerome Brunner (1960) mentions the need for research on almost every page, and more than once on several pages. The fact that educational practices lack, or might benefit from, scientific analysis is no condemnation of these practices. Educational practices arose and were modified in response to social needs, frequently as the consequences of social crises and emergencies, often against the better judgment of educators, and most commonly without the time and financial support for definitive research. Arbitrary judgments had to be made about class sizes, lengths of school terms, numbers of class meetings, passing grades, number of failures permitted, and so on. Practical solutions had to be attempted for problems that are not easily solved, especially at local levels, without risks to the educational development of the students involved. While everyone concerned, including parents, would probably endorse the principle that every educational practice should have a firm scientific foundation, few will be found who will endorse experimentation on their own children. School administrators can hardly be blamed for being reluctant to indulge researchers in experimental programs that might involve some risk to the educational advancement of their charges. To try a new method of teaching any subject might create more problems than the hoped-for potential benefits. It is no wonder that most research that has been attempted in education is fragmentary, safe, and undefinitive.

In the light of all these considerations, we approach the business of improving teaching through the application of findings from the psychology of learning not without some misgivings but with confidence that where so much needs to be done something can be done with the appropriate methodology. I need not remind the reader continually that our concern will be with goals, criteria, job analysis, and variables; such concerns should be apparent as we begin our search for "the better way."

LEARNING PSYCHOLOGISTS AND EDUCATION

The fact that many educational practices lack a scientific foundation is not solely the fault of educators. The very nature of their business, learning or teaching, is not really well understood even by those who have attempted to study it under refined laboratory conditions. The psychology of learning is marked by great gaps and theoretical controversies. The lack of scientific information about learning has resulted in a serious division of opinion about just how ready psychologists are to offer help to educators. The human engineers adopt, in general, a rather safe position. They are ready to admit ignorance and request permission to do the necessary research. This permission, as was just said, is not going to be easily obtained—despite the confidence of the human engineers that success will crown their efforts, that there is "a better way" if their methods are followed. Some psychologists, especially those associated with Skinner, feel that they already know enough useful principles to go to work almost immediately revising educational systems. Other psychologists, perhaps a great majority, have varying degrees of misgivings. The educational enterprise is a vast and complex one, involving as it does the training of people from kindergarten through graduate and professional schools in a wide variety of skills and knowledge. To apply the psychology of learning in its present state to such a tremendous field of activity should give even the boldest psychologist some pause. It is noteworthy, for example, that Professor Ernest R. Hilgard (1956) states, in his very valuable *Theories of Learning,* "There are no laws of learning that can be taught with confidence." By this generalization, Hilgard does not mean to imply that learning psychologists have nothing to contribute to education. On the contrary, he himself offers a number of suggestions that derive from learning theories that he believes are useful in education. What Hilgard means by his comment is that there is as yet no completely worked-out system of learning theory that can be readily applied. This view is shared by many other learning psychologists who as parents and citizens would like nothing better than to be able to offer a neat package of learning principles to the world of education if such a package were available. Arthur W. Melton (1959), who has long been concerned with training problems in the U.S. Air Force, echoes the Hilgard position in his comment that "While there have been impressive advances in psychology, and especially in our understanding of the learning process in the last 20 years, the fact remains that there is no unified science of learning—and this makes application difficult."

William Estes (1960) in his review of learning for the *Educational Encyclopedia* offered rather small comfort to educators. He found modern learning theory to be, as yet, in far too unsettled a state for application: ". . . no convergence is imminent between the educator's and the laboratory scientist's approaches to learning."

Perhaps the most disheartening comment about the feasibility of applying learning psychology to education was uttered by Donald Snygg (1954) at the Kentucky Symposium. Snygg stated: "The sad truth is that, after 50 years of careful and honest and occasionally brilliant research on the nature of learning, the only people who can be proved to have received any practical benefits from learning theory are the learning theorists themselves." He went on to describe the complexities of learning theory that makes it useless to educators and compared learning theorists to "the shipwrecked Scotsmen who made a good living by taking in one another's washing."

At the same symposium Kenneth Spence (1954), for the past three decades a leading figure in the psychology of learning, raised the question of potential applications of learning principles in real-life situations and answered it saying: "No definitive answer, of course, can be given at the present time, for as yet none of them [i.e., learning theories] is sufficiently abstract or complete to account even for all the laboratory findings." Spence did foresee eventual application, as with other sciences, but he was not ready to predict a date for transference of laboratory findings to the classroom.

From these comments it should be clear that not all learning psychologists are confident of any easy solution of classroom teaching problems. In fact, even to suggest such in the face of authoritative statements is little short of foolhardy. The teacher might well be wary of anyone who suggests some change on the basis of his knowledge of learning psychology. The reader should be reminded, however, that these are all general statements in response to the general question: Can learning theory be applied to education? It is true, as stated earlier, that there is no single, general, complete, ready-made system that can be taken over as a whole by educators? The field of learning is and has been riddled with controversy for decades. But, in spite of many basic theoretical disagreements, there is much common agreement on specific empirical findings and on some isolated principles. Some of the prominent figures in learning theory were, as Snygg said, brilliant investigators; they also wrote voluminously. In the course of their careers they discovered, one after another, practical operations or principles. Many of these are, unfortunately, more useful in the laboratory than in the classroom; a few do appear to have merit and considerable potential.

In this textbook we shall ignore the controversies and the broad systematic positions and concentrate on the occasional morsel of educational wisdom that appears in the writings of this or that theorist. Some of this wisdom will be basically negative (you will have to learn what you should not do as teachers), and some will have positive virtues in limited circumstances. In the succeeding chapters we will examine the educationally useful contributions of learning psychology, but first it is necessary to learn something about the everyday research operations of the learning psychologist in his laboratory and contrast these with the work in the classroom. Only by such a comparison can one judge effectively the significance of a given proposition and the limitations that must be observed. After the characteristic features of laboratory work have been noted, the remainder of this chapter will describe a learning psychologist at work in a real life situation. This sample should give further guidance for evaluating the contributions of theorists.

Learning in the Laboratory

Since 1880 psychologists have been experimenting with learning. The work began with the now classical experiments of the German psychologist Hermann Ebbinghaus, who tried to determine how to improve retention or "memory," one of the "higher mental processes," which most psychologists at that time did not feel quite competent to study. Ebbinghaus[9] began with the assumptions that retention was a function of effective learning (basically interpreted as a matter of repetition), and that by discovering the factors that governed retention and forgetting he would also find the principles underlying more effective methods of learning and the factors that lead to forgetting.

While Ebbinghaus was a practically oriented psychologist and was in-

[9] See the English translation of his 1885 work, *Memory* (1913).

terested in improving classroom study operations (which at that time
relied heavily on drill and rote memorization), his findings took him
rather far afield from the classroom. In order to compare the relative
effectiveness of different methods of learning Ebbinghaus found himself
in need of suitable materials for study. He recognized that such materials
had to be uniform in difficulty or the comparisons would be invalid. He
also recognized that some materials might have more inherent interest or
be more familiar than others. His search for comparable materials led him
to reject selections of poetry or any meaningful material and, of necessity,
to the invention of meaningless—that is, *nonsense*—material. To prepare
such material, Ebbinghaus hit upon the *nonsense syllable* as a working
unit. He created such nonsense syllables by following a pattern of con-
sonant-vowel-consonant or C-V-C. Thus, *j-i-k* would be a suitable bit of
nonsense to learn. Similarly, *m-e-l, v-o-f, k-e-z,* would be generally acceptable nonsense syllables. Any combination that happened to sound like an
ordinary word, e.g., *s-a-w,* would be rejected. Ebbinghaus now had a stock
of materials to use. Because one syllable could be learned quickly, simply
by looking at it, he decided that a learning problem could be developed by
combining eight, ten, twelve, or more syllables into a list. Such a list could
then be read over and over until the whole list was learned.

Ebbinghaus served as his own subject and memorized many such lists
of nonsense syllables following different arrangements and methods with
different lists. Any difference in efficiency of learning or retention he
would attribute to the differences in arrangements or methods of study.

The nonsense-syllable approach devised by Ebbinghaus became a rather
standard method for studying learning in the United States, and literally
thousands of experiments have been performed with nonsense syllables as
the learning material.

Although Ebbinghaus earned undying fame with his invention of nonsense syllables, he did not contribute substantially to the solution of
educational problems. His results were, of course, highly personal (since
he was his own subject) and applied only to lists of nonsense syllables
learned by one adult. There is, of course, some question as to whether his
results can be applied to the learning of meaningful materials by anyone.
The fact that Ebbinghaus used *lists* of material further restricts his findings to such lists. While it is true that schoolchildren sometimes have to
memorize lists of meaningless material (the alphabet, for example), they
do not follow the methods and procedures practiced by Ebbinghaus. In
classrooms, the alphabet is commonly learned to the tune of a simple
melody. Again, children are in part familiar with the alphabet long before

they begin to learn to recite it in sequence. For them it is not essentially novel material.

Reluctance of Learning Psychologists to Apply Findings

Although we must recognize Ebbinghaus as the father of learning psychology, we may question the value of his contributions to education. Succeeding generations of psychologists acted as if they had burned their fingers by premature efforts at application. They have stayed rather distantly aloof from practical problems of education, preferring to work on the theoretical level that they hope will yield far-reaching principles more quickly than will piecemeal attacks on specific empirical questions. Their ultimate goal is a scientific theory of learning by means of which practical problems can be solved quickly and efficiently. When a psychologist, such as John Dewey, has become interested in education practices, his attitude or approach has been based on philosophical or theoretical positions that are not actually supported by laboratory research.

The reluctance of psychologists to think in terms of practical applications of learning theory to teaching stems from two basic reasons. One has just been mentioned and will be explored more fully a little later, namely,

PEANUTS ●   *By Charles M. Schulz*

Reprinted by permission of United Feature Syndicate. Copyright © 1960

FIGURE 2. *The Motive of the Theoretical Psychologist*

that their interests have tended to follow the "pure" science or theoretical path. The second reason is that psychologists are not at all sure that teachers need any special training or even that the practice of teaching can be taught. This latter reason may appear strange and unconvincing, yet it is not unexpected if we consider the common experience of psychologists. Psychologists, for the most part, have taught at the college level where, traditionally, there have been no official standards for the ability to teach —not that standards at other levels are especially meaningful. The Ph.D. degree was considered a teaching license, and even working toward the Ph.D. degree was adequate justification for placing a graduate student in front of college students in the role of instructor. Thus it was possible for any graduate student, with no real standards to meet, to be a "successful" teacher; he was the only one who determined his own success. He usually developed his own techniques, probably on models of his own teachers. Whether he was popular (because of humor, lightheartedness, good looks, or easy marking) or unpopular (because "he had rigorous standards") was about all that anyone ever determined about him. Somehow some students learn something, regardless of who is teaching (or even if no one is).

This unsystematic and unstandardized operation at the college level may provide some explanation for the insecurity felt by most psychologists, at least, at the prospects of saying very much that is intelligent about teaching. Most learning psychologists are teachers as well as researchers. When they see young graduate students performing apparently adequate jobs as teachers without any formal training they cannot be blamed for having dim views about the benefits of such training. When they discover, as did T. S. Parsons, W. A. Ketcham, and L. R. Beach (1958), that students who are not assigned to any class at all do as well as students taught in formal classes, then they can very well begin to doubt the value of their own appearance before classes. The finding just mentioned is not an isolated one. Similar studies at Antioch College (R. Churchill and S. Baskin, 1958) and at Oberlin (C. McCollough and E. L. Van Atta, 1958) found no significant differences in learning between students working independently (no classes) and those who attended classes of various types. Clarence Leuba (1963) of Antioch College is so impressed by such findings as well as investigations of his own, that he now believes that "The instructor's main function . . . no longer is to impart his knowledge and his enthusiasms in lectures to students . . . rather, his function might be first, to suggest in a syllabus the resources—books, journals, films, recordings, projects, etc.—helpful for an understanding of the objectives, methods, and subject matter of an area."

It should be noted that in most such studies, success in learning is measured by objective tests on textbooks. The researchers cannot effectively control the amount of time spent by students in private study and there is no real basis for evaluating the efficiency of various methods of teaching. It is difficult, if not impossible, to evaluate by objective tests all that a student might learn in a classroom from an effective instructor. This matter will be considered later; for a moment we are concerned with accounting for the doubts of college psychology teachers about the usefulness of psychology in teaching. Perhaps their doubts are quite justified at the college or graduate-school level where they normally teach. By the time the students are old enough to become students of psychologists they may have been so trained as to make college instructors largely obsolete in courses that are evaluated by objective tests.

It should also be noted that when a psychologist, and especially a learning psychologist, is teaching, there is no basis for assuming that he is working in terms of some kind of psychological knowledge of useful teaching techniques based on scientific discoveries. Psychologists have not been trained as teachers and not too many of them have any great interest in teaching as such. In short, psychologists in their laboratories are not faced with the same kinds of problems, obligations, and duties as are primary and secondary school or college teachers. At the same time, teachers have not been trained as psychologists, although often enough they are expected to act like psychologists. There simply has been no basis for communication.

To return to the first difficulty mentioned earlier, we must recognize the psychologist, in his laboratory-teaching activities, has different immediate goals, objectives, and criteria for his activities from those of the classroom teacher. The learning psychologist in his immediate and direct work is usually occupied with *short-term* operations, even when working with human subjects. Traditionally, he schedules appointments for one hour or less, and selects learning tasks that can be mastered to a degree desired by the psychologist within such a time. He becomes familiar with certain procedures involved in the learning of such short assignments; commonly enough he does not care whether a subject learns or not or whether he learns quickly or slowly. These factors may not be important to his experimental design. The psychologist is interested in discovering *general principles*. These are his ultimate objectives. To get at these general principles he tries to control a situation to the point where only one factor of the many that could influence an outcome is allowed to vary. All other factors are held constant.

When the psychologist is finished with his experimental program, assuming success, he has a general principle or law of learning, but if this general principle can operate only in the laboratory under controlled conditions, with a captive population, it may not have *any* practical value. It may well be that several or many general principles that govern behavior are operating at the same time in a real-life classroom. Some of these may have mutually canceling or opposing effects, so that the net value of an understanding of the principles may be zero as far as doing anything about the learning behavior of the students is concerned. To appreciate this problem, the reader should learn a little more of how the learning psychologist works. The discussion that follows points up the difficulties of transferring laboratory principles into classroom practice.

Differences between the Laboratory and the Classroom

We need not spend time on minor differences between the laboratory and the classroom, but the following eight considerations are of major importance:

1. Laboratory Subjects. Usually, laboratory subjects are small animals (rats, dogs, monkeys) or college students (the latter are used largely because they can talk). Later the differences between college students and the rest of the world of man will be emphasized, but for the moment all that is necessary is to point out that college students are an unusual, carefully selected sample of humanity. They are normally of a much higher I.Q. level than the general population and have a successful history of prior learning—at least successful enough to get them into college. We will not worry now about the differences between animals and people. These are obvious enough, and certain important differences will be apparent in subsequent discussion. In the laboratory the psychologist has complete control over animal subjects, actually amounting to a life-and-death control. With human subjects his control is less perfect but still formidable if he is using students from his classes. The classroom teacher has certain limits in this respect that need no elaboration.

2. Freedom from "Past Experience." Laboratory "lessons," as already mentioned, are short-term projects—usually less than one hour in duration. Because the psychologist is interested in *principles*, not applications, he tries to create learning assignments that are completely divorced from prior experience. (It would not do to ask a college student to learn the

"Gettysburg Address"; he might have learned it before, at least in part.) The psychologist tries to devise a task that is completely unfamiliar to the learner. (Even though this is quite impossible with college students, the psychologist acts as if he has achieved this.) Not only is the task supposedly unfamiliar to begin with, but it usually will have no further usefulness for the learner in the future. In short, past and future are not taken into account as these might affect the learning—everything possible is done to exclude background and meaning. The same effort to place the learning task in a vacuum is made with lower animals. Sometimes, of course, the purpose of a study might be to discover the effect of one kind of specific experience on another as a problem in itself, but here *all other experiences* are, hopefully, excluded or ignored.

3. Criteria. Not only are the tasks short, meaningless, and isolated, but also the degree of learning is not usually high. If a subject runs through a maze twice or recites some nonsense material twice, it is considered learned. Of course, teachers sometimes follow such standards in a classroom in connection with, say, spelling or the multiplication tables. Imagine the consequences if a concert pianist appeared publicly after only two successful private renditions of a concerto. Naturally, criteria vary with the problem and often different measures are used, but typically the laboratory psychologist is not interested in the "long haul." He has a short-term operation and is content with rather limited mastery.

4. Subject Matter. Two of the most popular tasks have just been mentioned. For animals, these are mazes or simple discriminations—black from white, etc., or such other simple tasks as running, jumping, standing up, picking up a leg, or pressing a lever. For humans, the tasks have usually been divorced from meanings—the subjects memorize series of nonsense syllables, numbers, or bits of poetry. The most popular task of all in the laboratory has been the learning of a *group of pairs* of syllables like *KAL-MES,* where the first syllable is supposed to represent a "stimulus" and the second a "response."[10] The subject is to learn to say the second whenever he sees the first. Usually a fairly large number of such pairs, for example, eight or ten, are learned in terms of a series of exposures or trials. The experimenter shows the set of pairs, one at a time, for about three or four seconds. He then shows only the stimulus syllables and records the responses made by the subject. Such a precisely timed study of

10 This procedure is called "learning paired associates" in contrast with learning lists of syllables that follow a fixed order. The latter procedure is called "learning serial lists."

a fairly large number of items in a rigidly controlled practice session is probably not duplicated in a real life situation. If school-children are asked to memorize capitals of states or a foreign language vocabulary in such lists, they might be performing a task somewhat similar, but the similarity is more apparent than real. Whether it is wise for school-children to learn such lists is not our present question, but the operation of learning groups of pairs of items so arranged is probably a relatively rare classroom practice. Yet it is one of the most common laboratory operations.

5. Techniques. We have just mentioned the fact that in the laboratory learning time may be precisely controlled by the experimenter. He allows one second or five seconds or whatever he happens to select as appropriate as the time for a trial or exposure and adheres to this rigidly, frequently employing mechanical devices to control this time factor. He makes numerous other arbitrary decisions about the number of trials, when they are to occur, amount of material to be learned, etc., none of which have any bearing on what goes on in classroom operations. He also tries to confine all the learning or influences on the learning to the laboratory. There is no homework or interference (helpful or harmful) from other sources.

6. Individual Differences. The laboratory psychologist takes each subject as he comes (rat or man) and counts him as a unit. He does not try to become acquainted with the learner beyond the degree necessary for the task. Sometimes animals are "tamed" or "gentled," but this is only to eliminate fear factors. It is the working assumption of the laboratory psychologist that one subject is as good as or the same as another. This, of course, never proves true, but statistics take care of the differences. To the classroom teacher, no student should ever be a statistic, and individual differences of a wide variety must be considered if teaching is to be successful. (Later you will learn that in spite of this debonair equalization of subjects in the laboratory, the psychologist, paradoxically, will be in the van of those who advocate individualized instruction.)

7. The Number of Learners. The most important of all differences between laboratory and classroom concerns the number of learners. In the laboratory the psychologist usually works with one subject at a time. He may, of course, prearrange a lot of automatic equipment so that he can "run" many subjects at a time. But in these cases, the equipment serves as the teacher, and each subject is learning by himself, usually in isolation and rarely in a "social" situation where he can be aware of what or how well some other learners are doing or learning. When a psychologist is training a rat to run a maze he usually puts one rat in one maze—there have been rare exceptions for specific problems, but the basic rule is *one learner at a time.* Similarly with human learners. They come one at a time, learn their nonsense syllables, and leave. We have practically no useful information about how this isolated learning exercise differs from learning the same assignment in group situations, which is not surprising, since psychologists are in rather general agreement that they would prefer to teach or observe one subject at a time in a learning situation. The psychologist in the laboratory thus appears to meet the oft-quoted ideal teaching situation that called for Mark Hopkins on one end of a log with a student at the other. Actually, the psychologist frequently arranges his equipment so that he is screened from the learner, as if he were not physically present. He does not normally interact with his learner. The contrast with the classroom teacher could hardly be more marked! The classroom teacher not only attempts to interact but tries to do this with 20, 30, 40, or more students at a time. In the laboratory the psychologist is present primarily because he has been unable to "automate" all the tasks. Sometimes he is able to efface himself almost completely and let a tape recorder give instructions to the subject about the task. His only interaction with the student might be that of directing him to the room in which he will do his learning.

8. *Content as Reflected in Purpose or Degree of Usefulness.* In the laboratory the learning tasks are essentially meaningless, useless, and arbitrary. There is no value to the achievement. A subject might be asked to remember the kinds and positions of 20 items briefly exposed on a table. There can be no possible virtue to such knowledge; it is completely unrelated to any subsequent practice or experience. There is no long-term commitment here. Even the rat that is asked to learn a 14-turn maze will never find his food that way again. The laboratory calls for learning without a purpose, without an intent, without a future prize or penalty. No foundation is being laid for future learning situations. Here the difference from the classroom is too obvious to warrant further comment. Yet it is from just such operations that the principles of learning have been derived, to the extent that they have been recognized. It is true, of course, that some classroom students regard certain subjects as "junk" and ask "Why should I learn that stuff?", but even such a question is not based on a positive conviction that the "stuff" really is "junk"! There is an under-lying suspicion that it might be worthwhile to master the material, at least later if not sooner. You must recognize here an essential and proba-bly vital difference between the learner in a laboratory and learner in a classroom. The one learns some meaningless trivia with no concern over future retention or use; the other studies a long and relatively complex course where future achievement in some cases depends on present accom-plishment and where retention may be an important essential element.

Quite commonly the learning of college students and rats is equated by psychologists as following the same principles. It may be that the kinds of tasks selected by psychologists result in findings that support such conclu-sions, although we shall have occasion later to question this view (see pp. 143–146). For the present the reader should be warned that much of the work (and *principles of learning*) of psychologists refers to the learning of rather simple kinds of skills or "knowledge" and that more and more the great differences between the learning operations of a rat and of a college sophomore are being appreciated. Psychologists, generally, have come to recognize more and more that children differ from college students and even that rats differ from cats. More important, they have recognized more clearly in recent years that the learning of some kind of primitive task, some unfamiliar, meaningless material, is not the same as the learning of material dependent on some past experience or background. These are matters that will come up again.

Two Experimental Examples

The review of the differences between laboratory and classroom might be made more meaningful by examination of an actual laboratory experi-ment in learning. To spare my colleagues any criticism from the practi-cally minded, I will describe one of my own experiments (Bugelski, 1962). In this I had 100 college sophomores learn eight pairs of nonsense syllables presented as paired associates—that is, the subjects were to try to "antici-pate" and say aloud the second syllable of each pair when shown the first.

The subjects came to the laboratory one at a time and were seated be-fore an apparatus that exposed the "stimulus" syllable for two seconds. Then the "response" syllable appeared in view. The subjects had been assigned to five groups, 20 to a group, to which the response syllable was exposed for differing times. I had decided upon five different response syllable times, namely, 2, 4, 6, 8, and 15 seconds. The five different groups of subjects thus had different amounts of time to study each pair of syllables. As the time for study of one pair elapsed, the next pair in the set of eight pairs followed the preceding pair after a two-second delay. The subjects could, of course, continue to think about the pair just seen during this additional period when the pairs were being changed. Thus, the subjects were able to devote a total of 6, 8, 10, 12, or 19 seconds of "presentation time" to each pair of syllables, depending upon which group they happened to be in.

When the eight pairs were shown for the first time, the subjects could not, of course, demonstrate any learning. On the second "trial" they were free to announce any response syllable if they knew it. If they did not know all the responses, they were shown the set over and over (the pairs appeared in new positions on each trial) until they were able to give all the response syllables correctly.

It was expected (the experimental hypothesis) that the subjects who had the longest opportunity to study (presentation time) would learn the complete set in the fewest trials; after all, they had more learning time, they were not being rushed, they had a chance to look for possible cues or hints that would help them remember from one trial to the next. This expectancy was borne out (see table). In the table we note that the subjects with

Table 1
Average number of trials and total times
to learn eight nonsense-syllable pairs
under different presentation times

Group of 20 students	Presentation time in seconds	Average number of trials	Total study time in seconds
1	6	10.2	61.2
2	8	8.8	70.1
3	10	5.8	57.9
4	12	4.7	56.1
5	19	3.3	62.2

the 19-second presentation time required only 3.3 trials to learn all eight pairs. The subjects who had only a 6-second presentation time needed 10.2 trials to learn the same material.

If one multiplies the number of trials by the presentation time, however, one finds that the *total* time to learn each pair amounted to 61.2 seconds for the 6-second presentation time group. The 19-second presentation time group, despite its great advantage in number of trials, required just about the same total learning time. Some groups took a little more time, some a little less, but none of the differences was large enough to be "statistically significant." In short, the total learning time was about the same regardless of how it was broken up in the separate trials.

The reader may not be astonished by this finding. If he has been interpreting the results for himself in less laboratorylike language, he might be thinking something like this: It takes a certain amount of time to learn something, regardless of the length of the practice period. The reader should be cautioned that such a conclusion will be valid, if at all, for a continuous learning session (no rests), and only for the materials used and the methods followed. But even with these precautions in mind, we might raise the question of more general application to education. Can we now say that a fixed amount of time is required to learn something? Remember that the results are for groups of subjects. Some subjects learn slowly, some rapidly. Those who learn one kind of material slowly might not be so slow with other materials. It would, however, still take the subjects a certain amount of time to learn anything. If this is so, we might have a word of practical advice for curriculum planners. They should remember that there is only so much time in a school day (or school year). If something new is introduced, something else must go unless a more efficient method is introduced. Without a more efficient method there must, inevitably, be less learning time for both the old and new material or the old will not be learned so well as formerly.

At this juncture the reader might review the eight differences between the laboratory and the classroom. How much practical educational value can be distilled from an experiment such as the one just described? How must such applications be circumscribed in relation to the experimenter's materials and methods, his goals, subjects, and criteria?

Perhaps one experiment is not enough to get the flavor of the laboratory operation, and one more might not be amiss. In this second experiment (Bugelski, 1970) I tried to demonstrate in the laboratory what I knew to be perfectly true in real life, namely, that people can learn things they do not want to know. The reason for doing the experiment was a rather serious one. Too often we hear that motivation is the necessary ingredient of learning, that some students do not learn because they do not want to. Interest, it is said, is fundamental. But I am not at all interested in learning television commercials. I definitely do not want to know them; yet I know quite a few quite exactly. Nor do I want to learn about other people's troubles, bad news, and hundreds of items of information I possess. Is intention to learn really of any consequence?

When beginning my research I already knew about a standard finding from learning studies known as "Incidental Learning." In incidental learning experiments a subject is asked to help the researcher by reading a list of items to another subject who is instructed to memorize the list. The reading subject is not told to learn; all he is asked to do is read. When the "learner" has reached a certain level of memorization, the experimenter "springs" a test on the reader. It frequently turns out that the reader has learned a great deal, although he did not try to, want to, or need to; in short, he learned without intending to learn. Many psychologists working in this area believe that the incidental learners do develop some kind of interest or curiosity about the material or sense some competitive need and do *try* to learn. This is not, however, of concern here.

In another form of incidental learning a subject may be told to study some material for some particular purpose, e.g., he might be told to learn specific facts. After some study time has passed, he may be tested for general information and physical details of the arrangement of the material, misprints, etc. Again he might show that he has learned things he was not told to or expected to learn, and again, he might testify that he had no intention of learning such material.

Incidental learners, then, are not told to learn some kinds of material. In my experiment I deliberately instructed my subjects *not* to learn material that would be shown to them. They were then shown 32 common English words on a screen and instructed to say them out loud four times as each word appeared for 5 seconds. Half of the words had a plus sign. These were described as the to-be-learned words. The other half of the words had no sign and were described as "undesirable"; the subjects were told that, if they learned the unmarked words, they would suffer in the retention of the marked words and to do anything they could *not to learn* these words.

The subjects were divided into six groups—group V was a control group and had no instructions about the signs. They were told to learn all of the words, and their results are of interest only to prove that the marked and unmarked words were equally easy. In Table 2 you see their results. Group II was a simple comparison group for group V. These subjects were told not to learn the unmarked words. Notice that they could not refrain from learning some of them. The other groups are the really interesting ones. These groups, (I and IV) and (III and VI), were told to try to form images of the words, either all of them (I and IV) or only the marked ones (III and VI). Notice with group I that, when the subjects try to "image" all of the words but try at the same time not to learn some of them, they are unable to do this.

Table 2

Anti-intentional vs. intentional learning. Mean recall scores with and without imagery instructions. $N = 60$ (10/group). Words were marked (+) or unmarked (−).

Instructions

	Image (I) all words	No Imagery (II) instructions	Image only (III) marked words	Totals Marked	Unmarked
Inhibit marked words	+ 7.9 − 7.4	+ 8.9 − 4.2	+ 9.7 − 3.5	+ 26.5	− 15.1
(Totals)	(15.3)	(13.1)	(13.2)	(41.6)	
Learn all words	(IV) + 5.9 − 7.3	(V) + 6.7 − 7.2	(VI) + 8.5 − 6.3	+ 21.1	− 20.8
(Totals)	(13.2)	(13.9)	(14.8)	(41.9)	
(Totals)	+ 13.8 − 14.7	+ 15.6 − 11.4	+ 18.2 − 9.8	+ 47.6	− 35.9
	(28.5)	(27.0)	(28.0)		

Groups I, II, III > IV, V, VI, significant at > .05 for marked and unmarked words

  I > II   significant at > .05 on unmarked words

  I > III   significant at > .05 on unmarked words

Groups III and VI demonstrate that, when the subjects "image" a word, they remember it better than if they do not go through this exercise.

What does this experiment prove? To me it seems to demonstrate that, if you go through the motions of looking at and saying something and give it enough consideration or "attention" in the form of imaging it or thinking about it, learning will result whether you want to learn it or not. This is probably what happens with bad news. We hear it, say it to ourselves, attend to it, probably "imaging" the circumstances, and we then remember it. Remembering means that we have learned. (There is no other test, as yet.) The same thing happens with the abominable TV commercial; we look at it, hear it; the images are supplied if we do not indulge in our own, and we remember. We go through these operations because we are waiting for it to end so that we can resume watching the program and do not miss a moment. We will return to this subject later, but for now we can see that intention to learn may not be the crucial feature it has been made out to be. It does seem necessary that the teacher devise ways of making someone go through the motions and do some work on the material—such work may be no more than thinking about it, imaging it, or "attending" to it.

If the experiments just described are not too convincing of the learning psychologist's ability to develop practical applications, we can, perhaps, strengthen the case by taking a small step outside the laboratory into a more intimate learning situation. We can watch a psychologist attempt to teach an old dog a new trick. With some misgivings we can consider the next section a description of a psychologist at work in a real life situation.

LEARNING IN REAL LIFE

Earlier in this chapter the work of Keller and Moore was mentioned to illustrate some practical teaching applications of psychology. At this point, we might profit by a more extended illustration of what a psychologist can do by way of teaching. Skinner (1951) has provided a detailed description of how to teach a dog a trick. His original article should be studied carefully, but here I will simply outline the main steps and avoid critical comment. In a sense, the rest of this book deals with questions that might be raised in considering this particular illustration. That is why I have chosen it instead of a classroom study.

According to Skinner, the steps to be followed in training animals can be listed in a fairly fixed order.

1. First decide of what the skill to be learned consists and what it involves. In specific terms, what precisely is it that you want the animal to do? Here you are limited by the capacity of the animal. It must be able to do the required operations. A good way of determining this is to discover if it has ever been done by a similar animal. In Skinner's experiment he picks the behavior of a dog kissing a drawer knob. There is nothing beyond the dog in such a task. Dogs have been seen licking various objects, and there is no reason to question their capacity for this behavior.

2. Having defined the task, prepare the dog for learning. This means, get the dog ready to perform, to be active. This is accomplished, with dogs, by starving them for a while. (Skinner favors rather severe "deprivation schedules" for rats and pigeons and recommends that they be "reduced" to three-fourths of their normal weight. Such a weight makes animals eager learners in food situations.)

3. Plan on using immediate rewards ("reinforcers," in Skinner's language). This means, reward the dog *at once* for every movement made in a suitable sequence. The reward must be presented as soon as the desired behavior occurs. Skinner rewards the dog the moment he turns, even slightly, toward the drawer involved.

4. Because it is inconvenient to follow the dog around to feed it, teach the animal that some easily made signal (e.g., snapping the fingers) always precedes a reward. This is done by tossing bits of food onto a newspaper and snapping the fingers just as the dog is about to snap up the food. In time, such a signal will appear to work just like the food reward or at least "call" the dog to the feeding station. It is relatively easy to set up this "secondary reward" or "secondary reinforcer."[11]

5. Arrange a chest of drawers across the room from the trainer's position. With a supply of food bits available, and the dog probably watching, *wait* for the animal to turn its head in the general direction of the drawer. This will eventually happen. As soon as it does, snap your fingers and throw a bit of food onto the newspaper.

6. Now wait for the head-turning to happen again and repeat the reinforcement.

7. After a few reinforcements of the head-turning, wait for the animal to make a more definite turn toward the drawer, perhaps a step in the right direction, before snapping the fingers.

8. Extend this process of reinforcing desired actions gradually to the point where the dog takes more and more steps and eventually crosses the room before the finger snap.

9. Having selected a particular drawer knob, wait until the dog moves

11 Skinner's symbol for a secondary reinforcer is S^r.

its head at least slightly in the direction of that knob. Again the finger snap.

10. Specify more and more rigorously the head movements that merit a snap again until the dog's nose is touching the knob. The dog has learned.

If a verbal command, such as "Go kiss the knob," is given just before the dog starts each trial, it will now serve as a cue or signal for the dog to engage in such behavior whenever the trainer issues the command. Such a cue is called a "discriminated stimulus" or S^D.

This description of how to train a dog presumably applies to teaching tigers to jump through burning hoops and elephants to do a dance. Skinner believes that it may also apply to the teaching of many academic skills to humans. The procedure is called *shaping* by Skinner and is advocated for any kind of motor performance as well as for more intellectual tasks. Essentially, the procedure is one of rapidly rewarding an organism for every move or effort in the right direction but requiring closer and closer approximations of the correct sequence as the training continues.

You might test the practicality of Skinner's suggestions for yourself. It is not necessary to have a dog. A human will do. A simple stunt that might work out well is to follow a pattern devised by J. Greenspoon (1955). Ask someone to recite words aloud as rapidly as they occur to him, one after another. Decide for yourself that whenever the subject mentions some word that can be classified in some easily recognized category (e.g., plural nouns, transitive verbs, names of animals) you will murmur "good" or "mm." You should not be surprised to find such words appearing in greater and greater frequency. The same procedure can be followed in controlling a conversation by showing interest whenever the other party in the conversation mentions some special subject that you might choose to "reinforce." Whenever the conversation drifts away from the selected topic, you show boredom and unconcern. You might by now begin to wonder if you have not always been following Skinnerian technique in your normal, everyday human relationships. This would not be at all surprising inasmuch as all of us do a lot of teaching and learning in the process of getting along with others. Perhaps the only difference is one of degree of deliberateness with which we approach the task of modifying someone else's behavior.

THE PSYCHOLOGIST AND THE CLASSROOM: A RECAPITULATION

The considerations spelled out in this chapter force us to recognize that the construction of a bridge between the laboratory and the classroom is not an easy task. Psychologists, some bold, some wary and more modest, are in general agreement that *some* improvement in educational practice can be anticipated. One can reassert the human-engineering viewpoint, "there is a better way," and it will be found if there is sufficient discontent with present methods. No teacher is ever doing a perfect job. He can always do better.

Leaving aside human engineering, we can return to our major concern. We have seen something of the learning psychologists' work. We appreciate the difference between a laboratory and a classroom; and we also recognize that for a long time most psychologists who concerned themselves with learning were driven by a desire for theoretical advances. Now many of them are becoming interested in the workaday world. We can expect some of their activities to result in improvements. We can also expect difficulties and disappointments. It is not at all a certainty that psychology is ready for education or vice versa.

Perhaps the case can be stated most effectively by asking a learning psychologist just what he would do when faced with a real life educational situation. What would he really have to say? The reply of one learning psychologist to such a question is not too encouraging. This is the report of R. M. Gagne (1962) in which he reviews his experience with military training problems. Gagne addressed himself to the problem of how a learning psychologist might go about setting up training programs for three types of military tasks. He chose tasks involving *motor skills* (gunnery), *procedures* (turning on a radar set involving 15 switches in a sequence), and *diagnosing malfunctions* (trouble shooting in complex electronic equipment). For these three kinds of training, Gagne considered the possible usefulness of several widely recognized learning psychology assumptions (the virtues of practice and "doing") and learning principles (reinforcement, distribution of practice, meaningfulness, response availability, and increasing distinctiveness of elements of a task). As he reviewed and evaluated the evidence for their practical application Gagne found all such learning assumptions and principles were either less than helpful or largely inapplicable. Instead of relying on such laws of learning, Gagne finds that greater progress in improving efficiency can be made by (1) *task analysis*—that is, "identifying the component tasks of a final performance"; (2) *mastery or learning of the separate elements;* and (3) *"arranging the total learning situation in a sequence"* to benefit from all possible transfer or "mediation" effects. Gagne concludes "If I were faced with the problem of improving training, I should not look for much help from the well-known learning principles like reinforcement, distribution of practice, response familiarity, and so on."

Gagne's conclusion is not encouraging, to say the least, but it may be too broad in its implications. There are many principles of learning besides those he lists and possibly intends to cover by "and so on." Some of these may prove to be very effective in situations Gagne's analysis did not cover. In any event, his somber warning is well taken. We can face the problem of showing how some principles of learning may work in some conditions or for some tasks, fully aware that these or other principles may not work under other conditions or with other tasks.

It is time now to turn to such theoretical contributions and determine, if possible, what there is to work with, what the educator can hope to adopt and apply to a world of real-life learners. You must recognize, however, that the suggestions of psychologists may be somewhat difficult to accept by a world that is content with old and relatively easy ways. The psychologist is going to insist on defining standards, on criteria, on objective measurement. It will not be enough to say that "Johnny reads pretty well." We will have to be able to say *how* well is "pretty well." It will not be enough, either, to pass Johnny from one grade to another because he is too old for this group or that or because he has become a trial for the teacher.[12] From the human-engineering approach there can be only one standard for passing. The product is either good enough or not good enough, and "good enough" is defined in operational—that is, objective—measurement terms. Engineers have an expression for standards or criteria —"go–no go"—by which they mean that a product does or does not meet certain preset standards. If a bearing is supposed to drop through a hole, it must be small enough to "go"; if it is too large, it is "no go" and is rejected. If it is too small, it is also rejected by additional screening. From the human-engineering point of view, if a teacher finds a student not learning, there is no question about whose fault it is. It is the teacher's. He is not using an effective method. Although Skinner has never publicly aligned himself with human-engineering psychologists, he does express their attitude when he states (Skinner, 1958) that, under proper educational operations, all students will earn A's and if they do not the teacher is to be blamed.

Whether teachers, students, or their parents will accept such a position remains to be seen. Perhaps the whole effort to bring science to education is misguided. The educational process incorporates many situations and circumstances besides the instructional process. There are many problems

12 In New York City a child can be held back once in the primary grades and once in the junior high (seventh and eighth) grades. This virtually guarantees graduating from eighth grade by age sixteen.

of personality and social adjustment to consider. To control the educational situation to the point where all students earn A grades may require kinds of social control that are repugnant to a democratic society. At best, the kinds of control required would call for an upheaval or so drastic a change in the pattern of education that it is unlikely to find favor in the foreseeable future. There are unquestionably other values in education besides good grades. If, as John Dewey (1938), argued, education should be regarded as life and not as a preparation for life, it may be that "life" will rebel at efforts directed to "improve" it. The effort should not be prejudged, however. No great harm will come from increasing the efficiency of what we are now trying to do.

Chapter Two

Two
Theories
of
Learning

The objective of this chapter is to provide some of the background that the teacher needs if he or she is to appreciate the logic and evidence underlying the practical suggestions that psychologists have made for controlling the learning process. If this objective is to be met meaningfully, it will do no good to review in detail each of the many theoretical approaches to learning theory and attempt evaluations. Such reviews and appraisals have already been made elsewhere by other people, and teachers can read these with interest, even though they will gain little of practical value from theoretical discussions. Remember Hilgard's remark (p. 15) that "There are no laws of learning that can be taught with confidence."

The poverty of application of learning theory to education cannot be denied. When Hilgard (1956) tried to determine just what might be useful to a teacher, he settled for fourteen broad applications on which there might be general agreement. These fourteen are indeed rather global and common-senselike generalizations, such as "Learning under intrinsic motivation is preferable to learning under extrinsic motivation" and "The personal history of the individual, for example, his reaction to authority, may hamper or enhance his ability to learn from a given teacher." Teachers who had never heard of learning theory might have set down these suggestions. A similar list of practical applications was offered by L. P. Thorpe and A. M. Schmuller (1954), but this too is rather slim pickings from the vast learning-theory literature. Thorpe and Schmuller mention, for example, that "Learning is facilitated when it goes forward under conditions in which the learner also experiences satisfactory personality adjustment and social growth." Some years ago I reviewed these suggestions and presented an even briefer list (Bugelski, 1956), but that list (see p. 470) was scarcely an improvement.

One reason why these lists are so vapid is that their reporters were looking for uniformity of opinion or general agreement. While this might be a useful criterion for some decisions, it does not appear to be especially meaningful in this context. One theorist might be right on some particular matter and all the rest wrong (and/or vice versa). What is important for teachers is that some aspects of the work of most psychology theorists have potential value, even if other theorists have not indicated agreement or ever bothered about such matters. Consequently, the next five chapters will consider several learning theories that have some impact or meaning for educational practice. No attempt will be made to describe each theory in detail; rather a capsule review should suffice, with special attention to principles that appear relevant to teaching. Inevitably, the picture of the theory will appear distorted to the student familiar with learning psychology or to supporters of the theorist under consideration. This will not concern us. We are looking for what is useful in education; an important theorist who has nothing to say of value to this purpose will be quickly dismissed; some will not even be mentioned. The reader is cautioned, then, not to assume familiarity with a theory, even if he memorizes all that is written here about a given view. One paragraph here may represent a formidable library of writing. The procedure then will be, first, to present a short summary of the general theory; second, as occasion requires, to supply more detailed descriptions of specific principles that have some prospective utility for teachers; and, finally, to state the specific principles in terms of what appear to be reasonably practical applications in educational situations.

Theories in General

The discussions that follow presume that a *theory* means a set of interacting, interlocking, or interdependent principles designed to account for a wide array of observations or facts. A loose collection of independent laws is not a theory. The ideal theory would consist of the minimal number of laws (hopefully, two) from which all the rest of the generalizations (laws) that appear to summarize the observations in some area of interest can be deduced. Theories frequently consist of a series of *assumptions* or "postulates" that are then tested by experiment. Each positive outcome of a research helps to justify the assumptions involved in the deductions on which the research was initiated. The reader should recognize that all laws are really only assumptions or at least include the assumption that future events or observations will comply with the present generalization. If the generalization is hastily made without a great supporting body of fact, the *assumed* property of the generalization is somewhat more evident. In the subsequent pages the names of Ivan Pavlov and Edward Lee Thorndike will loom larger than the rest because, as stated by Hilgard (1956), learning theory in America really amounts to agreement or disagreement with, or alteration of, Thorndike's views. Hilgard might have included Pavlov's views to make the picture complete. Because Pavlov began a little earlier and because his famous dogs are known to everyone old enough to be reading this book, this chapter will start with Pavlov (1927).[1]

THE PRINCIPLES OF PAVLOV

The work of Ivan P. Pavlov (1849–1936) is an expression in objective terminology and laboratory work of the ancient doctrine of *association*. From the earliest Greek writings down to the present day (with an intensive and powerful assist from the British Empiricists) the doctrine of association has been the basis for explaining memories and how one idea leads to another. Aristotle provided the basic principle or law, that of association by *contiguity*. We remember or think of something because previously we had encountered that something together with something else. Seeing a sailor might remind you of being seasick or of travel or of the war, depending on your past history (and many secondary laws of association). If you are asked to report the first word you think of when someone says "chair," most likely you will say "table." To "needle," you will say "pin" or "thread"; "grass" will invite "green," and so on. In each instance, the two objects or experiences had, for you, occurred previously at the same place or time or both—that is, they had been experienced in contiguity. Aristotle and Plato applied the principle of *association by contiguity* to ideas, of which philosophers are so fond.

They were saying, in short, that one idea leads to another because the two ideas had been experienced in close succession or together at some earlier time. Notice that this is not an explanation. It is a simple assertion that seems so plausible as to be considered axiomatic. Such axiomatic-appearing statements can be thought of as postulates or laws.

The Law of the Association of ideas does not meet with great approval by modern psychologists. Psychologists are less enamored of the concept of "idea," and very few would use such a concept in their work. They prefer the more objective concepts of *stimulus* and *response* or *reaction*. In the case of Pavlov the term "reflex" was used to describe a unit of behavior or "response."

For Pavlov, the basic process in learning was the formation of an association between a stimulus and a reflex (response) because of their simul-

[1] Pavlov's monumental work, *Conditioned Reflexes* (Anrep translation), is now available as an inexpensive paperback volume. Dover Press, 1960.

taneous action or contiguity. For convenience, a stimulus (any energy change in the environment to which an organism reacts) will be symbolized by the letter *S* and the response involved, reflex or otherwise, by *R*. For Pavlov, then, learning consists of the formation of some kind of hypothetical *connection* in the central nervous system between an *S* and an *R*.

Conditioning

In Pavlov's scheme, the organism either is equipped at birth or develops through maturation certain natural connections between some *S*'s and some *R*'s. Some stimuli are normally or "naturally" followed by certain "natural" responses. Such normal or natural stimuli are called *unconditioned* stimuli, or *US*, and the natural responses to such stimuli are called *unconditioned responses* or *UR*. Thus a tap on the patellar tendon will result in a knee jerk. Such a response to an *unconditioned stimulus* or *US* is called an *unconditioned reflex*, or *UR*, because it does not depend on any special conditions; it is there as a given. If, however, some other *S*, say the sounding of a bell, occurs several times *contiguously* with the tap on the knee and if the leg should thereafter jerk when the bell is sounded without the knee being tapped (it is not likely to do so, by the way), then we could speak of learning. Pavlov preferred to speak of "conditioning" because his procedures consisted of establishing certain controlling circumstances or conditions in which a new stimulus (previously inadequate and irrelevant for the response) had come to "elicit" or "evoke" the response. Such a response, under the control of an extraneous *S*, he called a *conditioned response*, or *CR*, and the stimulus involved, a *conditioned stimulus*, or *CS*.

Pavlov did not work with knee jerks. The knee jerk is difficult, if not impossible, to "condition." Pavlov preferred to "condition" the salivary reflexes of dogs to a wide variety of stimuli. Later he and his hundreds of students explored other reflexes of the liver, stomach, circulatory system, the intestines, bladder, heart, and other visceral organs. Pavlov occasionally strayed outside the viscera to study what he called the "defensive reflex" (a dog is trained to raise a paw when a bell that will be followed by a shock is sounded—raising the paw saves the animal from the shock), but the vast amount of Pavlovian research was concerned with visceral organs and Autonomic Nervous System functions.[2] The reader should note this latter preoccupation; it will have an interesting interpretation in a later chapter (p. 117).

---

[2] The Autonomic Nervous System is a part of the central nervous system. It appears to function in an independent fashion and controls the visceral and glandular functions of the body.

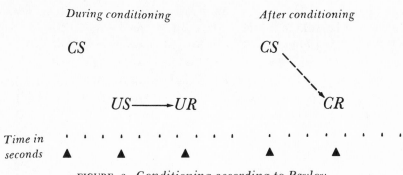

FIGURE 3. *Conditioning according to Pavlov*

Note that the *CS* during conditioning precedes the *US* that directly evokes the *UR* by about three seconds. After conditioning the *US* is no longer required. The *CS* has become a substitute for the *US*. It now evokes the response that is labeled *CR* because it is not exactly the same as the *UR*. Note also that the *CR* occurs earlier in time than the *UR* did originally as far as the *CS* is concerned. This coming forward in time is characteristic of a conditioned response and could be considered a defining condition for learning.

For Pavlov, conditioning consisted of pairing the *CS* and a *US* from time to time (eight or nine pairings were usually adequate) until the dog reacted to the *CS* before the *US* was presented. Essentially, what happened was that the trainer or teacher had substituted one *S* for another, and Pavlov's kind of operation can be thought of as *stimulus substitution*. Hence Pavlov has been called an *S-S* psychologist. Theorists frequently argue that the *CR* is not really and fully like the *UR*, but this is a minor quibble. There is no commanding reason why one should assume that a *CR* should be exactly like a *UR*. To get the full *UR*, you may need the *US*.

This is an important point for you to note. Only the stimuli are manipulated. The response itself need not occur, at least not in any observable fashion. Many experiments have been done on animals that have been paralyzed by the drug *curare* so that they do not move. Paired stimuli are then presented, e.g., a bell and a shock; the animal does not react in any visible way. After the drug effects wear off, a ringing of the bell may bring out a response, such as is given under routine conditioning without drugs. Textbook diagrams of conditioning usually show a connection between the CS and the CR. Such a connection must surely exist; the point, however, is that it may be an indirect connection with some intermediate neural center that is also activated by the US. For the purpose of keeping the theorists suitably defined, then, we will label Pavlov as an S-S theorist, meaning that he was concerned, operationally, with the pairing of stimuli.

The response, while of major importance, was only the objective, observable, or measurable indicator of the result of the pairing of stimuli.

What has just been described is the basic Pavlovian operation. Unfortunately, the exciting history of Pavlov's discovery of the conditioned reflex (about 1895) has had to be omitted as have all the elaborate laboratory details. These the interested reader can find elsewhere. If Pavlov's basic discovery is appreciated, all the rest is secondary.

Extinction

The most important secondary principle that Pavlov first described is that of *extinction*. He discovered that if the *US* is omitted in a series of what amounted to test trials, the *CR* begins to decrease and eventually fails to appear—that is, is extinguished. In his well-known saliva experiment with dogs, for example, a bell *(CS)* is rung just before food *(US)* is presented. After a number of trials, the dog salivates when the bell rings, just as at times your mouth waters when dinner is announced. If the bell is then rung repeatedly without food appearing, the salivating not only begins to decrease but eventually stops. Pavlov did not consider food to be a reward for salivating; the food normally came before salivation began—at least at first. He thought of the food as the evoking stimulus and spoke of it as a "reinforcing stimulus" in the sense of a "strengthener" and not at all in the sense of reward. You can think of extinction as a kind of "boy-who-cried-wolf" phenomenon. The shepherds no longer came when they found no wolf. The important point to note is that the shepherds *could* have come and the dog *can* still salivate. It no longer salivates to the formerly effective signal. The dog, of course, can be retrained quickly to salivate again when the bell is rung if food is presented along with the bell.

Spontaneous Recovery. Once a response is extinguished, it may, however, occur again after a rest. Pavlov called this *spontaneous recovery*. The mechanisms underlying spontaneous recovery became the subject of much theoretical speculation in America, but for readers of this book the fact of spontaneous recovery is only of minor importance. It does caution us against assuming too hastily that some response is not likely to occur merely because it has been "extinguished" once. Some responses may have to be extinguished repeatedly before they are really gone.

Generalization

Generalization was another important secondary principle described by Pavlov. He found that once the response was conditioned, it was not necessary to present the precise *CS* to obtain the expected response. A *similar* stimulus would also bring it out. The less similar the stimulus, the less the amount of response.

In Pavlov's laboratory the principle of generalization was studied intensively. A stimulus would be selected for conditioning purposes that could be varied in either quantity or quality, and the variations would be tested after a dog was trained to some standard value. For example, a common procedure in testing for generalization might start with conditioning a dog to salivate to a metronome beating 60 times per minute. After the dog was conditioned, Pavlov would set the metronome beating at a faster or slower rate and see what happened. Commonly, the dog would still respond but with diminishing amounts as the rate was changed more and more radically from the original training rate.

The principle of generalization is familiar to all of us from our everyday experience. We do not have to be specifically taught to avoid each and every kind of automobile as we cross streets; we do not have to learn how to sit down in every new chair we encounter or how to greet each new person we meet. Enough genuine or pseudo psychology has filtered down into our culture so that even children can give reasonable accounts of why we happen to behave in one fashion or another on the basis of our prior experience with similar stimuli.

The principle of generalization must be thought of as both useful and harmful to the learner. On the useful side we may note that a learner can respond to a stimulus even if it varies from time to time (it is rare when we are offered the same view of a visual stimulus, for example). To insist on a specific stimulus each time would mean that an organism would have to be conditioned to millions of stimuli. On the harmful side we may note that, if it is actually necessary to respond to one and only one stimulus, any response to a similar stimulus is an error. Professor Clark L. Hull (1943) illustrated the two-faced nature of generalizations by the plight of a monkey in the jungle which had had a narrow escape from a tiger. Thereafter the monkey would rush to safety when anything black and orange came into view. To rush up a tree when a black and orange butterfly came by would hardly be useful.

The erroneous responses resulting from generalization can be eliminated by instituting a procedure whereby undesirable conditioning is extinguished. At the same time the response to the desired *S* must be reinforced by supplying the *US*, because extinguishing a response to a generalized *S* will also generalize, and the desired response will disappear along with the undesired. Under these conditions we have *generalization of extinction*.

Generalization of extinction may be somewhat more difficult to understand than simple positive generalization. It must first be appreciated that extinguishing some conditioned response means that the response will no longer occur to the CS. This does not mean, however, that some degree of response will not occur to other stimuli that are similar to the original conditioning stimulus. Such responses to "generalized" stimuli, however, will not be so strong as they would have been if the response to the original stimulus had not been extinguished. The extinction effects will also spread to such similar stimuli, and the amount of response will be reduced. The spread of extinction effect will diminish with distance along the similarity continuum, however, and the more distant stimuli will be less affected than the more similar stimuli.

If we return to our metronome illustration the whole matter can be easily clarified. If the original CS is a beat of 60 per minute, we can expect, by generalization, to get some response to a beat of 90 per minute. This response will not be great, to be sure, and it will be less than that occurring to beats of 70 or 80 per minute. Now, if the response to the 60-beat stimulus is extinguished, we can expect to have a reduction of response to the 70-, 80-, and 90-beat stimuli. The reduction, in terms of percentage, however, will be greatest for the 70-, less for the 80-, and least for the 90-beat stimuli.

Discrimination

When the learner had been trained to respond to only one S and not to similar stimuli, Pavlov spoke of *discrimination,* and the controlling stimulus was considered to be a *discriminated stimulus.* Note that neither Pavlov nor any behaviorist psychologist ever implied that the learner *makes* a discrimination—all that Pavlov said was that a stimulus has acquired a specialized function in controlling behavior.

Pavlov's concepts of generalization and discrimination are concerned with stimulus factors—that is, with the range of stimuli to which the learner responds in about the same way. Educationally, a parallel concern would be: To how many different questions or variations of the same question will the student give the same answer? If similar questions evoke the same answers, the student may find himself in difficulties if society has decreed that different answers are required. Sometimes students will write long, even competent, answers to questions that were never asked. The student complains: "That's what I thought you asked for." Or he complains about "trick" questions. The teacher must take the potential dangers of generalization into account and train students to identify the specific stimulus features of questions, problems, maps, diagrams, and similar materials so that they do not make mistakes by "generalization." Discrimination will not normally occur by itself, although Pavlov did state that with prolonged training the generalization effects are reduced. It is safer to extinguish undesirable generalized conditioning effects.

Response Generalization and Discrimination. Generalization poses the question: To how many stimuli will the same response be given? A logically parallel question has been asked by American psychologists: How many different responses might be given to the same stimulus? This question has never really been answered effectively in the laboratory (see p. 48). There is always the possibility that the stimulus is not really the same. In the laboratory, for example, a rat might "press a bar" to "get food." The bar can be "pressed," however, by the rat's head, mouth, right paw, left paw, both paws, or in other ways—some rats use a kind of climbing motion. So long as the bar is moved, the rat eats. Can we say here that the rat is making different responses to the same stimuli? We do not even know what the stimuli are. (In a later chapter [p. 103] E. R. Guthrie argues that each response is actually a highly specific conditioned response to a specific stimulus.) We do know that in this example it is easy enough to require that the rat react in one and only one way, say, with a left-paw pressure of a specified number of grams. This specific movement can be called the "correct answer." Such a spelling out of the requirements can be enforced through reinforcing one set of movements and not another—that is, providing food only when the desired movement occurs.

In teaching humans it is important to spell out precise requirements where there is danger of such response generalization. If learners are permitted to "get away with" some rough approximations of the proper response, they will actually learn these approximations. In reading aloud a child may mispronounce a word, the teacher may correct the reader by pronouncing correctly, and the child is sometimes permitted to go on without having, himself, pronounced the word correctly. The net result will be that the teacher has learned to "correct" the students and the students learn that the teacher will correct them.

Commonly enough, the precise nature of the responses involved in some lessons is not spelled out and only approximations are learned. Children, for example, learning the national anthem may be too young and inexperienced to know what "o'er" and "ramparts" mean. They have been known to sing "or the ram parts" with great enthusiasm and patriotic fervor. In singing "America" children come through with "tizzadee" and may be quite surprised about the appearance of the words when they eventually come to read them. One child's reaction to a horror movie included learning about a mad scientist named Frank N. Stein. Only years later did she learn the scientist's actual name. Other children, and many adults, generalized along stimulus lines from this same movie. They call the monster "Frankenstein."

The Orienting Response

Before proceeding with an evaluation of Pavlov's principles, mention should be made of another potentially significant contribution of Russian psychologists, which is attributed to Pavlov but has only recently excited the interest of American psychologists through the work of E. N. Sokolov (1960). Observers in Russian laboratories noticed that the onset of a conditioned stimulus, e.g., a bell, would normally be followed by a characteristic reaction that could be described as "coming to attention." The dog would perk up, look about for the source of the sound, appear to become somewhat tense, and in general be on the alert. The response has been described by some as a "vigilance" reaction, but the term "orienting response" appears to have gained wide acceptance. More detailed studies of the orienting response have resulted in the finding that it is a rather complex reaction with neural, sensory, circulatory, and motor components. The alpha rhythm of the brain, for example, normally stops with the onset of the signal, more blood rushes to the head, pupils dilate, respiration stops momentarily, and muscle tonus increases. Sokolov reports that such changes, if not extreme, are a basic requirement for the process of learning. If the animal is too responsive to the CS, it will not learn; if, on the other hand, it does not notice the CS, learning will not take place either. The orienting response may be another word for *attention,* or it may include some other, still unknown, kind of central nervous system reaction that amounts to attention. In any event, we cannot afford to ignore the importance of what is already known about the orienting response itself, namely, that learning is unlikely in its absence. In later chapters the role of attention in learning will be considered at greater length. Here we have only paused to acknowledge another Pavlovian contribution.

A Summary of Pavlovian Principles

In the last few pages, Pavlovian principles were described in somewhat everyday language in order to underscore the fact that, although he considered himself first and last a physiologist, Pavlov did have rather strong views that his laboratory findings did apply to everyday life. He never hesitated, for example, to apply his principles to problems of behavior disorder and their cure. It is important, however, to remember that Pavlov persisted in describing his work as basically physiology, the physiology of the cerebral hemispheres, and that his own descriptions were couched in physiological-sounding language. Pavlov's work is full of references to hypothetical physiological processes, such as excitation, inhibition, positive and negative induction, irradiation, concentration, and so on. The principles presented here are only a fragment of the Pavlovian theory and were selected from the mass of his writings because of their potential applicability to education.

In consideration of the restriction to applicable principles, then, the important features of Pavlovian theory are essentially those described above—namely, the basic notion of conditioning as an adaptation or translation of the principle of association by contiguity from the realm of ideas to the area of behavior, the orienting response, the principle of generalization, the principle of extinction, and the extension of the principle of extinction to cover the extremely important matter of discrimination. In the concept of discrimination as a function of the extinction of undesirable generalized conditioning, we meet head on with some basic goals of education. The process of education might even be defined as the formation of finer and finer discriminations.

In the following section, some fairly immediate and obvious applications to education will be drawn from the principles described above. In the next four chapters you will be able to see how other psychologists have been stimulated by Pavlov into developing additional applications to education.

PRACTICAL ASPECTS OF PAVLOVIAN FINDINGS

In turning to the question of the meaning of Pavlov's findings for the classroom, we will need to indulge in some speculation about the meaning of his actual findings. It was mentioned above that Pavlov thought of himself as a physiologist, but his physiology has not found favor with scientific critics. What has survived from Pavlov are his empirical findings and not his theory. His careful laboratory work and his observations of behavior are his real monument. Among his most astute observations were his findings on individual differences in his dogs. Pavlov's insistence on taking the nature of the dog into account makes a good starting point for a consideration of applications of Pavlov's principles to education.

Individual Differences

Pavlov strongly emphasized the role of individual differences in temperament observed in his animals. Some dogs, he found, learned some kinds of response patterns well, others, poorly or not at all. It does not appear unreasonable that we should assert with equal forcefulness the existence of individual differences among humans and here emphasize, as Pavlov did, *temperamental* differences among learners. Some children will come to the learning situation eagerly, some will have to be dragged. Some will react effectively to some lessons and not to others; other children will react oppositely. While psychologists are not prepared to supply analyses of temperament of children, or indeed of adults, and further to indicate for what kinds of learning each temperament variety is suitable, the teacher certainly can take into account the factor of temperament and not expect to treat all individuals in the same manner. In saying this, I am not even including differences in capacity and background—although both are obvious difference factors—I am merely pointing out that any method of instruction that assumed uniform *reactivity* on the part of the learners is doomed to failure. It would be helpful, of course, to spell out for humans as Pavlov did for his dogs which breed and which individual is suitable for what, but this cannot be done. The first practical conclusion for the teacher then is:

Take the temperamental disposition of the learner into account, in relation to the kinds of responses (or content material) that are to be taught.

In connection with temperament it should be mentioned at this time that American psychologists, notably Spence (1958), have become much concerned with the concept of *anxiety* and its relation to learning. Although their interests are not Pavlovian, they find that the level of anxiety (as measured by personality tests) which characterizes a person has a bearing on his learning. Although there is some dispute about the facts, the common thinking on this relationship seems to be that people of high anxiety do well on simple tasks but do poorly on more complex problems. This specific problem need not be explored further except to note that a teacher may well find students who show this interesting reversal when tasks vary in difficulty. It is easy to be misled by high achievement levels on simple tasks.

Conditioning

Pavlov, as was said, confined his work to glandular secretions and other liquids of the body, or, in neural terms, he was working with functions that depend on the Autonomic Nervous System. Now, normally, these functions are of interest to teachers only in connection with emotion. It is possible that Pavlov's conditioning principles really apply *only* to emotional reactions. To say *only* does not imply something trivial. We commonly think of emotions as some kinds of relatively rare experiences, and we label behavior as "emotional" only when it appears to be extreme, as in terror, rage, or passion. More correctly, we should regard *all* behavior as "emotional" to some degree and even perhaps consider most of our lives as spent reacting, at least in part, emotionally. Here I am including such milder emotional patterns as those described in terms of "feeling good" or "feeling bad." How often we really feel neutral, if ever, is unknown. To the degree, then, to which we are emotional, Pavlovian principles can be expected to hold. We can condition our learners to like or dislike, to hate and to love, to fear, to enjoy, and so on. Later you will see how other psychologists introduce emotion into broader patterns of behavior. For the present you need only to know that a second practical Pavlovian application is:

Conditioning applies to emotional aspects of behavior. The learner can, in general, be conditioned to respond favorably or unfavorably to his teacher, the content material, the environmental surrounding, indeed to anything that can function as a stimulus.

This conclusion should not be taken lightly. It may turn out (see p. 127) that the teacher's role is perhaps restricted to that of a conditioner of emotions. If this should actually be true, the teacher should certainly be aware of this role and take steps to produce the appropriate emotional reactions to the stimuli under his control.

Extinction

From the Pavlovian principle of extinction comes another practical application to education. When we have good reason to believe that some undesired emotional response is learned, we can extinguish such behavior by withholding the *US,* if this is within our power. While this withholding often may not be possible and other methods of extinction may have to be used (see p. 52), where possible it is indeed effective.

Fear of lightning might serve as a useful example. Perhaps most people are more afraid of thunder than of lightning—thunder or any sudden loud noise is an unconditioned stimulus for a startle or fear reaction—but many people do get to fear lightning. It is easy to imagine why this is so: the lightning always *precedes* the thunder, a necessary relationship of stimuli for conditioning to occur. Shortly after the lightning, which we can now consider a *CS*, the *US* of loud noise occurs. Conditioning of fear can readily result. Because there is no way in which we can control the thunder—that is, have it not occur—there is consequently no way in which we can institute extinction procedures. We cannot eliminate the *US*. A child afraid of lightning cannot have this fear extinguished because we have no control over the presumed unconditioned stimulus of thunder. Other methods for controlling the fear will have to be employed.

But a child who is afraid of another child or teacher can be helped if we prevent the other child or teacher from actually harming him. In practice, it is often necessary to prevent the *US* from eliciting its usual response by introducing some interfering stimulus or situation. Extinction then occurs as a result of a competing reaction. In one experiment[3] a timid and submissive monkey was placed in one side of a box. A glass window separated this monkey from a more aggressive monkey who normally bullied the timid one. When a light was turned on in the timid monkey's box, a shock was given to the bully monkey. Every time the bully saw the timid monkey he received a shock. After a few trials the bully became completely cowed and retreated respectfully from the once timid animal.

In a somewhat indirect application of extinction technique, Mary C. Jones (1924) was able to "cure" a little boy of fear of rabbits by introducing a rabbit at a considerable distance from the boy while the boy was given chocolate. Every day the rabbit was brought closer and closer while the chocolate was effective in distracting the child or at least in preventing the fear reaction from developing. Eventually the child could pat the rabbit fearlessly. His fear had been extinguished. Actually, while the principle of extinction is practical enough, application calls for special control and knowledge of both *CS* and *US*. In a later chapter another variety of control over undesirable habits will be presented with another interpretation of extinction. For the moment, the practical application is:

When an emotional response is recognized as a *CR*, it can be extinguished by withholding the *US* or reducing the strength of the *CS* below the level effective for evoking the emotional behavior.

3 See J. Murphy, R. E. Miller, and I. A. Mirsky (1955).

Generalization

It has already been remarked that generalization is a two-edged sword, an observation that suggests a number of practical applications. On the negative side, teachers can appreciate that learners will respond to similarities in stimuli and, if these are undesired, teachers must take care to set up extinction operations for the undesired generalized *CR*'s. Sometimes teachers confuse students by bringing up exceptions to rules. They should realize that there are no exceptions to rules. In these supposed cases, the rules are not truly rules. Students should be exposed to such alleged or apparent exceptions and trained to avoid the impending disasters under favorable conditions.

On the positive side, generalization can be expected to generate appropriate behavior (perhaps in less strength) to similar stimulus situations. When a student is expected to react to a broad range of stimuli he *should be given adequate practice at several points along a continuum.* Practicing archery, for example, in your basement may make you competent at hitting targets 20 yards away. To hit 60-yard targets you should practice at that distance. D. Wolfle (1951) suggests that practicing at 30, 60, and 90 yards might make one competent throughout a reasonable range. In the areas of spelling and reading, pupils can gain a great deal of competence if the teacher groups words that contain the same sounds—if there are no tricks involved in the spelling. When a child is learning to spell *round,* he might as well learn all the other *o-u-n-d* words at the same time—*around, found, bound, sound, ground, mound, pound*—but *wound* (in the sense of *injure*) should be extinguished as an *o-u-n-d* word and given discrimination training. Similarly, frowned and other *o-w-n-e-d* words must be eliminated. The practical conclusion here is:

Take advantage of generalization where it is safe. Always consider the range of stimuli that may be operative. Watch for undesirable generalizations.

It is also necessary to recognize the limits of generalization and to avoid the assumption that learning will "transfer" to widely different situations. Children who learn to hang their "wraps" in school may toss their "clothes" on chairs or the floor at home. Perhaps the word *wraps* is a *CS* that is favored in school but never used at home. A child may learn to hang "wraps" but not "clothes" or "your coat." In general, habits of neatness demanded in school do not transfer to nonschool situations. The stimulus continuum does not reach that far.

The Orienting Response. Practical Applications

Not much has been done with the orienting response in terms of school room application possibilities. A study by Zaporozhets (1961) is sometimes cited as an illustration of the potential application. In this study children were asked to look at and feel the corners in a maze prior to learning it, and they did better than other children who had to learn without such preliminary exposure to the physical features of the maze. Perhaps we can only conclude that calling attention to the critical components of a task is important, without relating this to the orienting response as described earlier. There is, however, considerable importance to be attached to the concept of the orienting response per se as far as teaching is concerned. It is essential that the teacher be sure that the student is reacting to the key stimuli or their features and not only looking attentive. If the teacher knows what stimuli are affecting the student, the battle is half won. The other half, the factor of *time,* has already been considered in the first chapter, and we will return to it later.

This is not all that Pavlov has to teach, but for the present these applications of Pavlovian experiments to the classroom are enough. In Chapter 4 the reader will find other psychologists spelling out practical lessons from modifications or extensions of Pavlovian theory.

Soviet Education and Pavlovian Principles

Before we turn to Pavlov's great American contemporary, this seems a good place to comment briefly on Russian application of Pavlov's principles, since what is going on in the Soviet Union sometimes arouses the fears of American educators. Certainly Pavlov's popularity and authority in the Soviet Union is undisputed, but Communist philosophy has difficulty digesting the whole Pavlov doctrine. On the one hand, it approves of the basic emphasis on environment or stimulus control and the general view that anyone can be educated (conditioned) to become anything. This is no different from the view held by the American founder of Behaviorism, John B. Watson, who heartily espoused conditioning and believed (see p. 4) that he could make any "dozen healthy infants" into doctor, lawyer, merchant, thief, and so on by controlling the environment or stimulus world. (It is highly improbable that Watson really could have got enough help to make good his boast.) The Communists hold that all social institutions (and behavior) are a consequence of the methods of production and distribution of the world's goods. Because these are environmental operations, the Communists must be environmentalists.

On the other hand, the Marxian cry "Workers of the world, unite!" is a most unenvironmental plea. Clearly, the workers who do not unite cannot unite because their environment has conditioned them otherwise. The Communists insist on their power and capacity to change the world and exhort their followers and the "workers of the world" to believe as they do and thereby to change themselves by rational decision and choice. No good behaviorist can subscribe to this possibility. From the behaviorists' views, capitalists are capitalists because they cannot escape their environments—they cannot even want to.

This basic contradiction is not all that Communist leaders have to worry about. As was pointed out earlier, Pavlov strongly emphasized the role of individual differences in temperament in his animals. Pavlov would not even undertake to produce a given response in some dogs, and he was not about to make doctors, lawyers, merchants, or thieves of the Russian citizens—Communist theorists to the contrary.

At the present time, and since 1957, the Soviet Union is introducing a form of educational control designed to produce the "new Soviet man." In these new schools children are enrolled at the age of three months and kept in school for full days (till the parents pick them up after work) or boarded for weeks. The children are constantly in the company of other children and are trained to work together cooperatively ("collectively"). Games and toys are designed that call for mutual efforts and any individualistic tendencies are "extinguished." All children are regarded as basically alike or potentially equal. The Soviet Union, in general, frowns on "psychometrics" or intelligence testing, ability grouping, or any procedures that might enhance individual distinctiveness. Children are trained to do their best for the benefit of the collective to which they belong and, ultimately, for the benefit of the State.

The results of this great mass experiment in behavioral control will not be known until at least one generation of children is reared in this fashion. For the present it appears that Soviet educators engaged in these schools are satisfied with developments. It should be noted that, while group efforts and mutual criticism are continually stressed, the actual methods of teaching in classrooms have not been altered from traditional procedures. Teachers will lecture or transmit information in authoritative styles while students listen and recite. The changes to be looked for will appear more in character and personality than in academic or other achievements if the new techniques of behavioral control through environmental control are effective. Some Pavlovian principles are being put to work in the areas where they might actually work most effectively: the field of emotion. What will emerge from the effort cannot be foretold. We must wait and see.

THE THEORY OF THORNDIKE

Edward Lee Thorndike (1874–1949) did more to affect American education than any other man. As the great authority for many years at Teachers' College of Columbia University, he trained more educators than anyone before him and perpetuated his thinking through his students, presumably for generations to come. Thorndike never did recognize Pavlov as one having anything to say about education. Conditioning, for Thorndike, was an interesting laboratory curiosity. What was important to him was what he saw in the behavior of his own laboratory animals: the overwhelming influence of reward.

At the time of Thorndike's early thinking, the basic Western philosophy was based on the pleasure-pain principle: We do that which brings us pleasure; we avoid activities and situations that bring us harm. Under Darwinian influence and pressure to objectify mentalistic terminology, Thorndike sought to translate the hedonistic pleasure-pain view into some kind of scientific credo. He hit upon the substitute terms "satisfiers" and "annoyers" (these are necessarily objective things or events in the outside world), defining the former as "things we do nothing to avoid and frequently strive to attain." Annoyers he defined as the reverse of satisfiers: "things we do nothing to attain and frequently strive to avoid." Thorndike was now ready to describe what went on in learning.

Thorndike (1898) conceived of learning as basically a matter of problem-solving. To study learning, the learner must be given a problem. For this purpose Thorndike invented the "puzzle box"—a cagelike container in which an animal could be locked. Food was placed outside the box where the animal could see it through the bars. The food could be "attained" by the animal if it opened the door by operating a device that would release it. Such a device might be a string looped over pulleys and available to the animal inside the box. When a hungry cat was placed inside the box, it might learn to get out by pulling the string if it moved around actively and eventually caught a claw in the string. The opening of the door would lead to escape and food.

The Three Laws of Learning

With his box for equipment and animals (usually cats) for learners, Thorndike pursued the experiments that led him to his three laws of learning. Of the hungry cat in the puzzle box, he offered the following explanation of behavior:

At first the cat behaved aimlessly, at random, stupidly (*trial and error*); then it came upon the correct response by accident (*chance success*); finally, it was rewarded (by consuming the *satisfier*). Attainment of the satisfier or satisfying state of affairs strengthened the connection between whatever stimuli were present and the response made just prior to the appearance of the satisfier. This, for Thorndike, was the basic principle that governed learning and from which he derived his *Law of Effect.*

The *Law of Effect* states that: When a connection between a stimulus and response is made and this is followed by a satisfying state of affairs, the connection is strengthened; if the connection is followed by an annoying state of affairs, the connection is weakened. Thorndike stated the *Law of Effect* in many ways. He was fond of remarking that "bonds" are "stamped in" by satisfiers and "stamped out" by annoyers. Regardless of the care in choice of language in order to be objective, the law has generally been interpreted to mean that if something is to be learned, a reward must be presented for the desired behavior and if something is to be eliminated, punishment must follow the response.

If the cat were replaced in the box, Thorndike found that it would usually take less time than before to get out. With additional trials (as many as 20 distributed over several days), the time would normally decrease more or less regularly until the cat would emerge almost as soon as it entered the box. This improvement in escape time Thorndike attributed to additional strengthening of the connection or "bond" between the stimuli and the response. Such improvement through practice led him to formulate his *Law of Exercise:* Connections are strengthened with use, and weakened with disuse. The use or practice referred to here involves continued rewards. Practice without reward is meaningless. It is important to emphasize that Thorndike saw no virtue in practice as such. Each practice trial had to result in a success or it was of no significance. Blind repetition without rewards would not affect the learning. In later years, after 1930, Thorndike virtually repealed the *Law of Exercise* in order to discourage any belief in the virtues of practice as such. Practice does not mean repetition. It must include satisfying aftereffects for correct performances.

The third basic law pronounced by Thorndike was the *Law of Readiness.* This law was originally stated in terms of an impossible physiology that involved the readiness of neurones to conduct and to make connections. For our purposes the law can be restated to incorporate the importance of attention and/or motivation for learning, because what

Thorndike was really describing was a preparedness, a "set," for making the next response in a sequence. Fulfillment of such preparations was considered satisfying; failure of fulfillment was annoying. While Thorndike was not at that time thinking of *capacity* or readiness in terms of growth and development, there is no harm done to his thinking if we incorporate such a capacity aspect in the *Law of Readiness*. We can then note that in the puzzle-box situation the cat had to be able to do what was required in the situation. It had to have the capacity to perform the desired response. To be sure that someone can learn to do something, we must be sure that he is likely to engage in the necessary activity. He must be big enough, strong enough, old enough, and in the proper state of motivation. In the experimental demonstration just described, you can be fairly certain that the cat is hungry, that it is likely to catch its claw in a dangling string, and that it has the appropriate sensory equipment for the satisfier to affect it.

The first law, that of *Effect,* is perhaps the most important for teachers and amounts to an abbreviation of what was suggested above: that learning depends on the consequences of behavior. If the behavior is followed by satisfiers, it will be "stamped in"; if it is followed by annoyers, it will be "stamped out."

This stamping in or stamping out of behavior involves the concept of neural action as did Pavlov's conditioning. But unlike Pavlov, who postulated various processes of "irradiation" and "concentration" in the cerebral hemispheres, Thorndike presumed that the central nervous system was a static connecting system: connections or "bonds" exist between sensory neurons and motor or action neurons. Behavior thus amounts to the initiation of motor activity as a consequence of sensory stimulation. Thorndike thought of the units of behavior as distinct stimulus-bond-response patterns, which can be summarized in the formula

$$S \longrightarrow R$$

where the arrow represents a connection or bond joining the stimulus S and the response R. Thorndike never gave a satisfactory explanation of why a satisfying aftereffect would strengthen and an annoying aftereffect weaken a bond.

In later years Thorndike modified his original *Law of Effect*. He had decided that the negative side of the law did not really work—that is, that punishment did not weaken bonds. Following some experiments of a rather equivocal nature, he came to the conclusion (Thorndike, 1932) that if punishment had any effect at all, it was not to weaken old bonds but rather to force the learner to try other responses that might be strengthened by rewards. His experiments were not especially convincing as they involved saying "wrong" to college students who were trying to *guess* the meanings of foreign words or what number (from 1 to 10) should "go with" some word in a purely chance situation. That the student felt any chagrin, remorse, or pain at being told he was "wrong" seems dubious. Yet, despite the inadequacy of the research, Thorndike's conclusions were rather generally accepted. For his part, he eliminated the punishment half of the *Law of Effect* and took a more positive approach: *Only rewards can bring about learning.*

As a result of his numerous experiments on number-guessing by college students, Thorndike came to believe that if an individual is in a situation where he makes a *series* of responses and only one of these is rewarded, other responses close in time to the rewarded response will also be learned to some degree. Thus if an individual makes seven responses in a situation and the fourth response is rewarded, then the third and fifth responses are likely to enjoy the benefits of the reward, and perhaps to a lesser extent so will the second and sixth responses—even if all these responses had been punished by "wrong." Thorndike named this finding the *Spread of Effect*. It was a highly controversial principle and was widely criticized, but L. Postman (1962), after reviewing all the critical studies, seems satisfied that it has some merit.

Implications of Thorndike's Laws

Thorndike's laws of learning involve certain assumptions that need to be spelled out.

The first of these is that learning is blind, dumb, and mechanical. The animal appears to react at random; one random reaction is followed by the attainment of a satisfier. The animal need not, in fact does not and cannot, "understand" the relationship between the stimuli, the responses, and the effects. In the Thorndike puzzle box there is little for the animal to "understand"; it cannot even see the pulleys and the connection of the string with the door.

The second assumption is that responses are not really random. The organism is born with a repertoire of responses that are likely to occur in given situations. When one of these is rewarded, the bond between the S and that R is strengthened. Thus, in contrast to Pavlov who found learning to be a substitution of one stimulus for another, Thorndike found learning to be a substitution of one response for another. Unless we are willing to accept the existence of two kinds of learning, one of these men (if not both) is wrong.

Other Thorndikian Laws

Over the years Thorndike experimented with various kinds of animals and college students and came up with a number of additional principles or beliefs that are of some interest but not of great practical value. For example, he proposed a principle of *Belongingness* as of importance in the formation of connections. If a stimulus and a response "belonged" together, a connection could be quickly learned. What makes stimuli and responses belong together Thorndike never spelled out. He suggested as an illustration that first names "go with" last names better than last names go with other last names. Perhaps for fifth-grade boys baseball batting averages go with decimals. While some kinds of evidence can be mustered in its support, the principle of *Belongingness* is difficult, if not impossible, to apply in education with any foresight (if some connections turn out to be learned poorly, we might argue that the stimuli and responses do not "belong" with each other) and needs no further consideration here.

Another Thorndikian suggestion was that of *Vividness* or *Prepotency*. Those items or elements in a stimulus situation that stand out or are especially exciting will be more quickly incorporated into behavior or learned than will less noticeable elements. For some species there may be a selective aspect or attention-getting aspect to stimulus elements that would not attract other species. Such a principle may have some *post facto* virtue in explaining why something was learned, but it has little practical value for teachers who can hardly make every stimulus item vivid, prepotent, or exciting.

A third principle, that of *Associative Shifting*, is actually a recognition on the part of Thorndike that some learning involves stimulus substitution and not response substitution. By including this principle, Thorndike, without recognizing Pavlovian conditioning, actually admitted that some learning goes on which, in effect, amounts to conditioning. According to Thorndike's description, some responses that occur in varying situations may eventually come to occur in situations that did not originally call them out. The procedure for bringing about such learning calls for slowly changing the stimulus situation by additions and subtractions of stimulus components while the desired behavior is maintained. Eventually the response may occur in a new stimulus situation. Thorndike used his principle of *Associative Shifting* to account for the ability of learners to solve new problems rapidly on the basis of past experience. Because it is essentially a principle of conditioning, which has already been discussed, this principle need detain us no longer.

Summary of Thorndike's Views

Although Thorndike continued to revise and extend his views throughout his long and distinguished career in education, he remains identified by his emphasis on the original laws of *Readiness, Exercise,* and *Effect.* Actually, the modifications he introduced made both *Readiness* and *Exercise* rather meaningless and unimportant propositions and left only the *Law of Effect* to carry the burden of explanation of learning. Even the *Law of Effect* was drastically modified by the elimination of the punishment component.

What remains from Thorndike's writings is an emphasis on learning as a function of rewards. Rewards, if given immediately, would increase the probability that the response performed just before the reward was given would be given again in the same situation.

Perhaps the more important feature of Thorndike's thinking was his emphasis on the chance or accidental nature of the responses that do occur. Learners learn by trying one response after another. Some of these responses are successful, others are not. No attention is given to the other aspects of a response (how logical it might be, how appropriate, or how sensible). All that matters is that the response is successful, and this is a matter of social decision. The experimenter or teacher (society) decides whether a response is to be rewarded or not—that is, whether it is to be considered successful. All that the learner can do is try blindly and make errors until he finally does what has been decided by others to be right. Thorndike's emphasis on "trial and error and chance success" makes out of learning a blind, mechanical process that leaves no room for "insight," "understanding," or "intelligence."

PRACTICAL APPLICATIONS OF THORNDIKE'S THEORIES

Although he played a leading role in the development of American education, Thorndike's success as an educator cannot be traced to any immediate practical applicability of his theoretical writings. Such applicability as there is consists largely of matters of attitude or approach (for example, treating learning as problem-solving). Much of the advice to teachers is negative—that is, teachers are told what not to do. This section will point out for teachers possible uses of his laws of *Exercise, Readiness,* and *Effect,* and, in addition, have something to say about his theory of intelligence and how this affects educational philosophy.

Exercise

In the discussion of the *Law of Exercise* it was pointed out how practice must be differentiated from mere repetition. Teachers sometimes assume that writing out something "50 times" somehow insures learning. Unless such repetition is accompanied by satisfiers or rewards, the mere repetition will presumably be ineffective. It can, of course, produce fatigue, irritation, and negative emotional effects. A first practical rule or suggestion then might be:

Make sure that every time a correct response occurs some kind of satisfier or reward follows.

In a later chapter you will see that some kinds of behavior will persist longer if rewards are occasionally skipped. For the present it is enough to recognize that sheer repetition is probably a meaningless activity without educational merit.

Readiness

A learner must be ready to learn. Thorndike's rather vague principle of Readiness means that the response which is desired is indeed available and likely to occur. The organism is mature enough to make the response and is not in some condition (tired, asleep, sick) that will prevent the occurrence of the response. It also means that various prerequisites have been met. In general, the principle of *Readiness* means that one does not try to teach an organism a response it cannot make. If chimpanzees, for example, do not possess the neural structure necessary to produce human-like vocalizations, they cannot be taught human speech.

You must remember that Thorndike's concept was not the current, widely accepted maturational interpretation of readiness. The latter view has been imposed on Thorndike's view, which really was concerned with attention. If you keep in mind that we are dealing with a learner's attitudes and sets, his preparation for reacting to presented stimuli, and his current state (in a sense we are asking: Is the learner ready to pay attention to this material?), no real difficulty will arise from the present practice of identifying readiness with capacity as a function of age or growth.

The principle of *Readiness* is extremely tenuous and circular. If an organism learns, it is or was ready. If it does not, perhaps it was not ready. The most satisfactory meaning to be found in the *Readiness* principle is that teachers must be sure that a response is available before they start to teach. Sometimes the question of readiness concerns limitations on the part of the teacher and not on the part of the learner. We cannot normally teach children to read until they reach the age of five. We say that they are not ready until they reach that chronological level. Yet, as was pointed out on page 8, some teachers have succeeded with three-year-olds, by using special methods. If *no* method will result in success then the organism may not be ready. I have to be cautious even when I make this statement, because new methods may be discovered by which the response can be made to occur.

The success of new methods of teaching reading to youngsters has led to some rather strong criticism of the *Readiness* principle. Jerome Brunner (1960, p. 32), for example, states "We begin with the hypothesis that any subject can be taught effectively in some intellectually honest form to any child at any stage of development." Brunner, himself, calls this a "bold" hypothesis and certainly does not wish to suggest that chemistry can be taught to a day-old infant. What "intellectually honest" means may be difficult to define. There is always some danger in letting children think they are studying biology when they are only feeding rabbits. There may be even more danger, in terms of efficiency, when children are taught certain skills before they need to learn them or before they have actually matured to the point where the learning has been efficient.

Psychologists today sometimes overlook the extensive work done in the 1930s in the area of *maturation*. Many researchers were able to show that babies and youngsters could be taught or otherwise "trained" to do little exercises like stair-climbing, roller-skating, use of scissors, and various games. Untrained (control) children might not do well if tested along with the trained children, but the almost uniform finding was that the now older, untrained children could learn to perform to equal levels of efficiency in a much shorter time. The study of B. D. Wood and F. N. Freeman (1932) is a sharp reminder for those curriculum enthusiasts who are urging the introduction of early training in skills and subjects on the grounds that these *can* be learned. Wood and Freeman describe a program in the teaching of typing in the primary grades. Second-graders were able to type after a fashion, but not so well as fifth-graders after one year of practice. The important finding, however, was that after two years of practice, children were no better than their age mates who had been given only one year of practice.

In concluding this consideration of *Readiness* I suggest that mere capacity for performing at some rather ineffective level is no reason to institute training, if such training is going to be largely wasted. Waiting until the capacity for benefiting from training is at a higher level might be far more suitable. There probably is no great need for nursery tots to be reading the latest best-sellers; perhaps they should be mixing mudpies, but in the latter case, they should not be described as "taking" elementary chemistry.

The difficulty with this suggestion is that we do not really have available catalogues of ages and maturity periods that spell out what any individual is ready to learn efficiently. We do not even know what efficient learning would be at particular ages. Until research answers such questions I might hedge my suggestion by a somewhat more permissive statement: Students should be permitted to try their hands at any legitimate study for which they show inclinations, and they should be permitted to continue *if they can match the progress of those selected for such studies by current methods.* Such permission, however, should not be granted at the expense of other requirements. Typing is not a substitute for geography, nor is reading a substitute for tying one's shoes.

Effects

The *Law of Effect* was by far the most important emphasis or principle introduced by Thorndike. Regardless of theoretical problems and interpretations of how rewards work in learning, American learning psychologists have generally agreed that rewards *do* work. Because of this agreement, the practical suggestion having some popular support among learning psychologists in general can be advanced:

If you want someone to learn something, wait until he does it and then reward him.

Because Thorndike defined his satisfiers (or rewards) so loosely, he was quite safe (and circular) in concluding that learning occurs only if a reward is supplied *after* the desired behavior occurs. Cats are rewarded by fish and milk. Humans are rewarded by being told they are good, smart, correct, and so on. Thorndike was the first learning psychologist to include "knowledge of results" as a reward. Of course, for him this meant "knowledge of being correct." Such knowledge was considered a satisfier because it was effective with college students in the way that fish is effective with a cat. Similarly, when a dog learns and the only reward is a pat on the head or a "good dog," such effects are taken to be satisfiers. The impact of Thorndike's reward psychology was to make learning a function of pleasant student-teacher relationships, of permissiveness, of the introduction of a whole range and variety of rewards, awards, stars, pins, and honors. Punishment was ruled out, and the teacher was left with only one device: the reward.

Rewards must be immediate. Thorndike emphasized as a practical, empirically supported operation the practice of immediate reward. A reward will be ineffective if even a few seconds intervene between the desired response and the presentation of the reward. You will find this emphasis on immediacy expressed by virtually all theorists. It may be important on the animal level, but on the human side, with the capacity for labeling and the ubiquity of knowledge of results, the operation of the principle becomes slightly less clear. Thorndike based his conclusion on results from line-drawing experiments. A blindfolded subject would be asked to draw a four-inch line. Immediately after the subject stopped drawing, Thorndike would announce "right" or "wrong." Subjects in such situations learned. When the announcement was withheld for 10 or 20 seconds, no learning occurred. Recently it has been shown, however, that subjects can and do learn in just such situations even if the reward is withheld for 20 seconds (Bilodeau, E., Bilodeau, I., and Schumsky, D. A., 1959).

We will return to this principle again, but in the meantime a practical rule is:

Reward immediately any desirable response in the teaching situation.

An illustration of the efficacy of immediate reward is learning music. If the student has an "ear," he knows immediately whether or not he is playing the right note. A student who does not know that a note is correct will never make a musician.

It is recognized, of course, that to reward immediately one must be there, at the elbow of the performer, so to speak, ready to reward as soon as the desirable response occurs. The necessity for immediate rewards appears to demand individual instruction. Actually, a whole group can be rewarded if every member makes the response at the same time. Such group learning and reward occur when the learners chant in unison. Group learning can also occur when one person recites or performs and everyone else in the group is attentive and reciting silently. In a spelling class, for example, if one pupil is called on to recite, the rest should be told to write or recite quietly. The reward of "right" can then be shared by the whole class. Such a procedure creates the problem of attention control, but this is a separate problem and need not detain us here.

The principle of immediacy of rewards means, of course, that whatever rewards are given to students at graduation exercises or at the end of the month, week, day, or even minute are of no value whatsoever as far as having any bearing on the learning. Gold stars or honor rolls or any other kind of delayed recognition may have value for other reasons. Perhaps they are *motivational* agents. They are not rewards of the kind that can strengthen learning. This conclusion is not meant to suggest the elimination of gold stars or blue ribbons. If such devices are used, the teacher should know why he is using them. He is not rewarding any specific learning as such.

Avoid the trap created by the Spread of Effect. The reader will recall that it is possible for the effects of a reward to spread over some time preceding and following the desired behavior. If a learner has been engaged in a series of steps and finally has attained a goal after an error or two, the introduction of reward may strengthen not only the correct response but also any erroneous behavior that took place in the temporal vicinity of the reward. The best way to avoid such a spread of effect is for the teacher to space out the steps in learning so that undesired responses do not benefit from a subsequent reward. It is also desirable for the teacher to delay introducing any new activity just after a reward; if an error occurs in the new task, it may be learned because of the persisting effect from the previous reward. The teacher must know what it is that he is rewarding.

Do not punish learners if your intention is to weaken some habit. Only reward is effective in producing learning. If punishment is used at all, it should be directed toward forcing the learner to try other responses, one of which will be rewarded. Punishing the learner and leaving the situation at that will achieve nothing.

Intelligence

Thorndike styled himself a "connectionist." He meant by this that he considered that learning resulted from the strengthening of connections or bonds in the brain. If an individual has the right experiences (and this is a matter of luck), he will strengthen more connections, or at least different ones, than persons who do not have the right experiences. The more we learn, the more connections we have, and the more connections (of the right and useful kind) we have, the more educated and intelligent we are.

In his work on intelligence-testing and vocabulary-building, Thorndike emphasized the value of words. The more words one could use appropriately (the bigger one's vocabulary), the more intelligent one was. While this view may strike some readers as limited, it should be obvious that the person with the greater vocabulary in any given sphere is better equipped *technically* to work in that area. An auto mechanic who can accurately define a carburetor is more intelligent about carburetors than a professor of philosophy who can only point to that "gadget" or "thingamajig." The chemist's vocabulary of chemical terms enables him to work effectively in a chemical laboratory. He might be quite stupid in a biology laboratory if his vocabulary there is limited. Besides vocabulary, Thorndike, in studying intelligence, also tested for completion of sentences, arithmetical skills, and ability to follow directions but loaded these sub-tests with verbal-usage skills. Intelligence, for Thorndike, was a matter of how many words the learner knew, and this, in turn, depended on how often the learner had been rewarded for using appropriate terminology.

Whether or not one uses correct terminology is itself a matter of learning or experience. If one is rewarded for using a precise vocabulary one will, in this sense, learn to be intelligent about at least those areas in which correct terminology is employed. If teachers are content with some vague approximation and allow saying it "in your own words," there will be little or no student advancement in either knowledge or intelligence. One quickly runs out of his own words. I am not suggesting here that students should not be asked to state or restate various propositions in different ways—only that they should not be credited with real knowledge when they do not really have an appropriate grasp. A student who has a "rough idea" cannot be expected to perform effectively. Sometimes teachers give credit or partial credit for using the right method even if the answers are wrong because of computational or other errors. Such rewarding for ineffective work strengthens the habit of disregard for precision. Teachers who practice such methods do not appreciate the impact of Thorndike's basic principles and apparently believe that somehow the student will sooner or later rise above himself through the operation of some mysterious or miraculous agencies. Nothing could be more un-Thorndikian. For Thorndike there is nothing mysterious or miraculous about learning. Students learn what they have been rewarded for doing. If they have not been rewarded, they will not learn.

At this time it might be profitable to remind you that in Thorndike's view learning is a blind, mechanical result of the functioning of rewards. Students learn if they are rewarded and do not learn if they are not. The student deserves absolutely no credit for what he knows and, correspondingly, he deserves no blame if he is slow, stupid, and unknowing. Many teachers are fond of taking credit for the work of their good students even if they really had nothing to do with the achievements of these people. At the same time they absolve themselves of any responsibility for the dull and failing students. Such remarks as the following are common enough in teacher circles: "You just can't pound anything into his head" or "She's bound to fail if she doesn't straighten out." For Thorndike such remarks would be a confession of inadequacy on the part of the teacher and an admission that the teacher really had no comprehension of his role. A student is stupid because he has not been taught to be bright.

From the discussion of intelligence presented above, a final practical rule can be derived from Thorndike's writings.

Do not be content with rough approximations where specific answers or responses are essential for subsequent success.

In other words, do not hope for intelligence to generate spontaneously. Intelligence must be taught, and, even after it has been taught, it will operate blindly.

PAVLOV AND THORNDIKE: A COMPARISON

When we considered Pavlov's work I pointed out how the desire on Pavlov's part to study physiology objectively led to his objective psychology and to the emphasis on environment as determining changes in behavior. The fact that the Soviet government adopted Pavlov's views as supporting its own ideology was also mentioned. The views of Thorndike are not so different as one might imagine. Thorndike, too, was in search of an objective methodology, even though his major work was done before the advent of the Behaviorists. For Thorndike, learning was a blind, mechanical matter of chance. If one were lucky and if the environment were favorable, learning would occur as a matter of chance successes.

The only real difference between Thorndike's procedures and those of Pavlov were that Thorndike approached the problem in a typically American way: he arranged a situation in which learning could occur and then left it strictly up to the learner. It does not appear to be stretching the point if we say that Thorndike was following a philosophy of rugged individualism in his laboratory work. Where Pavlov, in essence, forced his dogs to salivate, Thorndike left it up to the cats to pull strings or not to pull. Whether this difference in laboratory procedure was really a meaningful difference I have questioned elsewhere (Bugelski, 1956), but it does represent a difference in viewpoint that might be paralleled on a much higher level of national ideologies. In any event, although two different schools of thought developed around the views of Pavlov and Thorndike, both theorists can be described as objectivistic and as believing in learning as the necessary result of environmental manipulation. Pavlov manipulated stimuli; Thorndike manipulated rewards.

In the next chapter the followers of Thorndike will be considered. In Chapter 4 we will return to examine the work of Pavlov's "psychological descendants." Later chapters will take up more eclectic contributors to the psychology of learning in different contexts.

Chapter Three

The
Thorndike
Tradition

By the early 1930s, Thorndike's interest in learning theory had begun to wane. He had taken the *Law of Effect* about as far as it would go and more and more was preoccupied with other activities. His interests in dictionaries and word books are well known; less familiar are his studies in numismatics and other somewhat esoteric matters that may be found in his extensive bibliography of more than three hundred titles. If learning theory was to prosper, then someone else would have to take up the task, and that someone appeared almost immediately.

THE POSTULATES OF C. L. HULL

The outstanding learning theorist in the United States during the 1930s and 1940s was Clark L. Hull (1884–1952). While Hull was not directly concerned with applications of learning, he was intensely concerned with building a general theory of behavior. He felt a strong need to affiliate psychology with physiology and also an equal need to make progress rapidly. For the latter reason, he decided to risk falling into error (so long as the errors could be discovered and corrected) by setting up a *deductive* procedure of theory-building. A deductive theoretical system amounts to a set of postulates[1] that can be logically arranged to develop theorems (as in Euclid's geometry). Hence, Hull built up a theory from a set of postulates or hypotheses that described the more-or-less factual generalizations he could make about behavior. Because psychology was not sufficiently developed to provide the necessary basic laws in the decades of his activity, Hull felt justified in guessing at their nature and stating them as if they were true, knowing of course that they would have to be proved by experiments that would establish the truth of the deduced theorems. Hull postulated (guessed at the nature of) about eighteen such laws that he thought would cover the area of his interests.

[1] For Hull, postulates were guessed-at laws.

Hull believed that it was possible to reconcile the views of Pavlov and Thorndike, because he saw the great overlap in the generalizations drawn by these two geniuses. He and his students (R. E. P. Youtz, 1938; D. G. Ellson, 1938) were able to show that many Pavlovian principles could be demonstrated in Thorndikian situations, for example, generalization, discrimination, extinction, spontaneous recovery. Indeed, Hull believed that Pavlov's situation was really only a *special case* of Thorndikian learning, because what Pavlov described as an unconditioned stimulus (usually food) was also and really operating as a reward. Pavlov had ignored the reward feature, and Hull saw this as a major error on the part of Pavlov. Hull proceeded to describe Thorndikian principles in more-or-less Pavlov-like language in his various sets of postulates. Many of these are of no concern to this book, and the immediate aim of this section is to show that Hull thought of himself as a somewhat more scientific objectifier of Thorndike.

Primary Reinforcement

In his famous postulate dealing with primary reinforcement, Hull (1943) restated Thorndike's *Law of Effect* roughly this way: *Whenever a response is closely followed by a diminution of a drive or a drive stimulus, there will be an increment in the strength of the bond between the response and the stimulus (or stimuli) present at the time the response is initiated.*

Underlying this principle of *Primary Reinforcement* are three assumptions that must be appreciated in order later to evaluate some practical applications of Hull's postulates. First, according to Hull's view, there will be no learning unless a drive (some physiological need) is reduced, and for a drive to be reduced, a drive must be present. Consequently, motivation is fundamental to learning and must be established first. How motivation is to be established on a human level is a problem. With animals it is only necessary to deprive them. We will return later to this problem of establishing motivation, because it is of major importance.

The second assumption is that a drive need not be fully eliminated. It need only be diminished. Nothing is said about how much it needs to be reduced. Turning this around, we recognize that rewards for learning need not be large or magnificent. Even a tiny reward will do, although we do not really know what we mean by "tiny."

A third assumption is that the learning will proceed in increments—that is, by steps of some unspecified size. The size of the steps might well vary from small to huge, depending on what is to be learned. Hull had the notion that each increment would be in some pattern of relationship to every other. For example, the increments probably would not be equal (most learning "curves" appear to indicate that the major part of the learning occurs in the early stages of practice and that less and less is learned in later trials). Such "negative acceleration" suggested to Hull that perhaps one learns in percentage units. On the first trial one might learn, for example, only 10 percent of the total skill or behavior pattern. On the next trial one would learn 10 percent of what was left to be learned, or 9 percent (10 percent of 90). On the third trial, with 81 percent of the learning to be accomplished, the learner would pick up 10 percent more, or 8.1 percent, and so on. Eventually, the amount learned on the final trials would be too small to notice, even though, according to this view, nothing could ever be learned perfectly.

The Continuity Hypothesis

The view just described can be thought of as a *Continuity Hypothesis*. According to this hypothesis, learning is continuous and cumulative. Every reinforcement adds strength to the learning. Sometimes, as with small children, when we fail to see any learning taking place in spite of our best efforts, the *Continuity Hypothesis* suggests that learning is going on but that the behavior involved is so weak or low in the array of competitive responses that it does not occur as readily as we want it to. In Hull's terms, the response strength is still below a hypothetical threshold. If we can get the behavior to occur and reinforce it (diminish a drive), we will add to its strength on each such occasion, and eventually it will be strong enough to appear first on a test trial. This assumption that learning occurs even when it cannot be seen is difficult for some teachers to accept. There are indirect proofs of the *Continuity Hypothesis,* but this is not the place to investigate them. We can temporarily accept the assumption with suspended judgment.

One implication of the *Continuity Hypothesis* is that there is a regular, progressive increase in any learning process. Logically, we should also expect some decline in the *rate* of increase even though the learning continues. Such speculations are reflected in what is commonly called *the learning curve.* Learning curves when drawn from individual learning data rarely look like the so-called "learning curve" of the textbooks. Individual patterns tend to be erratic with many ups-and-downs. Thorndike's cats showed *more* or *less* regular drops in the time to escape from their puzzle boxes. It is appropriate to emphasize the more or less-ness rather than the regularity.

In recent years psychologists have become disenchanted with the notion of a learning curve. They find that there are too many variables influencing the course of learning. K. J. Hayes (1953) found little reason to believe in the "typical" learning curve. If there is a "typical" curve, it is not like those published in earlier textbooks. The course of learning depends upon what is being learned, the readiness of the learner, various individual difference factors, and such features as the drive state, incentive values, complexity of stimulus situation, and even the features of the performance being measured. K. Spence (1956) has found it necessary and useful to divide learners into slow, medium, and fast groups in order not to distort the *group* learning picture.

At the present time, teachers might well be advised to reserve judgment about the typical curve of learning or its specialized features, such as plateaus that are still fondly described in some textbooks as inevitable stages in the course of learning. A presumed plateau might be an excuse for poor teaching or failure to recognize obstacles to progress.

I would point out here in anticipation of later discussion that these remarks about the learning or acquisition curve apply with equal force to the alleged forgetting curve. There is no more basis for assuming a typical forgetting curve than for its opposite. Again, as will be seen later, there are too many variables involved to permit some preordained course to prevail.

Secondary Reinforcement

Hull formulated another postulate that has more direct bearing on human learning than that which restated Thorndike's Law of Effect. This is his principle of *Secondary Reinforcement*. From the principle of *Primary Reinforcement* we have already learned that any stimulus can become associated with a response that is followed by primary-drive reduction. Such primary reinforcement is presumed to account for most basic kinds of animal or human learning related to bodily needs. It is quite clear, however, that most socially important or academic learning, even in kindergarten, is not learned in terms of primary-drive reduction. Teachers do not reward children with food and water. For human learning we must look for other kinds of reinforcement if we want to stick with a reinforcement principle.

To help solve the human learning problem Hull postulated *Secondary Reinforcement*. According to this principle: *Any stimulus that is present when a primary reinforcer is being supplied will take on the characteristics of the primary reinforcer.* In other, and perhaps simpler, words: If some stimulus is present just before the object or condition (the reward) that reduces the primary drive is presented or attained, that stimulus will take on reinforcement characteristics. To illustrate: If a mother talks to a baby while feeding it, murmuring endearments, these tender words will become secondary reinforcers.[2] Such secondary reinforcers can then add increments to the strength of *S-R* bonds just as primary reinforcers do.

The range and variety of secondary reinforcers is unlimited. For Hull, all that was required was that some stimulus accompany a drive reducer. Any kind of word, noise, light, smell, or other stimulus would serve. A pat on the head, a smile, Thorndike's use of "Right"—all illustrate secondary reinforcers. In a child's history, verbal promises eventually may serve as effectively as real reinforcers. If such promises are not kept, their secondary-reinforcement value will extinguish—and so will any other kind of secondary reinforcement if it is not followed up, at least occasionally, with a primary reinforcer.

A study of I. J. Saltzman (1949) nicely illustrates the operation of secondary reinforcement. Saltzman trained rats to run down a short alley to a goal box. The alley was painted gray; the goal box white. The animals were always fed in the white goal box. Later the same animals were tested in a T-maze situation. They were placed on the starting leg of the T-maze and watched to see if they would turn left or right at the choice point. If they turned left, they would arrive at a black box; if they turned right, they would arrive at the same white goal box in which they previously had been fed. Neither goal box contained any food for the hungry rats. Under these conditions, in 15 test trials, the animals showed a preference for entering the white goal box, even though there was no food reward to be gained. Saltzman concluded that just being in the white box had some positive effect on the animals. Secondary-reinforcement effects of this kind have been demonstrated frequently with animal subjects. On the human level clean-cut demonstrations are almost impossible to arrange because of the difficulty of excluding potential secondary reinforcers. Human subjects beyond the child level normally observe the effects of

---

2 The example of the feeding child is especially pertinent because it is obvious that a "drive" is being reduced. The baby acquires a repertoire of secondary reinforcers even before it begins to talk. Because mothers talk so much while feeding babies, mothers, their voices, and the words they say become powerful secondary reinforcers and last a lifetime.

their own behavior. They usually have "knowledge of results." Such knowledge, as will be seen later, is considered to have secondary-reinforcement value.

Secondary Drive

Just as humans are not given food or water for learning, so they do not learn academic material because of hunger or thirst drives. Yet Hull felt impelled to pursue the principle that there must be a drive if learning is to take place. He found it convenient to assume a postulate of learned or "derived" drives; he thus paralleled his principle of *Secondary Reinforcement* with a principle of *Secondary Drive.* To describe this, Hull merely indicated that: *Any stimulus that is present at the time a primary drive is activated (and rapidly reduced) can take on the properties of the basic drive and serve as a basis for future learning.* Thus, if some neutral stimulus precedes some painful stimulus (a drive of pain is presupposed), that neutral stimulus will come to cause a drive that functions like pain. In this case, it is assumed that pain is accompanied by an emotional reaction (fear) and that this fearful reaction will then be aroused by the stimulus that accompanied pain. Fear of fire or sharp knives would illustrate such a derived drive of fear. Sometimes Hull referred to this fear as "anxiety," reserving "fear" for the direct reaction to a painful or harmful stimulus.

The reader is reminded that Hull found it highly useful and necessary to include both secondary drives and secondary reinforcers in his system. Without them, he would have been helpless to handle the problem of human learning. As mentioned above, it is obvious that people cannot be starved like rats in order to get them to learn, nor do we feed human learners in order to reinforce correct responses.

Reactive Inhibition

Besides the postulates of primary-drive reduction and secondary reinforcement and secondary drive, Hull's postulate of *Reactive Inhibition* (I_R) has some interest for teachers. According to this, every action results in the generation of some negative aftereffect, analogous to fatigue. Every time a muscle is contracted, some degree of presumed *Reactive Inhibition* substance or state is developed. If the action is repeated, this negative state builds up cumulatively until it is there in sufficient strength to prevent any further reaction. The learner must rest. During the rest *Reactive Inhibition* presumably dissipates. If there is not enough rest between trials or performances to dissipate accumulated I_R, any stimuli that are present will become conditioned to the resting response because the *Reactive Inhibition* functions as a drive. This drive is reducible by rest or by doing nothing. Such nonaction or inactivity, because it is followed by drive reduction, can be conditioned to the stimuli present that originally initiated the response involved. In this way, a learner who is pushed beyond a certain stage of fatigue or I_R will learn to make resting responses rather than the responses we want him to learn.

Other Concepts Developed by Hull

Hull developed some interesting concepts that were not strictly tied to his systematic postulates. Three of these—the *Goal Gradient,* the *Fractional-antedating Response,* and the *Habit-family Hierarchy*—should be considered here because they have some practical applications.

The *Goal Gradient hypothesis* may be expressed simply: *The closer the learner approaches a goal, the more active (eager?) he becomes.* For Hull, the important point was that in a sequence the responses that were closest in time to the reinforcement were most effectively learned. Responses earlier in the sequence were thought to be reinforced also, but the delay in reinforcement prevented their developing great strength. There have been various disputes and alternate views about the *Goal Gradient.* For this book, the importance of this hypothesis by Hull lies in the notion that sequences are, in a sense, learned backward, the last steps being learned first and best, and so on, back toward the beginning. According to this, we have an interesting paradox. The first step in a sequence is the last to be learned.

Hull's *Fractional-antedating Response,* or r_g in Hull's notation,[3] is of more general interest for teachers. According to Hull, learning is evidenced by the antedating nature of behavior. We know somebody has learned something if he does it before he is prompted or pushed or otherwise forced to produce the response. In learning a foreign vocabulary, for example, the learner may have to look at the translation a number of times after the stimulus word is presented. Later he responds correctly without looking it up. If he has to look it up, it obviously has not been learned. All learned behavior has this antedating quality. In Pavlov's experiments, the dog began to salivate sooner and sooner after the bell was sounded until finally it salivated *before* the food was presented. At this

[3] The r_g is thought of as *part* of a major or final goal response or R_G. Hull pronounced r_g as "Little Argie."

point we say the dog has learned. Hull argued that in most, if not all, learning this kind of antedating occurs. There may be tendencies to do *parts* of the final response (the goal behavior or R_G) before it is necessary or even desirable. Thus, "there is many a slip 'twixt cup and lip" simply means that we started to drink before the cup was brought to the final position. In typing a word like *t-h-e*, I may type *h-t-e* because I am, to some degree, antedating the goal response. Hull believed that any part or fraction of a goal response could and would come forward in time as learning developed. A Pavlovian dog would not only salivate but would begin to chew, swallow, and smack its lips before the food arrived. Such fractional-antedating goal responses are of great importance for explaining many aspects of behavior. For Hull, they were "surrogates" (substitutes) for ideas, thoughts, wishes, impulses, foresight, purpose, indeed for knowledge.

The last of Hull's concepts of importance here is the *Habit-family hierarchy,* which he elaborated not only to take care of the basic nature of learning but also to account for the flexibility of behavior. This concept involved an appreciation of three structural-functional aspects or features of the *Habit-family hierarchy,* as follows.

1. Organisms naturally (from birth or through maturation) are likely to vary in their responses to any single stimulus. The variability may be extremely limited, as with a reflex, or quite extensive. The organism may respond in one, two, three, or more ways to any stimulus (see Figure 4). The likelihood of any specific response (without learning) is limited, and each response has its own probability rating. The probable responses can be thought of as comprising a *hierarchy* from high to low probability. In teaching an organism we do not usually try to teach the most probable response; that already is most likely to happen. Education itself really involves only those situations where society has decided that some less-likely response should be performed. To take a crude example, a tickle in the throat would normally (naturally) involve a releasing response in the form of a cough. Society frowns on coughs and requires that the unfortunate victim muffle or stifle the cough with a handkerchief along with a murmured "Pardon me." Such responses are not high in the hierarchy. Learning would amount to reinforcing the selected lower member of a hierarchy until it gained superiority over the several other members, eventually exceeding the most natural in potency. A person who muffles a cough with a handkerchief has been "educated." One who coughs in your face has not. In short, education consists of changing relative positions in a hierarchy.

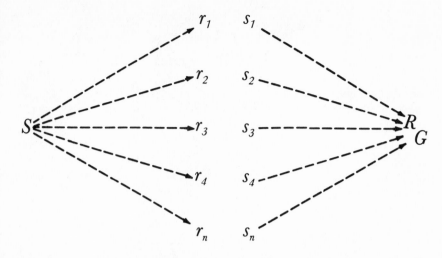

FIGURE 3. *The Habit-family Hierarchy*

A stimulus (*S*) may lead to more than one possible response. On the left, responses are shown as lower case *r*'s because most behavioral acts or responses would involve a chain of successive responses, or steps, along the way toward a final consummatory response, or R_G. The R_G, too, would occur to many of a variety of stimuli generated by the responses occurring earlier in the series. The intervening steps are not shown here.

Note that the originally most-likely-behavior possibility is not lost. It is merely displaced.

2. The second feature of the *Habit-family hierarchy* is observed on the goal end of a sequence of responses. The goal response or "consummatory" response can be arrived at or result from a number of possible alternate pathways or sequences (see upper part of Figure 5). To illustrate simply, it may be possible for you to get to some destination by walking, running, swimming, flying, riding on one of a variety of conveyances, or being carried in a sedan chair or other container. All these alternate ways of arriving at a goal have to be learned separately.

3. In every instance, however, we recognize the fact of the third component, the r_g, which, because it is a part of the common goal, will be the same for every different alternate route or method. Such r_g's make the *Habit-family hierarchy* a true family because all sequences follow the same initial stimulus and have the same final goal and have a common (family-tie) component, the r_g (see Figure 5).

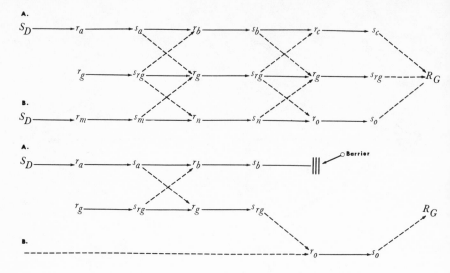

FIGURE 4. *A Two-member Habit-family Hierarchy*

The upper portion of this Figure shows two separate ways, or paths, leading from a stimulus to a goal response. Assume that S_D represents some drive or need for a drink of water. Such a drive generates stimuli that in the normal course of life will lead to various ways of securing the desired drink. Consider method A. The drive stimulus evokes the response of going to a sink (r_a). This response arouses stimuli from the sight of the sink and water tap (s_a). These stimuli lead to turning on the tap (r_b). The flowing water is a stimulus (s_b) for holding a cup under the tap (r_c). The sight of the filled cup leads to drinking (R_G). On another occasion, B., the need for a drink occurs at some spring or brookside and initiates going to the brook (r_m). The sight of the water (s_m) leads to dipping the hand in the brook (r_n), which, in turn, generates the stimuli of feeling the water and seeing the hand in the water (s_n). These stimuli lead to r_o—cupping the hand. The sight of the cupped hand of water (s_o) leads to drinking (R_G).

The lower portion of the Figure shows what can happen if sequence A. is blocked or interrupted. Suppose that s_b, the stimulus for reaching for a cup, cannot initiate r_c. There is no cup. Instead of giving up, the experienced individual readily reacts with r_o, because the same stimulus (r_g) has been conditioned to both r_c and r_o. The r_g's and their action-produced stimuli Sr_g have become conditioned to both members of the hierarchy in that the r_g's have come forward in time and occurred at the same time that other stimuli, both external and response-produced, have been occurring in previous drinking experiences. Because the r_g's are common to both members of the habit-family they provide the means by which one can solve a problem by another route if a first, more preferred method does not or cannot work.

Some further points about the r_g need to be noted. "Little Argie" is, first of all, a response. As such it can be conditioned to other stimuli. Second, like any response, it generates stimuli from its own action. Such response-produced stimuli are stimuli in their own right and can become attached, as conditioned stimuli, to other responses. Third, once such r_g's are aroused, their stimuli can (because the r_g is common to several sequences) initiate any sequence at all in the hierarchy. In short, it is quite possible (see lower part of Figure 5) to start some action and take one route and find that you have switched over, in midstream as it were, to another that is just as good or better. While man may be a creature of habit, his habits, if he has enough of them, can provide considerable flexibility and even apparent ingenuity if he has the proper background. To illustrate, you might find yourself in need of a match (really in need of a small controlled flame). Not having a match might settle the issue if you had a small and inadequate background of experience with heat and flame. A more experienced (in this area) person could use an electric light bulb to light his cigarette by having suitable r_g's and their stimuli associated with heat from light bulbs.

PRACTICAL APPLICATIONS OF HULL'S POSTULATES

Hull's output was tremendous, and if the practical applications that follow seem few, I can only remind you that Hull almost studiously avoided the practical. He was too concerned with arriving at general laws to worry over immediate returns in the classroom. In the following pages, however, his work may prove to have been more applicable than he would have admitted. Remember, too, that others have built on Hull, and in later chapters their work will be seen to have greater classroom application.

The Continuity Hypothesis

If we assume that Hull's *Continuity Hypothesis* is substantially correct, as teachers we should not be discouraged at the slowness and even apparent failure of learning. So long as a response is made at least occasionally it can be reinforced and thereby learned. For a specific student, the threshold for a specific response may be extraordinarily high. We should keep on reinforcing every appearance with confident expectancy that eventually the behavior will become stronger. We should continue the practice of evoking the desired behavior, by whatever means, and rewarding the child immediately thereafter. For example, a child should be made to say "Thank you" on every appropriate occasion, even though he does not seem to be learning to do so. The "Thank you" should then be followed by a reward (a smile or a "good boy" will do). Sooner or later the child will say "Thank you" when the conditions call for it.

To take another example that may seem extreme, music students can be trained to recognize piano tones and name these accurately if they are trained intensively. So-called "absolute pitch" seems a natural gift because some people can perform the tone-naming task almost without training, and others because of their slowness are labeled "tone-deaf"; yet the skill is learnable. The required training may be too expensive or time-consuming to merit the bother; this then becomes a question of economics and not of psychology.

Of course, if Hull's *Continuity Hypothesis* is incorrect or inadvisably applied, we will waste much teaching time and energy.

The Habit-Family Hierarchy

With this concept, Hull provides an extremely practical insight into teaching. If learning consists of strengthening a member of a family of responses that response must be there to begin with. We never really learn *to do* anything that we do not already know how to do. All that happens is that we now do it under other than natural conditions, when special stimuli are present. Learning consists of rearranging the probabilities of responses. Instead of doing the most probable thing, the learner is required to do something less probable. If a response has no probability of occurring, learning cannot take place. In short, we cannot teach anyone anything he cannot already do. While this sounds paradoxical, it is really not at all self-contradictory. Elephants cannot be taught to fly by flapping their ears. The flying response is simply not there. Given the appropriate sense organs and response mechanisms, learning can proceed. Learning, then, means that responses we are fully capable of producing come to occur to stimuli that, at first, were more likely to be followed by other responses. If a behavioral routine consists of a sequence or series of responses, then each step involved must be available and learning amounts to the rearrangement of the time sequences in which such responses might normally occur. This may also involve bringing responses under the control of stimuli that are produced by earlier responses (movement-produced stimuli) which do not originally have a high probability of appearance. In terms of a practical approach we can conclude

If there is reason to believe a certain response pattern is possible, that

pattern can be brought under the control of other stimuli—that is, it can
be learned.

As a simple example, a child who can pronounce the letters of the alphabet can be taught to spell.

The *Habit-family hierarchy* concept has another immediately important
application to education. If learning consists of strengthening a lower
member of a hierarchy, then the learning can also be thought of as *displac-
ing* higher members. These higher members, with their greater probability
of occurrence, will prevent learning so long as they keep intruding. In
teaching some new response pattern a double attack can be launched by
the teacher in terms of attempting to extinguish competing habits while
reinforcing the new. One practical possibility is to fatigue the competing
response out of existence while the desired response is reinforced. Another
possibility is physical restraint or prevention of the competing response. If
a child at a piano lesson is sitting in such a fashion as to be unable to
strike the keys in some desired manner, the teacher should eliminate the
competing postural response before worrying about the key striking. In
general, a learner who is preoccupied with something else (for example,
thoughts of baseball instead of spelling) must have the competing activity
eliminated by one means or another before the lesson is started. If this is
not done, the lesson cues or stimuli will become attached to the competing
behavior instead of the lesson.

College teachers of chemistry and physics sometimes complain that students come from high school with incorrect information or shoddy techniques. Frequently they claim that more harm than good has been done
to the student; they must now undo the harm before progress can be made.
Psychology instructors commonly start their courses by trying to discourage students from thinking about behavior in the ways in which they have
been taught by previous experience. In teaching any advanced course a
teacher should start out by testing or otherwise determining what the student already knows and what he *thinks he knows.* If the latter is incorrect
information, the first step in teaching is to eliminate such misinformation.
The golf professional who starts his teaching procedure by helping his
student not to raise his head as he swings the golf club is an excellent
model for any teacher. The golf pro begins by eliminating bad habits.

While this advice to "eliminate the negative" may be nothing new to
teachers and while teachers may be more concerned with *how* to eliminate competing responses, it is necessary to recognize the role of competition. The teacher should not begin to teach without the awareness that
competing responses are more than likely to be present. With animals
this presence may be more obvious than with humans, but even with

humans the wise teacher starts with observations of what the learner does initially or naturally and then begins to eliminate this natural response, if it is a competing one. In a sense, if all competing responses were eliminated, the desired behavior would be all that was left. The anecdote that Michelangelo said he found David locked in the block of marble and all he did was chip away the undesired stone makes the point. The soprano who sings through her nose might benefit by being asked to hold her nose tightly closed to become aware of the nasal effects. High tones might be helped by squeezing parts of the body that are normally held relaxed— this relaxation actually representing a competitive response. A practical observation then is:

The first step in learning is to identify and eliminate competitive responses.

The *Habit-family hierarchy* concept has the additional value of highlighting the importance of teaching a variety of methods for reaching the same general goal. The flexibility and adaptability of humans depends on their being able to "switch horses in midstream." To do this, the other horse must be there. In other words, if we expect our learners to adjust readily to novel situations or to surmount obstacles and difficulties, we must prepare them for such occasions by deliberately instituting alternate routes to goals wherever possible. To teach only one habit, to practice only one routine, results in intellectual rigidity. Foresight and insight on the part of the learner can result only from foresight and insight on the part of the teacher who plans on deliberate instruction in various techniques and methods for achieving certain ends.

A simple illustration of this might be teaching a person to prepare coffee. The learner should be made to brew the drink by percolating, dripping, boiling, steaming, using "instant" mixtures of various kinds, and any other method that is effective. On a later occasion, the learner will not be at a loss because he does not have his automatic electric percolator at hand, or if the electric current has been cut off by a storm.

More practical advice then can be:

Avoid rigidity in teaching. Introduce a variety of techniques for solving problems. Ingenuity can be taught. It does not spring from an empty head.

The Goal Gradient and "Backward Learning"

Many response patterns that we learn consist of a series or chain of separate responses, steps, components, or unit reactions. A child learning to tie bows in his shoelace or, later in life, learning to tie a bow tie goes through a series of separate movements with one movement preparing the stage and supplying the stimuli for the next. Such tasks will be reinforced only at the end of the activity, when the sequence of steps is completed. Under such conditions the reinforcement will be closest in time to the very last movements made. These last movements, then, will be best learned. The early stages will be relatively longer removed from the reinforcement and will be learned less well. The teacher will do well to examine each skill being taught to determine whether it is of any importance that all parts of the task be equally well learned. If so, the earlier phases will require more practice or, perhaps, separate reinforcement.

When a student learns a poem or speech we can expect a similar course of differential learning. The last part will be learned best, the middle part next best, and the beginning only poorly. Of course, if the student does not recite the entire "piece" through on each occasion but stops as soon as he makes a mistake and goes back to the beginning on every such occasion, the beginning will be overlearned while the end will suffer. In either event, it is clear that unless special pains are taken to insure equal practice and equal reinforcement at each step along the way, the learning will be uneven with the end of the operation relatively better learned. It might even be possible with some tasks, for instance, tying a bow, to begin with the end or final action and teach the whole task backward, taking advantage of this goal-gradient effect.

The practical advice we can derive from Hull's concept of backward learning then is:

Determine the relative need for practice at each step in a sequential act and schedule such differential practice, including the separate reinforcement of each step until all parts of the task are equally well learned.

Reactive Inhibition

For teachers, Hull's postulate of *Reactive Inhibition* means that there is a limit to the amount of effective practice at any one time. To continue practicing beyond the point where efficiency is being curtailed by fatigue is folly. Not only are the learners wasting time in the sense of getting less return for the investment of energy, but they are actually learning to avoid the learning situation. The student who tries to study when sleepy will learn to become sleepy in the presence of books. In general, practice periods should be only so long as they are productive. Rests and breaks are important for learning but these, too, should be no longer than required to dissipate the accumulated reactive inhibition. Unfortunately, there are no general rules for identifying the time limits of both work and rest that apply to any individual or any activity. A ten-minute "coffee break" is not unreasonable. For the present we are limited to laboratory results that in general show a greater efficiency in learning when practice is "spaced" (that is, when a rest period is interpolated between work periods) rather than "massed" (continuous practice).

The postulate of *Reactive Inhibition* is intimately related to the practical educational problem of lesson length. At present there is no really meaningful data that can be applied to cover all situations. About all that we can be reasonably sure of is that the 50-minute hour is probably not an appropriate time for any continuous activity. Adults, of course, can carry on for much longer than children. Teachers dealing with groups of children might well introduce "stretch" or exercise periods or change activities when signs of boredom, restlessness, or fatigue appear. A change of activity is often as effective as a rest. In Hull's writings, rests are presumed to reduce or eliminate *Reactive Inhibition,* but there appears to be no objection to some change of activity as a possible eliminator of *Reactive Inhibition* so long as different muscle groups are used. Hence, a practical rule might be

Do not try to teach when the learner is tired, fussy, cranky, sleepy, or otherwise avoiding the learning situation.

This rule, too, may seem no more than common sense, but it is frequently violated by the agitated teacher or parent who is determined to "teach him if it kills me." The anxious student on the night before the final examination pushes himself beyond the point of efficiency in his "cram session." Of course, if he has not studied at all prior to this time, he should cram; he will learn something, in all probability, even if at great expense.

At the beginning of this section, it was mentioned that Hull possibly contributed more to educational wisdom than he himself recognized. His own interests were so strongly theoretical that he tended to concern himself with broad generalizations from which, eventually, more practical theorems could be deduced. Yet the principles discussed above, such as those of continuity and the implied advice of patience with the learner, of extinguishing competing responses, of teaching a variety of methods of problem solving, the principle of *Reactive Inhibition* with emphasis on "spacing"—these all appear very down-to-earth and practical propositions.

The *Habit-family hierarchy,* similarly, seems loaded with meaning for the teacher. It includes the advice to teach only what is teachable and to teach a variety of behavior patterns if "insight" is to be expected. The Goal Gradient principle calls attention to the need for equalizing practice over the component parts of a lesson and for considering the possibility of teaching some patterns or sequences "backward." All these appear to be practical and effective suggestions and meaningful guides for teachers, even if it is impossible to spell out the numbers for each task for each individual. Like Pavlov, Hull had a great respect for individual differences and was careful to include a postulate about them in his systematic theorizing.

THE SYSTEMATIC VIEWS OF SKINNER

The current representative of Thorndike's views is Burrhus F. Skinner (1904–   ). Skinner's (1938) systematic views (he claims that these do not comprise a theory) were developed in the 1930s and thus parallel in time the work of Hull. But, in contrast to Hull who was preoccupied with theoretical problems, Skinner embraced an empirical and practical orientation. For him the important question is: How can behavior be controlled—that is, modified toward different ends?

Skinner has never stayed aloof from values. He has wanted to improve the human condition which, one hundred years after Thoreau, he found still to be one of "quiet desperation." Like Thorndike, Skinner has always been ready to attack practical problems of everyday life to bring about improvements in man's happiness, efficiency, adjustment, and creativity. He has always considered himself a Behaviorist and probably would list himself at least in some ways in the camp of J. B. Watson (who, as the next chapter will show, was also a practically minded man) rather than in that of Thorndike. But Skinner's work can be discussed here because of its basic resemblance to that of Thorndike. Watson had no use for the Thorndikian reward, and the only learning principles he endorsed were *frequency* and *recency.* Today, Skinner's name is virtually synonymous with reward psychology.

The "Reinforcement" Situation

Skinner's views can best be described in terms of his basic laboratory procedure. For studying the control of behavior, he devised a situation in which an animal can perform an operation that it is likely to do; as soon as the desired response is performed, the experimenter presents a reward, or, as Skinner calls it, a "reinforcer." The laboratory situation is much the same as that of Thorndike except that in his original animal experiments Thorndike required his cats to get out of a puzzle box to food on the outside. Skinner arranges for food to be dropped into the box and saves himself the trouble of recapturing the animal for another trial.

In his laboratory at Harvard, Skinner concentrated on two experimental situations. In one, rats were required to push down a lever at one end of a box. Depressing the lever released a small pellet of food automatically. The rat could eat and be ready for another lever-press in an instant. In this way many trials could be observed in a short period. In the other situation, a pigeon could peck at a small target on the wall of a box. Pecking at the target disk would be followed by the introduction of a little food bin into the box for a few seconds. Again an enormous number of trials could be observed in a short period. As Skinner stated it, his concern was to determine the conditions under which the rate of bar-pressing or target-pecking could be changed at the desire of the experimenter.

Before considering what these conditions are, the reader needs to note that Skinner views his work as "operant conditioning" in distinction to the "respondent conditioning" he ascribed to Pavlov. As Skinner sees it, the difference is that in operant conditioning the organism operated on its environment,[4] changing it in some way (such as bringing food into sight), whereas in Pavlov's "respondent" conditioning, the environment (in the form of stimuli) operates on the organism. Skinner believes that most human behavior is of the operant type; that we "emit" responses in various situations; they are not forced out of us or "evoked" as Pavlov's views might suggest.

Skinner is sometimes accused of not being interested in stimuli. Clearly this is not so. He is interested in stimuli but regards them not so much as evocative of behavior as setting a stage on which the behavior can or will occur. A rat might be trained to press a bar, for example, only when a light is turned on. Responses made in the light are reinforced while responses in the dark are not. The animal will eventually press more actively under light conditions than under dark. Skinner holds that the light is not the *cause* of the bar press; it is merely one of the conditions under which the behavior occurs. If the animal does not press in the dark but does so in the light, the light, according to Skinner, is a "discriminative stimulus" or S^D.

---

[4] Operant conditioning is commonly called "instrumental learning" by many learning psychologists, who see the responses as *instrumental* in changing the environment.

Secondary Reinforcement

Like Hull, Skinner made extensive use of the concept of *Secondary Reinforcement*. It will be recalled that Hull defined a secondary reinforcer as a stimulus that had acquired reinforcement characteristics because it had been present at the time a primary reinforcer was functioning. Skinner, too, attributes reinforcement characteristics to stimuli that accompany primary reinforcers. The work of Skinner's supporters led him to make some important modifications of the concept, however, and these should be carefully noted. In the first place, before a stimulus can become a secondary reinforcer it must not only accompany a primary reinforcer, it must precede it. If the stimulus in question occurs *after* a primary reinforcer has been attained, it will not acquire reinforcing properties. The fact that the secondary reinforcer must occur before the primary reinforcer makes it difficult to distinguish such secondary reinforcers from discriminated stimuli. In the illustration in the previous paragraph, for example, the turning on of the light was described as a discriminated stimulus or S^D. Animals would learn to press bars whenever the light was turned on and desist when it was off. If the experimenter now arranges for the animal to turn on the light briefly whenever the bar is pressed, he is likely to find the animal pressing the bar repeatedly even though no primary reinforcer (food) is presented. The animal appears to be working and keeps on working (longer than animals without such lights) because of reinforcing effects of the light.

Whether a stimulus is to be labeled a discriminated stimulus (S^D) or a secondary reinforcer (S^r) then becomes a matter of a procedural distinction. The S^D is presented *before the response;* the S^r is presented *before the primary reinforcer.* The reader will appreciate that the S^D will also and necessarily precede the primary reinforcer. Because of this temporal relationship an S^D can also come to function as an S^r. The reverse operation, that of an S^r coming to function as an S^D, is presumably impossible by definition, although, in practice, it might be difficult to determine just what was the role of a given stimulus. Confusion can be avoided if we remember that it is possible to arrange for one stimulus, say a light to serve as an S^D and a buzzer, bell, or any of a large number of possible different stimuli to function as S^r's.

The Role of Punishment

Skinner has consistently decried the use of punishment or "aversive stimulation" as a means of behavior control. He believes that positive reinforcement is a far more effective operation without undesirable side effects.

Skinner argues that the only real effect of punishment is to temporarily "suppress" a response. No permanent weakening of the punished behavior has taken place, and, when the suppression effect wears off as it is bound to do in time, the behavior will recur.

Perhaps the best way to appreciate Skinner's views on punishment is to contrast it with that of Hull. Suppose that some experimental animal is given an electric shock after some response in some situation or in the presence of some otherwise innocuous stimulus. For Hull, the shock would be a primary-drive inducer, the drive itself being pain. Any stimulus accompanying the shock stimuli, it will be recalled, would take on secondary-drive-inducing characteristics and presumably come to arouse drives that accompany pain, presumably fear or anxiety. Because Skinner did not wish to treat behavioral problems in terms of drives or other hypothetical internal conditions, he had a problem in handling such stimuli as those that accompany shocks. The problem was solved by classifying stimuli from which animals withdraw or retreat "aversive" stimuli. All punishment situations are considered "aversive." Any stimulus that accompanies the onset of some aversive stimulus might take on the properties of the aversive stimulus it accompanies; it would thus parallel the procedure for the development of secondary reinforcers. Because the stimuli are followed by avoidance behavior, such stimuli are labeled "secondary aversive stimuli." In Skinner's usage, the removal or disappearance of a secondary aversive stimulus can be reinforcing.

Skinner, it should be pointed out, bases his views of punishment on a series of rat lever-pressing studies (Estes, 1944). At first, a rat was reinforced for pressing the lever. Later, the lever was so wired that touching it would result in a shock to the rat. The rat usually withdrew quickly and stayed away from the lever for various periods of time depending in length upon the strength and frequency of the shocks. Sooner or later, however, the rat returned to the lever and pressed again. Because of such returns, Skinner argues that the behavior has merely been *suppressed* and has not been eliminated. When the punishment was no longer continued, the rat began to press again as if nothing had happened. Of course, if the shock were sufficiently strong and continuously applied, the behavior could be suppressed more or less permanently.

The Emphasis on Responses

The basic emphasis in Skinner's work is on the response. How to control and manipulate conditions that will alter response rates is the only real question. The stimulus feature, while important (see above, the S^D), is secondary. The important factor is the response itself. If this occurs, then, says Skinner, a reinforcement will increase the probability of its repetition or recurrence. If a reinforcer is not supplied, then the probability will remain unchanged. If a response has been reinforced in the past and now reinforcement is withheld, the response will tend to drop in probability or *extinguish*. The crucial events according to Skinner's psychology are the occurrence of a response and the immediate consequences —that is, reinforcement or failure of reinforcement. The teacher, by manipulating reinforcements, can bring behavior of many kinds under control.

Conditions for Behavior-rate Changes

What are some of the conditions under which Skinner has determined that behavior rates can be altered? With animals, the first of these is *deprivation*. Before a rat or pigeon can be trained, it must first be deprived of food or water. This, of course, is what makes food or water a reward or reinforcer. In general, we might suppose that all reinforcers depend upon some kind of prior deprivation. Skinner avoids the use of such words as *need* or *drive* because they are difficult to handle in a purely empirical approach. We may believe that a rat that has had no water for 48 hours is thirsty, but we do not really *know* this. All we do know with certainty is that it has had no water for 48 hours. With humans we find that many kinds of objects or circumstances can work as reinforcers, and we might be tempted to speculate about some deprivation history. If a student is reinforced with a kind word, must we suppose that he has been deprived of kind words? Skinner would prefer to stick to observables and accept the fact that the kind words are reinforcing. Such an approach has its dangers. We might find the same student not reinforced by the same words spoken by someone else or under different conditions. This would leave us with a problem that can be skipped for the present (see p. 182).

A second condition that Skinner has found effective to control response rate is the pattern or *schedule* of reinforcement. At first it is desirable for the teacher or trainer to reinforce every single response the organism makes. Once the response is well above the "operant rate,"[5] it is possible to skip occasional reinforcements and gradually reduce the number to almost any desirable frequency. Skinner has found valuable two general

5 The "operant rate" is determined by observing how frequently in a fixed time period some response occurs without reinforcement.

procedures; one of these he calls the *ratio schedule* and the other, the *interval schedule*.

The ratio schedule involves the gradual reduction of the reinforcements. As an example, say that an animal responds five times for four reinforcements. After it has maintained this 5:4 ratio for a while, the reinforcements are reduced so that the ratio is 5:3, then 5:2, 5:1, 6:1, 8:1 or 10:1 or whatever is desirable. With care (reinforcing again in case the animal shows signs of response extinction), a pigeon or rat can be brought to the point where it will respond hundreds of times for one reinforcement. The interval schedule calls for delaying the reinforcement until some specified time has elapsed since the previous reinforcement, say, 15 seconds, 30 seconds or more. A response made after such an interval will be reinforced. What happens when an animal is being reinforced under an interval schedule is that the animal tends to decrease its response rate immediately after a reinforcement and then gradually begins to increase the output of responses as the time for reinforcement approaches. Skinner likens the ratio schedule to the "piece rate" paid to some kinds of factory workers and the interval schedule to working on a salary.

By switching from ratio to interval schedules or by mixing the schedules, Skinner has been able to alter the behavior outputs of pigeons and rats as he pleases with some truly remarkable refinements of control. He is of the opinion that the behavior of any organism, including man, can be rather completely controlled by providing or withholding reinforcements. He has some rather remarkable curves of response patterns produced by various kinds of animals (Skinner, 1956), and it is probably impossible for the reader to detect any meaningful differences in the patterns.

With both the ratio schedule and the interval schedule, Skinner's procedure calls for two patterns of reinforcement: *fixed* (regular) and *variable*. Thus, with a fixed ratio schedule, an animal might be reinforced for every tenth and only every tenth response. With a variable ratio or a variable interval schedule, the animal might be reinforced at almost any time, depending on the desires of the teacher. In general, Skinner finds that the variable ratio or variable interval schedules tend to result in more persistent activity. Extinction is delayed far longer with variable patterns of reinforcement than with fixed patterns.

As is true for the other important figures in the field of learning, the work of Skinner is much too involved, detailed, and complex to summarize completely here. In Chapter 10, "Programed Learning," Skinner will be given his proper due for launching a very important movement in education. For the present, this summary of some of his work must suffice.

PRACTICAL APPLICATIONS OF SKINNER'S BASIC VIEWS

Skinner, as was said on page 87, has always been ready to attack problems of everyday life, and hence it is not too difficult to find several practical applications of his basic views to learning situations.

Reinforcement and Punishment

Skinner's opinions and conclusions about the strength and value of the rewards that he prefers to call "reinforcers" are probably of most interest to teachers, although the first practical application here is put into negative terms:

Do not use punishment to foster learning.

Skinner objects to punishment, or "aversive control," because he has found that punishment is actually ineffective and accompanied by undesirable complications. Where another might use punishment in the hope of eliminating undesired behavior, Skinner uses *extinction procedure*. In his Utopian novel *Walden II* (1948a), Skinner suggested a way to eliminate the habit of telling off-color stories. All that is necessary (with control over potential listeners) is to make sure that no one laughs. Lacking the reinforcement that had previously sustained this behavior, the off-color storyteller soon stops his recitals. In general, extinction procedure is looked upon as the one sure way to get rid of unwarranted behavior. Assuming control over reinforcers, we can then draw another practical application from Skinner:

Do not reinforce undesired behavior.

In the classroom situation, a student can be discouraged from raising his hand to volunteer answers when the teacher persists in not recognizing his plea. Punishment is not necessary.

Obviously, the source of reinforcement sometimes is unknown or uncontrollable. In such cases, the extinction procedure cannot be initiated. Punishment, however, will merely suppress the response temporarily, according to Skinner. If one chooses to take the risks involved and repeats the punishment frequently, the repression can be made relatively permanent. But Skinner would say: "The behavior is still there, ready to emerge after the suppressive effects have been dissipated."

It is important for the reader to recognize that Skinner's advice on extinction in preference to punishment does not imply that we should ignore undesirable behavior. If the behavior is being reinforced at all by someone else, ignoring it will be of no value. If a child is throwing spitballs in class, ignoring this action will not result in a cease-fire. The culprit can readily perceive that the teacher is only pretending to ignore him. The common advice to parents to ignore the attention-getting behavior of their children rarely works. Children know very well that they *are* getting the attention they want.

To get rid of undesirable behavior, such as the use of foul language or ungrammatical expressions, the teacher must see to it that no reinforcement follows such speech. It might be possible, when a child utters some remark like: "I don't want nothing," for the teacher to say: "I don't understand you. What do you mean?" Pretending that there has been a failure of communication might amount to nonreinforcement and aid extinction. The child might not come up with "I don't want anything," but he is less likely to keep repeating an expression that is apparently useless for communication. If other people could be impressed into cooperation and similarly pretend a lack of understanding, the extinction could be made complete. Similarly, children can be discouraged from referring to members of minority groups with derogatory labels.

As was said before, in many situations it is difficult, if not impossible, to discover the source of reinforcement. Reinforcement can come from too many other people or in circumstances over which the teacher has no control. In such instances, extinction will not occur except in one specific classroom or with one specific teacher. Our ordinary language habits testify to such discriminated learning histories. In different situations, all of us differ in our expressions, tones of voice, and verbal mannerisms.

Impact of Teacher Authority

Teachers frequently influence students in the formation of attitudes towards politics, races, and governments by rewarding (smiling or otherwise approving) remarks made by students. They may not even realize that in so doing they are engaged in teaching. The results could be disastrous if the teacher's own opinions are not sound.

Recently a colleague and I (Bugelski and Hersen, 1966) were able to influence hundreds of students in their attitudes toward Cuba, Alaska, old age (and I would not restrict any issue) by asking them to read a series of statements about the topics mentioned. As they read each statement they were told to write T (true) or F (false) after each statement and to guess if they did not feel sure. As each statement was read we would announce "True" or "False." For most of the statements the students had no real information, e.g., "The average annual rainfall in Alaska is 23 inches."

Other items would be obviously true or obviously false, e.g., "Cuba is an island." The point of the experiment was that, if the item were ambiguous, we would say "true" for some students, "false" for others. After a number of such experiences, the first group of students began writing "true" whenever they came across an item about which they had no information. The other students could be developed into doubters of ambiguous statements. The tendency to believe an item (or disbelieve it) if they did not know the answer transferred to a psychology test taken by the students three weeks later when a test containing ambiguous items was given. The students never knew they had been trained to adopt their now controlled behavior. Teachers should beware of this great power to teach things they might never intend to teach. Taking strong stands on matters about which we are ignorant might well be taken as speaking gospel truth by young students who find the teacher to be so correct on other matters.

Random or Unplanned Reinforcement

Skinner (1948b) pointed out that where there is no control over reinforcements but where reinforcements are likely to occur at random or by chance, organisms will learn to do whatever they happen to be doing at the time of reinforcement. Many human superstitions may arise in this way through chance reinforcements of behavior. If we can refer to normal human behavior as "nonsuperstitious," we can recognize that normal behavior differs from superstitious behavior only in that the reinforcement of the former is more closely related to the behavior. Educators and parents make certain reinforcements *contingent upon* certain responses. This is the only difference between what we consider logical and what is termed "superstitious," however, and, in agreement with Thorndike, Skinner finds learning to be blind and mechanical.

Unless reinforcements are controlled carefully almost any kind of behavior may be strengthened by adventitious or capricious reinforcement. The teacher must know what he is rewarding. Praising a plagiarized paper may well encourage further plagiarism or other irregular methods of preparing assignments. A haphazard policy of praising or rewarding an entire class when some of the members have not actually earned their shares of the general recognition may encourage such slackers or noncontributors to pursue their former behavior.

The general conclusion to be drawn from Skinner's observations on superstition is that learners can learn many things, right things, wrong things, irrelevant and immaterial things. The only necessary and essential operation is to supply reinforcements. The learner will learn whatever he has been doing just before the reinforcer was supplied. Frequently enough he learns wrong and meaningless responses. He might as well be guided in his learning and learn those responses that have some merit in civilized life.

Skinner was courageous enough to spell out the significance of this view (1955) and expressed it this way: *If a learner fails to learn, it is the teacher's fault. With appropriate instruction all pupils should get A grades—"must all have prizes."* I doubt that this proposition is of sufficient use to teachers to offer it as a practical suggestion, but it merits some consideration, if only as a kind of attitude a teacher might well adopt. Hence I will risk rewording it as

When a student does not learn, the teacher fails the course.

Reinforcement Schedules (Partial Reinforcement)

From Skinner's findings about the influences on performance of different schedules of reinforcement come two more practical applications. The first of these is

In the early stages of training it is important to reinforce every desired response.

If this is done, the learning will proceed smoothly.

Sometimes teachers get carried away with the idea that rewards are vital for learning and that an omission of or failure to reward may be of drastic influence. Actually,

Once the learning is well under way, it is advisable to begin to omit reinforcements from time to time.

This is the second application. Skinner argued that it is virtually impossible to be sure that the learner will be reinforced for certain behavior outside the training situation. Such failure of reinforcement might lead to extinction. It is better to control the learning history in such a way that the learner adjusts to the reality of a frequently nonreinforcing world. In *Walden II* (1948a), Skinner even describes formal training for "frustration tolerance." The essence of such training involves the careful withholding and delaying of reinforcers; in short, manipulating the reinforcement schedule.

Secondary Reinforcement

Skinner does not emphasize the distinction between primary and secondary reinforcers as much as does Hull. You will recall that Skinner emphasizes a strictly empirical approach to behavior study. For Skinner anything that reinforces is a reinforcer. New stimuli that accompany previously proven reinforcers take on the capacity to reinforce—these are just another class of reinforcers.

In many training situations it is difficult or awkward to employ such reliable reinforcers as food or water even in teaching animals. On the human level such reinforcers are rarely if ever employed, and secondary reinforcers must be substituted. Fortunately, on the human level such things as smiles, pats on the head, and noises like "that's fine," "good," and similar expressions work most effectively. Such reinforcers must be learned, however, and will not work unless there has been an appropriate foundation of learning. In most cases, by the time children come to school they have a rather broad experience with secondary reinforcers learned at home. Teachers need only take advantage of these built-in reinforcing procedures.

Only one practical recommendation needs to be made in connection with secondary reinforcers, and that is to suggest to teachers that they *use them*. There appears to be so much aversive control employed in schools, so much threatening, scolding, derision, and other forms of punishment, that this simple suggestion does not appear to be amiss. Perhaps the advice should be extended to read:

Use secondary reinforcers more often; restrict or eliminate the use of secondary aversive stimuli.

Shaping. In Chapter 1 Skinner's method of teaching animals was described. Most meaningful and important behavior consists of more than simple, single responses. In the illustration in Chapter 1, a dog was taught to walk across a room and kiss a drawer knob. This complex chain of events is similar to many human behavior patterns that can consist of rather long chains of responses. Whenever a serial pattern or chain of behavior is being taught, it might be necessary to introduce reinforcers all along the chain. This might prove awkward and disruptive. In such situations secondary reinforcers can be most effective. It will be recalled that the dog was first trained to seek food at the sound of a finger-snap; this was a secondary reinforcer that could be administered quickly and easily. In the case of the dog the finger-snap was used to insure the immediacy of reinforcement. On the human level immediate reinforcement is also desirable, but usually it is desired that behavior continue toward the goal of the sequence. It would not do to interrupt the behavior of spelling, for example, after every letter to introduce a secondary reinforcer. For such patterns it is enough merely to nod the head slightly or to show positive interest as the spelling progresses. Such attentive behavior of the teacher is secondarily reinforcing.

Whenever a behavior sequence is being shaped, the teacher must manipulate the secondary reinforcers in such a way as to control the separate steps in the process, withholding the reinforcer until the proper step has been taken, waiting for the next step, reinforcing again, and so on, until the final step has been concluded. To manipulate complex chains of behavior successfully the teacher must know what a secondary reinforcer is for the particular learner and be in a position to administer such when needed. This last remark can be stated as a final practical suggestion from Skinner:

Establish convenient secondary reinforcers that can be introduced rapidly at any desired stage in a sequence in order to keep a learner actively engaged after a preliminary step has been taken.

As suggested above, Skinner is the most practical-minded of all learning specialists, and Chapter 10 will describe others of his contributions that are not so closely related to his laboratory principles.

Chapter Four

The
Pavlovian
Tradition
in
America

Pavlov's influence has by no means been confined to the Soviet Union or even to Europe, and while Hull and others were developing Thorndikian principles still other psychologists in this country were working along Pavlovian lines. This chapter will discuss briefly the work of three such American representatives of Pavlov.

THE THEORY OF WATSON

In the United States, the work of Pavlov was first utilized by John B. Watson (1878–1958), the founder of Behaviorism. Watson (1930) did not explore the details of Pavlovian theory or add to it in any significant extent, but he did make use of Pavlov's theory in accounting for changes in behavior. From Watson's point of view, man is born equipped with certain responses, and learning amounts to attaching different stimuli to these basic innate responses. Pavlov, it will be remembered, thought of the conditioned and unconditioned stimuli as somehow being drawn to the same locus in the cortex and there forming some kind of association by virtue of which one stimulus would replace the other. Hence he can be called an S-S psychologist.[1] Watson, instead, considered that the associations which occur are between stimuli and responses and that the response to any given stimulus can be conditioned. He is, therefore, considered an S-R psychologist. As far as Watson was concerned, learning took place because of conditioning. The strength of habits was determined not by reward but by frequency of contiguous association with stimuli.

Watson considered that among the responses with which man is born are the emotions of fear, anger, and love, and that emotional development therefore consists of conditioning these emotions to new stimuli.

[1] It will be recalled that in psychological jargon, S-S stands for sensory-sensory or stimulus-stimulus association. S-R stands for stimulus-response association. (See p. 43)

Watson's inclusion of emotions as conditioned responses may be considered an advance over Pavlov, who apparently did not go beyond the concept of *reflexes* in his thinking. Just how important Watson's emphasis on emotion turned out to be will become evident in Chapter 5 where the work of Mowrer is discussed.

In a study that has now become a psychological classic, Watson (in Watson and Rayner, 1920) described the conditioning of fear in a child. Little two-year-old Albert was conditioned to fear a rat. The child, sitting in his high chair, was allowed to reach for a white rat that was offered to him. Just as the child was about to touch the rat, Watson, standing behind the boy, struck an iron bar and produced a loud noise. The boy was frightened by the sudden noise and shrank back. After six more such trials (spread over a week's time), the boy showed signs of fear and panic whenever the rat or any white furry object (generalization) was shown to him. From this and similar observations, Watson argued that all our complex emotional life is developed through conditioning ever-increasing numbers of stimuli to fear, anger, and love responses.

While Watson apparently never did anything about little Albert's fears, other psychologists have simply reversed his technique and attempted to decondition or extinguish already acquired fears. One of the earliest efforts, that of M. C. Jones (1924) who "cured" Peter of his fear of rabbits, has already been mentioned (p. 52). More recently, J. Wolpe (1962) has elaborated the extinction technique into a complete system of therapy with very favorable results in fear elimination. Wolpe teaches his subjects to relax under instruction. While training is proceeding, he discovers the kinds of stimuli that arouse fears in a subject, beginning with the most minor fear stimuli and mentioning these while giving instructions to the subject to relax. After some trials, the subject is able to relax when some former fear-provoking stimulus is mentioned or introduced, and Wolpe then proceeds to more serious fear stimuli.

Watson became a controversial figure in the critical atmosphere of the 1920s, when he advocated rather stern, objective, aloof attitudes and measures in bringing up children. He was criticized (and unfairly) for making behavior appear to be nothing more than a bundle of conditioned reflexes, and his psychology was contemptuously referred to as a "muscle-twitch" psychology. Although he was strongly interested in practical applications of psychology (he later left psychology to enter the advertising field), he had little to offer that is really practical in the sense of being well supported by research. In psychological thinking he was quickly superseded and hence is today more famous for his strong stands and vigorous support of Behaviorism than for any practical applications of his own or Pavlovian theory.

THE SYSTEM OF GUTHRIE

The work of Edwin R. Guthrie (1886–1959) has always appealed to students of learning who have read his charmingly and effectively written books (see Guthrie, 1952). While Guthrie's style of writing may appear simple, his psychology, as is commonly reported, is "deceptively simple," because a system that allows a psychologist to explain in many instances (as Guthrie does) any outcome to any learning experience must be complex. Guthrie's system is neither easy to demonstrate nor easy to establish, and the most frequent criticism is that he had little or no supportive research. One reason for this is that his theories are not easily reduced to testable statements. As with the other theorists, this book can include little more than a thumb-nail sketch of Guthrie's views, highlighting what appears to have some practical potential.

Guthrie's central proposition was: Learning consists of conditioning responses to stimuli. While this *sounds* Pavlovian, it emphasizes the association or conditioning of a stimulus to a response whereas in Pavlov's system one stimulus was conditioned to substitute for another.

Acts and Movements

Guthrie oriented his theory toward the "muscle-twitch" far more specifically than did Watson. For Guthrie, behavior consisted of complex combinations of specific movements. When other psychologists use such terms as "response," they are really dealing with what Guthrie called an *act*. For him, an "act" was an abstraction; it did not really have a concrete existence. Where Skinner (p. 88) speaks of a rat pressing a lever, Guthrie would argue that this is too gross a description of what the rat "does." The rat's behavior consists only of *movements*. And the net result of these movements may be described as an "event" of some kind, an *act*. The rat does not *press* levers or anything else; it only moves its various body members about. Whether the bar goes down depends on the bar, not the rat. The rat could make the very same movements if there were no bar present. Any act is a complex affair; frequently the same name or label is attached to a whole variety of ways in which the "act" is performed. The closing of a door, for example, can be accomplished by kicking the door, butting it with the head, nudging it with the elbow, etc. The net result is a closed door, and it is in that we as citizens or house dwellers are interested. As psychologists, says Guthrie, we should realize that each and every set of movements that can occur in door-shutting had to be learned as separate conditionings of specific stimuli. Why do we close a door with an elbow nudge? Only because the stimuli at the time call out for that specific response just as they did when we originally learned this particular movement. The implications of this view for education should be apparent but will be spelled out a little later in this chapter.

One-trial Learning

Guthrie had little use for the concept of exercise or "frequency" that Pavlov and Watson considered to be the basic operation in learning. According to him, learning was an all-or-nothing affair. Learning takes place in one trial and no further trials are needed. While this principle appears to fly in the face of common sense, Guthrie offered this argument to support it:

Whenever a response is made—that is, of course, some movement—the response is at once, then and there, learned or conditioned to the stimulus or stimuli that are present at the time. Here Guthrie introduces an important specification for learning. The stimuli that preceded the response must now be eliminated or somehow disappear. If the stimuli remain, the learner will make new movements and continue to do so until the stimuli do disappear. If a movement is made and the stimuli leading to it are no longer about or active, the movement made will have been learned once and for all to those stimuli. There is no need for practice.

There are two reasons why we appear to need practice. The first is that the same stimuli are not likely to appear again in exactly the same form. We have to learn each individual response to a great many variations of stimulus patterns. Here Guthrie can feel confident, because it is highly improbable, as was pointed out earlier (p. 45), that a stimulus situation ever recurs exactly. *How exactly* it must recur Guthrie does not specify. He might have said, as a last resort, that the learner has changed and is no longer the same once he has had a given experience. What we think of as "practice" really means learning many separate movements in response to many separate stimuli. The more such stimulus-response patterns we acquire in any given area of behavior, the more expert we become in handling ourselves in various situations that are loosely described as "about the same." Thus, the more nails we pound with various hammers, from various angles, into various kinds of wood, the better we are at the *act* of hammering nails.

The second reason why we need and apparently benefit from practice, according to Guthrie, is that, commonly enough, the movements made in response to a given stimulus do not change the stimulus situation—it may still be there. In effect, *many responses are errors;* they are of no value to the learner. New movements are likely to occur, and making new or different responses involves action. Such action may be mistaken for "practice." In effect, what Guthrie says is that if you do something right the first time there will be no need for practice.

Postremity

With the just described all-or-nothing principle of learning Guthrie found himself committed to the controversial yet intriguing principle of *Postremity.* The word *postremity* was coined to emphasize the end of a series or the last movement in a sequence. The principle of *Postremity* states: *We always learn the last thing that we do in response to any specific stimulus situation.* We keep on learning new responses so long as we continue to react to whatever stimuli are present. Thus we are always learning. The only time we stop learning is when no stimuli are at hand. Another way of putting this is to say that, in any given stimulus situation, we learn whatever we do. If the stimulus disappears (or we are removed from it), we will have learned whatever we did when the stimulus was present. If the stimulus remains, we keep learning new things to do until it is removed.

As we learn literally thousands of *S-R* connections, we gradually come to have enough habits to fit a great variety of situations. We are then thought of as intelligent and capable. Yet all that has happened is that we have learned many thousands of separate muscle movements to distinct stimulus patterns.

Rewards

For Guthrie rewards and punishments were equally irrelevant for learning. Such activities as rewarding or punishing someone always occur *after* a response has been made. If it was already made, it was learned *ipso facto,* and the learning could not be affected by some subsequent events. If this is so, how does Guthrie account for the universal appreciation that rewards are apparently important in learning? For Guthrie there simply is no problem. Rewards or punishments are only techniques for eliminating the stimuli that preceded the response. The learner, having just done something in response to some stimulus, will do something else if that stimulus is still present and active. Introducing a reward (or punishment) will force the learner to react now to this new stimulus situation (e.g., candy for a child) and effectively terminate the influence of the original stimulus. Thus rewards (or punishments) *protect* the learning that has just occurred. They have no other role, and any other form of distraction will be equally valuable. Rewards and punishments are good distractors, and Guthrie has no objection to their use so long as they are not given some incorrect theoretical evaluation as having a bearing on the learning itself, which is a simple function of contiguity.

PRACTICAL APPLICATIONS OF GUTHRIE'S SYSTEM

Guthrie's central proposition that learning consists of conditioned responses to stimuli and the other principles discussed here lead to some exciting and controversial practical applications. Teachers may be reluctant to accept them (and the evidence is not weighty for their support), yet they may prove helpful in guiding instructional effort; at worst, they can do no harm.

Specific versus General Instruction

It has become so common for us to think in terms of "acts" that we no longer remember our own painful educational experiences in acquiring our, literally, vast arrays of habits. All too often, as a result, we teach children by general edicts instead of specific instruction.

A mother is likely to tell her child: "Don't be so sloppy. Eat like a lady." To eat like a lady, a child must learn the thousands of response patterns that make up ladylike eating. When a child drips ice cream from a soda over her dress, it will do no good to scream "Be careful!" The word *careful* is really an abstraction; it has connotation but no denotation. As far as behavior is concerned, it is quite meaningless. To analyze the ice cream soda example further, if the child is instructed to slide the bottom of the spoon over the rim of the glass and follows instruction, the syrupy substance will form a coating over the spoon and remain adhered to the spoon during the short time needed for the child to get the spoon into her mouth. The child is no longer sloppy and is now "careful." A new habit has been acquired.

Similarly, with specific instead of general instruction any other desired habit or trait can be taught. We do not teach children to be polite. We teach polite habits in specific situations. As was said earlier, children will hang up their "wraps" in the schoolroom but will not hang up their "clothes" at home. You hang "wraps," not "clothes." Children will even learn to wash their hands for lunch but not for dinner if they are taught to wash for lunch but not taught to wash at dinnertime.

According to Guthrie, all learning tasks must be broken down into the movements that make up the "act" to reveal what response patterns are to be learned in what situations. Whatever the learning task is, be it driving an automobile, writing one's name, or doing arithmetic, each task consists of multiple subtasks—the specific units or movements—and these must be associated with specific stimuli. The teacher must know the units and must always refrain from the general attack. The first step in teaching is job analysis. The job analysis should reveal all the specific movements involved. When all the possible movements in response to all the possible stimuli of a certain category have been learned, then we may say someone has learned to do something. This can be stated as a rule:

Break down any given assignment into its finest units. Teach the units. For example, Don't try to teach children *to be good*. Teach them good habits.

With this rule in mind, the teacher can see a second application of Guthrie's system to the matter of specific instruction. Pavlov developed the concept of *response generalization* (p. 47), whereby he meant that one stimulus or situation might be followed by a variety of responses. If the teacher is not sufficiently demanding, students may "get by" with responses that are only approximations of the correct "answers." Guthrie, in his writings, emphasized the speed and finality with which whatever is done is learned and, as we have just seen, insisted that learning takes place in one trial. Hence teachers should scrutinize all answers or responses that students make to questions to see their real adequacy. Such teacher remarks as "Well, I guess you have the general idea" represent more tolerance than teaching. Teachers frequently give "partial credit" when some of the steps in an answer are correct. From Guthrie's standpoint, this is unwise. In one sense, spelling the word *teacher as t-ee-cher* is partially correct; in another, it is totally wrong. Too many students are rated as "knowing what to do" without being able to do. "I just made a minor error in my calculations" is a commonly heard remark offered less in apology than in self-justification. The burden of requiring precise performances before certifying a student may be extremely onerous for the teacher, but to Guthrie's way of thinking it is obligatory for proper learning. Hence another rule would be

Specify the answer as well as the question and require the precise response desired.

If this is not done, the result will be incompetent or inadequate learning. Having the general idea never baked a cake. The importance of this rule will become more evident after reading the next section where the emphasis is on another of Guthrie's principles.

How to End Lessons

If you remember Guthrie's principle of Postremity, that the learner always learns or retains as a habit the last action he has taken, any teacher is immediately forced to conclude that the most undesirable kind of teaching (and the most often practiced) permits the learner to leave a lesson without performing the desired response correctly. Again, a common example is the spelling class. One child is asked to spell a word, does so incorrectly, is told to sit down while the next child takes a chance with his version of the word. If he is wrong, he sits down, and a third version is attempted. As their last response to the verbal command to spell the word, the first two children spelled that word incorrectly. They are, according to Guthrie, doomed to respond in the same incorrect way on the next occasion. Here teachers can also see the folly of allowing children to do homework without having the answers supplied. Such homework is not training or practice. It is a *test*. If the purpose of the teacher is to provide home tests, well and good. If, however, such homework is supposed to provide a learning experience, it is unlikely to be of such value.

The astute teacher, athletic coach, parent, or whoever is in charge should always see to it that the learner's last reaction is a correct response or a desired one. When a child slams a door in anger, then and there he has learned to slam doors in anger. The wise parent does not sigh with relief because the child is out of sight; he opens the door and sees to it that the child closes the door softly, even in anger—assuming, of course, that it is desired that doors not be slammed. The practical application is easily stated:

Never allow a learner to leave a learning situation with a wrong answer or incorrect response. Let the last response that occurs be correct.

Learning and Doing

According to Guthrie, we learn what we do. Stimuli become associated with movements. This principle lends itself to some meaningful negative advice and some less applicable positive advice. To start with the negative, the teacher is advised that it will do little good to present stimuli which the teacher hopes to associate with one kind of behavior if the students are already engaged in another kind of activity. In Guthrie's illustration, one should never call a dog that is busy chasing a cat. The dog will merely learn to run away when called. The time to call a dog is when the dog is approaching. This last remark is the positive side of Guthrie's advice. As stated above, this is not often easy to do. The learner must be caught in the act of doing what is desired and new stimuli can be associated with such behavior. Even if the positive aspect is not especially useful, the negative advice can well be taken seriously, particularly in situations involving classroom discipline. Shouting and yelling at disorderly groups merely adds a new set of stimuli for such disorderly behavior. The teacher must wait for a class to quiet down before beginning to talk. If necessary, someone else might be enlisted to establish the necessary peace and quiet. The teacher might then make his appearance and begin in a quiet atmosphere. In the military services when an officer is about to enter a room in which a group of military personnel is busy about its own affairs, someone may be sent on ahead to shout "Attention." When the officer enters he can begin his business at once.

The practicality of this advice may be underestimated by those who have never worked with animals, small groups, and even large audiences such as those at political conventions. The successful teacher knows when to teach and when not to teach. We can conclude our study of Guthrie with this typically Guthrian advice:

The teacher must be in charge. He does not try to teach when he is not in charge, when he has reason to believe that the behavior he is looking for will not occur.

TOLMAN'S SYSTEMATIC THOUGHT

Like Watson and Guthrie, Edward C. Tolman (1886–1959) always considered himself a Behaviorist (1932). On occasion he also admitted to having some Gestalt[2] sympathies, and more often than not he resorted to subjective-sounding language abounding in mentalistic terminology, such as "purpose," "bias," "hypotheses," "expectancy," and the like. Tolman

2 Gestalt psychologists belonged to an antibehaviorist, antianalysis group, which preferred a *phenomenological* approach involving such "mentalistic" concepts as "insight" and "understanding." Gestalt psychology was developed in Germany in the early 1900's, but the movement did not become popular in the United States until the 1930's.

considered these terms to be meaningfully translatable into a behavioristic approach within his systematic thought.

Although Tolman felt a great need for practical applications of psychology and made suggestions for curing even such great social problems as war, he never set out to propose applications of learning theory to education. Indeed, in his famous 1937 presidential address to the American Psychological Association (Tolman, 1938), he indicated that psychology, far from being ready to guide man's behavior, was not even ready then to predict the direction in which a rat in a maze would turn when faced with a simple right-or-left choice.

The S-S Principle

Tolman was one of the first behavioristic psychologists to face up to the fact that the $S \longrightarrow R$ approach with its preoccupation with simple behavior of simple animals provided only a limited account of human behavior. It took little or no account of individual differences, and, in general, could not account for many interesting, if complex, aspects of behavior. Tolman believed that additional elements had to be interposed between the S and R in the $S \longrightarrow R$ formula. What he wanted to insert was a complex assortment of factors and specifications that he labeled "intervening variables," and which he expressed as mathematical notations. "Intervening variables" were for Tolman various kinds of influences on behavior besides the behaviorist's environmental stimulus, such as motivation, skill, kind of learning situation, past history, and the kinds of responses required.

Like Pavlov, Tolman was a contiguity psychologist, and, like Pavlov, he thought of associations as being formed between stimuli. Thus some new or novel stimulus (*sign*) became associated with some already meaningful or important subsequent stimulus (*significate*) through a series of paired experiences. In Tolman's view, the Pavlovian experiment would be described as follows: Pavlov's conditioning stimulus or *CS*, for example, the sound of a bell, was a sign; the unconditioned stimulus *US* (food) was a significate. To be a sign, a sign had to be followed by a significate. Sometimes one merely waited for a significate to show up after a sign appeared. On other occasions one had to do something before the significate occurred. Whatever one did, whether waiting or acting, Tolman called a "behavior route" and the pattern involved was

sign—behavior route—significate.

Because of the sign-significate orientation of his theory, Tolman came to be known as an *S-S* psychologist, in contrast to Watson and Guthrie who we noted were *S-R* psychologists, and for this reason is a better "representative" of Pavlov than the other two.

Like Pavlov and Guthrie but unlike Hull, Tolman saw no need for reward or reinforcements to be introduced to establish learning. Learning would occur readily enough if a significate followed a sign. *Frequency* of pairings was the only learning principle. The nature of the significate was irrelevant—that is, as far as being good or bad. An animal that was whipped every time a certain person approached would soon learn that a whipping was about to be administered. Tolman liked to refer to his *S-S* learning as the learning of "expectancies." What an "expectancy" was he never clearly defined, but we can assume that it covered the kind of operation usually described by the expression "I was led to expect. . . ." A shock that followed the sound of a bell would quickly result in simple *S-S* learning: the significate would be the pain or shock. If the bell sound were followed by food, it would still be a case of *S-S* learning, but the significate would be food. Of course, a significate would have to be of some importance to the animal in the sense that it would be noticed. But this only means that a significate would be a *stimulus*—that is, something that the animal sensed in some way.

Tolman's *S-S* Expectancy principle can be stated simply: *When a stimulus (sign) is followed by a second stimulus (significate), the learner will acquire an association between these stimuli.*

If a given sign or stimulus is frequently paired with a negative consequent stimulus, there is no question but that this combination of events will come to be learned. Where at one time Thorndike believed that punishment weakened "bonds," we can appreciate that, for Tolman, punishment strengthened a bond. Of course, Thorndike was talking about another kind of bond—that is, one that invoked a change in response. Tolman was talking about learning to expect punishment itself, something Thorndike had not considered.

Latent Learning

Tolman's emphasis on *S-S* learning led him to a distinction that eventually was adopted by most psychologists except the confirmed Guthrians, the distinction between *learning* and *performance*. Most readers of this book already are familiar with this distinction, in the sense that they have always identified learning with *knowledge* and not with action. From a common-sense point of view, all of us learn things (have the knowledge) but do not continually display this knowledge. It is somehow "stored" and called on when needed.

This distinction between learning and performance led Tolman to the concept of *Latent Learning* (*latent* meaning hidden in contrast to manifest) for which he found convincing support. This concept of *Latent Learning* first arose from experiments by H. C. Blodgett (1929), who had found that if rats were given a number of trials in running through a maze when there was no food in it, they would almost immediately run through correctly once they did find food placed there. Such almost-perfect performances would be observed even though the rats had made numerous errors for some seven previous unrewarded trial runs. On the basis of this and similar findings, Tolman believed that it was possible for anyone to acquire a great deal of knowledge without ever showing it unless he had some appropriate occasion or need. The old joke about the farmer's son who did not speak for 12 years and was regarded as a mute until the day he shouted "For heaven's sake, Dad, jump!" when a bull was charging his father, illustrates the concept. When the father had jumped to safety and asked his son how it was that he had never spoken before, the lad replied: "I never had anything important to say before."

PRACTICAL APPLICATIONS OF TOLMAN'S PRINCIPLES

Tolman himself would not have expected to be cited as a contributor to practical education, but in even this limited account of his psychology we can find something of value for the teacher today.

The Importance of Significates

Tolman's S-S principle immediately raises the possibility of learning without preoccupation with rewards.[3] Teachers should recognize that unpleasant and negative consequences will be learned as readily as pleasant and positive ones. Learners can and do learn negative "expectancies" (as Tolman preferred to call his S-S combinations). This is something teachers have known all along. Psychologists have had a little more difficulty than

---

[3] The concern over rewards can *only* be felt by S-R psychologists. A reward can only be given for something—that is, before he can be rewarded, the learner must *do* something. Without action there is no meaning to the concept of reward.

perhaps was necessary in accepting such a view because of other preconceptions or obstacles they placed in their own paths. In any case, a practical corrollary to Tolman's principle stated on page 111 might be:

It is not necessary to reward learners in order to secure learning. It is only important that something "significant" (meaningful, important) happens after a sign (a signal, stimulus) occurs.

Knowledge and Performance

The concept of *Latent Learning* should lead teachers to recognize that performance is not always to be depended on as an indication of how much has actually been learned. There may be many obstacles or blocks to a satisfactory performance that must be removed before the knowledge can be exhibited. Tolman's own later experiments indicated that rats "knew" how to get to a goal without error when it appeared a desirable thing to do. Although the reality of such learning was disputed for many years, latent learning is now generally recognized as real learning, even if the basic operations underlying it are not clearly understood or agreed upon. Putting aside theoretical disputes and accepting the reality of latent learning then leads to this practical suggestion:

The degree of learning (acquisition, achievement) may not always be evident under fixed operating conditions. A change in incentive (reward, punishment) upward or downward may reveal a change in performance.[4]

As teachers, frequently enough we find ourselves in the position of having to say "I know he knows it" or "He can do it, but he just won't." In such situations, if the knowledge is to be made manifest, it may be necessary for the teacher to experiment with rewards, punishments, or other conditions, such as the needs and fears of the learner (Tolman called these "demands"), before we can get the performance we desire.

Tolman's contributions to education go beyond what has just been said. His views are, clearly, at variance with the active-participation project methods so strongly advocated by the Dewey-Thorndike philosophy. Tolman asserts that it is possible to learn by being told or being shown: the learner need not personally perform every bit of behavior he will learn.

---

[4] In this suggestion I have taken advantage of other research (L. P. Crespi, 1944; D. Zeaman, 1949) that indicates that the performance of rats can be readily altered by increasing or decreasing the amount of food they find at the end of the runway.

We all can agree that physical skills will not be achieved without action,[5] but not all learning involves physical skills. There is little we can *do* about learning such content material as history and geography, yet many people have learned these contents. Even in such learning there is, of course, some action. The nature of this action is left for examination in the next chapter.

[5] But see p. 135.

Chapter Five

Integration
of
the
Two
Traditions

The last of the important learning theorists whom this book will consider is O. Hobart Mowrer (1907–   ). A few years ago Mowrer would have been listed among the followers of Thorndike, but today he is looked upon as a builder on Pavlov. What led him to change his ideas during the 1940s and 1950s need not be gone into here. Important is that Mowrer's thinking represents the convergence of both previously described lines of learning theory, and his work is an effort to reconcile the conflicts and disagreements that developed over 50 years of thinking in the psychology of learning.

THE MOWRER THEORY

Mowrer (1960a, 1960b) today believes that, essentially, learning amounts to Pavlovian conditioning. But for him, Pavlovian conditioning is not the broad inclusive explanation of learning that Pavlov considered it to be. For half a century, Pavlov and his students were devoted to measurements of conditioned responses in the form of salivary secretions. Over the years they did examine other response patterns, but primarily these were also secretions of body fluids. Mowrer conceives the vast Pavlovian theory as resting entirely on the functions of the autonomic nervous system, a system that controls the reactions of the visceral organs and of the circulatory system. It is generally agreed that the autonomic nervous system functions as two systems: the *Sympathetic* and the *Parasympathetic*. The *Sympathetic* nervous system appears to be dominant in emergency functions, the *Parasympathetic,* in the routine vegetative processes of the body. When dominant, either system tends to inhibit the other. Psychologists for many years have identified the autonomic nervous system as the "physiological agency of emotion." If you will think of the *Sympathetic* (emergency) system as operating or dominant in such "negative" emotions as fear and anger, and the *Parasympathetic* as dominant in the more positive states of joy and love, you will have available a wide array of patterns of emotional behavior to consider in terms of degrees of involvement of either system and of changes from one state to another.

It is these emotional states that Mowrer believes Pavlov was conditioning through all those productive years. In Mowrer's view, the salivary response is only a partial reaction of a more complex emotional pattern that a dog undergoes when a bell "signals" food.[1] What happens under such conditions is that the dog has been conditioned to "feel good" or "feel hopeful" when the bell rings, and that the saliva is merely the accompaniment of this emotional reaction in the stimulus circumstances present. Mowrer recognizes, of course, that the dog, in a sense, has no business "feeling good" until the food is in its mouth. But, you will recall, all conditioned responses are characterized by antedating or coming forward in time. The dog feels good, then, *before* it actually should, and such an antedating positive emotional reaction Mowrer labels with the word *hope*. Hope is just one of the emotional reactions susceptible of conditioning. If a conditioning stimulus is usually followed by pain or disagreeable stimulation, Mowrer argues that a sympathetic nervous system action resulting in a negative emotional state will develop and become conditioned to the *CS*. Because in Mowrer's view pain and other unpleasant states have a large component of fear, it is this fear response that will be conditioned whenever the fear is evoked in the presence of some conditioning stimulus. If someone is shocked every time a bell rings, and if the shock hurts, we can expect the subject to become frightened after the bell-shock combination has been presented a number of times. The point to note is that the conditioned response is an emotional one, that of fear, and not a motor response of escape or avoidance. Such overt behavior, as you will see, is not conditioned, nor is it conditionable. Thus, for Mowrer, conditioning will follow the general lines of Pavlovian principles as they have already been described, but the responses that are learned or conditioned are strictly emotional and primarily of two general categories: hope and fear. Various interacting patterns can emerge from conflicting patterns of stimulations or changes in stimulation. Picture, for example, "hope" giving way to "disappointment" as it changes into "fear" if the stimuli are appropriately changed. "Fear" can change into "relief" as the inciting stimulus is withdrawn or disappears. And so on.

When a person is quietly resting, any sudden painful stimulus can be thought of as an increase in stimulation. Such a change in the direction

---

[1] Hull (1943) thought of the salivary response as a typical r_g.

of more stimulation or excitation Mowrer describes as *incremental*. Because painful stimuli can be used as unconditioned stimuli for fear, they can be considered, in Pavlovian language, as reinforcers. Note that there is no question or problem of rewards here. Pavlov equated unconditioned stimuli with reinforcement. If a painful stimulus is employed in a learning situation, Mowrer considers it an "incremental reinforcer." If some stimulus leads to or is followed by relaxation or decrease in stimulation (for example, food when hungry), Mowrer describes it as a *"decremental reinforcer"* because a net decrease in stimulation has occurred.

Mowrer's use of the terms *incremental* and *decremental* in connection with the term *reinforcement* may be somewhat confusing. If you remember that reinforcement is being treated simply as *strengthening* a learned connection and has nothing to do with rewards in the Pavlovian scheme, you should have no difficulty. Mowrer is simply trying to emphasize the fact that a great deal of learning goes on in connection with pain as well as in connection with more pleasant consequences to stimuli.

Mowrer starts his theorizing with an assumption of "homeostasis"—that is, that organisms, generally, do not behave in any way unless there is some kind of stimulation present. Behavior, again generally, amounts to coping with or getting rid of the stimulation so that a state of quiet balance or homeostasis is resumed. Under normal conditions of life the balance is constantly disturbed either from the outside world or from inner conditions, such as growing hunger, for example. If the stimulation rises in amount or intensity, it is proper to call it *incremental*. If the stimulation declines (for example, hunger stimulation disappears with eating), the term *decremental* is suitable.

Mowrer thus provides for two types of reinforcement, both of which are common enough and both of which serve as bases for learning in that incremental reinforcers are unconditioned stimuli for fear and decremental reinforcers are unconditioned stimuli for hope.

The Control of Behavior

We come now to the crucial question. If all that we can learn is to fear or hope, how can we account for the apparent learning of a whole repertoire of responses, content, meaning, and skills? The answer is that we do not really learn such things—we already know how to do them. If we learn to swim or play the violin or answer "1066" when asked when the battle of Hastings was fought, Mowrer says all these responses are responses we were fully capable of performing at the time we performed them. Remember

Hull's *Habit-family Hierarchy?* You can only learn what you are already able to do. Mowrer's position is similar to Hull's in this respect. We can all play a violin in the sense that we can hold both violin and bow in the proper position and we can draw the bow across strings. What is missing from our education if we do not actually perform well on the violin is that we have not been conditioned to feel good or hopeful when certain (correct) sounds we produce strike our ears; more correctly, we have not been conditioned to begin to feel "hope" or "fear" as the stimuli begin to occur that develop from our movements, which produce correct or incorrect sounds (movement-produced or "feedback" stimuli).

When we "learn" to swim the Mowrer analysis is the same. We already have in our habit hierarchies responses that keep us afloat as well as responses that lead to sinking. Learning consists of making responses that lead to feeling hopeful (afloat) and inhibiting the other kind. Similarly, we are fully capable of spelling *cat* as *c-a-t* or *k-a-t*. We have learned to spell *correctly* when saying *c-a-t* is followed by "hope"; if we also have come to feel badly when we say *k-a-t* we have learned even more.

The argument presented above may not yet sound convincing because the central concept or crucial mechanism has received only a mention and not an explanation. This important concept, in reality the key to Mowrer's theory, will be described as soon as the basic issue has been restated thus: *We can only learn emotional responses to stimuli. All other "learned" behavior consists of performing certain responses we are already able to perform, voluntarily or otherwise.* A child who cannot say "four" cannot answer the question of "How much is two and two?" Teaching such a child consists of making him feel good when he does eventually reach the level of maturation or language control that permits him to say "four."

Feedback and Feedback Stimuli

The omission referred to above can now be remedied. You should have been worried about what the appropriate stimuli are that initiate (after conditioning) the emotional reactions that are involved in the acquisition of skill or knowledge. Let us return to the example of swimming. What stimuli can there be that will initiate hope or panic in us? The stimuli in question are those that are produced by our own movements. Every time we move a muscle or bend a joint, tiny sense organs imbedded in our muscles, tendons, and joints are excited or stimulated, and these movement-produced stimuli enter the central nervous system where they function like any other stimuli to which we are sensitive. These stimuli are called "kinaesthetic" or "proprioceptive" stimuli, to give them a name, and their role in learning can now be appreciated. The swimmer makes a movement of arms or legs, proprioceptive stimuli pour into the nervous system from the contracted muscles. Immediately, there are consequences to these movements (the learner begins to sink—a sufficient stimulus for fear or panic). We now have the classical procedure for Pavlovian conditioning clearly before us: there are proprioceptive stimuli to serve as *CS*, there is the visual stimulation from going down beneath the surface *(US* for fear). The fear reaction becomes conditioned to the feedback stimulation from the muscles that have just contracted in a particular way. Now, according to Mowrer, assuming the novice has survived, the next time he begins to contract the same muscles in the same way the proprioceptive stimuli will begin to initiate fear; the fear, in turn, will lead to inhibition of further such contractions and the learner will contract other muscles or the same muscles in other ways. These new contractions may be followed by staying afloat, a completely different state of affairs accompanied by an emotional reaction Mowrer calls "hope." The learner will continue to do what leads to hope and more hope and will cease and desist from doing what leads to fear and more fear.

At this point an analogy to a thermostat may be of some help. A thermostat is essentially a feedback device. The thermostat that controls the heat in your home is so wired to a temperature-detecting device that, when the temperature falls below a desired standard (fear), a switch trips to start a furnace. More heat is generated (hope). When the indicated temperature is reached, another switch trips to shut off the furnace (homeostasis) for a while. Air-conditioning devices and refrigerators work in the same way. They are activated to more or less of some activity, depending upon information that is fed to detection devices (sense organs) from the present condition or state of affairs. The point is that the conditions (responses) produce the information and feed it back to the regulating equipment.

Applying this analogy to human behavior, we can consider some desired state of the organism (homeostasis) as analogous to the desired temperature. As this state alters, emotional behavior ensues (more fear, for example) and the musculature becomes active. The contractions of the muscles lead to a new condition—it might be of more fear or less fear (less fear can be interpreted as more hope). If the emotional reaction is one of hope, the same kind of movement is continued, and stimuli generated by the movement become conditioned to the emotion of hope. More similar movements generate more of these same kinds of proprioceptive stimuli that keep the learner repeating or continuing the same movements. In Mowrer's view, behavior is controlled, motivated, and guided by emotions, but the emotions, in turn, are guided by or result from behavior and its self-produced proprioceptive stimulation. In this sense, behavior guides itself or controls itself, more or less automatically, just as does the thermostat.

The heavy emphasis on proprioceptive or kinaesthetic stimulation should not mislead us into ignoring the other senses. The eyes and ears also operate as feedback devices in that we hear ourselves talking, singing, or playing music (well or badly) and see what our hands and legs are doing. In reaching for a pencil, for example, our stretching movements are continually under visual observation and our reaching movements are adjusted to the distances involved. If the pencil is rolling, we match movements with the speed and direction of the pencil. Such changing visual inputs, as we observe something we are doing, are essentially feedback stimuli.

The importance of the concept of feedback stimulation in Mowrer's theory is so great that additional illustrations may not be amiss. Suppose that a boy is trying to "shoot baskets" with a basketball. He stands somewhere near the target basket and flexes his arm muscles, sets his leg muscles, adopts a posture, sights the basket, and releases the ball. All this time stimuli from the various muscles involved are pouring into his nervous system. The ball either falls through the hoop or it does not. Depending on the result, the boy has an emotional reaction, either one of hope or one of fear. By simple Pavlovian conditioning, the stimuli generated by the muscular responses become conditioned to whatever emotion occurred. On the next occasion of throwing the ball, as these movement-produced stimuli begin to occur, they will initiate either hope or fear, depending on their resemblance to the stimuli that had existed on the prior throw. If the boy now is becoming fearful, he will not throw the ball but will readjust arms, legs, posture into some other position that results in less fear. If he has been successful, he will adjust his musculature until the returning stimuli from the contracting muscles are more like those that were present on the occasion of success. The same kind of analysis can be applied to any kind of motor skill from pole-vaulting to playing polo.

A second example can be drawn from Mowrer's theoretical account of how we learn to talk. Mowrer based his theory of human speech acquisition on some observations of talking birds and how they acquire language. According to Mowrer, a parrot or Mynah bird can be most effectively taught to mimic human speech by having someone talk to the bird when it is being fed or otherwise cared for. A hungry bird presumably feels better when eating. If someone says something to the bird at such a time, it will become conditioned to feel better when such sounds are heard. Because the bird (in the case of talking birds) can and will utter sounds, some of these sounds will approximate human speech. When the bird hears itself make such speech sounds, it will feel better. The more such sounds it makes, the better it feels. Mowrer, at one time, suggested that the bird falls in love with the trainer; more likely it gets conditioned to feel better at the sound of the voice of the trainer, and the whole operation could probably be accomplished by mechanizing the feeding in conjunction with a tape recording of some human speech sounds.

The important lesson from this illustration is that the bird is not rewarded for talking. It need not say or do anything while food is being presented. All it has to do is listen. The learning that occurs can be considered "latent" as, indeed, Mowrer considers most learning to be.

It might be of value to apply the analysis of talking birds' acquisition of speech to children. The following remarks represent Mowrer's theoretical account of how babies learn to talk. When a baby is being cared for—fed, fondled, changed, or otherwise being made to "feel good"—the attending parent normally keeps talking, singing, and murmuring. Such human sounds then become associated with "feeling good" or "hope." They become "secondary decremental reinforcers." The child, if not deaf, will, of course, hear these sounds and gradually come to feel good whenever he hears them. Sooner or later the child will engage in vocalizing activity of his own. As he hears these self-produced sounds, he will "feel good" to the degree that they approximate, in form, the sounds previously made by the attendant. The best "feeling" comes from the exact duplication of human sounds, and this self-stimulation from the consequences of his own vocalizing will result in the child's continued activity of a vocal nature, constantly "guided" and "controlled" by the emotional consequences. Mowrer also explained that if a child hears only loud, angry, fearful sounds from his parents, any vocalizing on his part will be inhibited and, accordingly, he will not learn to talk.[2]

The Role of Imagery

It is to Mowrer's great credit that, in 1960, he had the courage to revive the interest of psychologists in the concept of imagery as an essential factor

---

2 Sounds by themselves would not be fearful or angry. A prior history of negative consequences is necessary in such a case.

in the learning process. In 1913, Watson had outlawed the concept of imagery as an empty subjective mentalism, useless to a scientific psychology. From then on "imagery" became a "dirty" word. Mowrer, honestly facing the issues in learning, recognized that his feedback model required the thermostat-like control already described to provide some standard or reference level with which the feed-back stimuli could be compared. The ancient concept of the image seemed to him to serve just such a purpose. Thinking of the image as a "conditioned sensation" (Leuba, 1940) helped Mowrer to complete his picture of learning. He had already adopted a Tolmanic-Pavlovian S-S view. Such a position, you will recall, allows for the possibility that one sensory reaction, e.g., the sound of a bell (and its neural consequences), could be conditioned to some other stimulus, e.g., the lighting of a lamp (to the sensory consequences of the illumination). On a subsequent occasion the sound of the bell could conceivably revive, at least partially, the kind of neural activity that had originally been initiated by the light. Similarly, any two sensory experiences could be conditioned to each other. The idea is not at all novel; it goes right back to Aristotle and his doctrine of the association of ideas. In 1960, however, it was indeed novel for a psychologist to talk about imagery in relation to anything other than history.

The revival of imagery allowed Mowrer to provide the necessary "thermostats" in learners' heads. Now, as had been done before with any so-called instrumental behavior, he could have a model to match with the feedback stimuli developed or turned up by his own actions. As a simple example, consider the arrival of some acquaintance. You respond to him as someone you know, e.g., his appearance stimulates the running off of neural patterns that have been run off before and have been appropriately channeled. Such revived neural patterns are the essence of images. If you have never seen a particular person, there are no prepared patterns to run off, and you have no ready or suitable reactions. You can, at best, call him a stranger. The sound of a voice over a telephone may be enough to run off a formerly active visual pattern, and you "recognize" the caller.

Mowrer did not develop any practical educational applications from his treatment of imagery, but his work led to a revival of interest in imagery that became noticeable in the late sixties. Some of this work will be considered in later chapters where appropriate.

Mowrer's theory of learning is far more complex and detailed than this summary might suggest, but these essentials are enough to generate some meaningful implications for the teacher.

PRACTICAL APPLICATIONS OF MOWRER'S THEORY

Mowrer's interpretation of Pavlov and Thorndike does not affect seriously the practical applications discussed in the preceding chapters. What Mowrer has accomplished is to provide a formula or explanation whereby Pavlov and Thorndike can both be made more meaningful and applicable. In actual practice of applying psychology to learning, we might not, for example, be too concerned with the fact that a boy throwing a ball through a basketball hoop "feels good." Thorndike would have said this is a "rewarding situation," with the knowledge of results representing the reward. Mowrer helps us to appreciate *how* the reward might work.

Similarly, Mowrer explains how Pavlov was correct in explaining behavior as a matter of conditioning even though Pavlov was right for the wrong reasons. The failure to condition gross motor behavior had led many Americans to dismiss Pavlov as unimportant. Once we see that Pavlovian conditioning is restricted to emotional reactions, we can accept the impossibility of conditioning motor responses as one of the facts of life.

Rewards and Punishments

As teachers, all of us recognize the great role of emotion in learning or in behavioral guidance and control. We take the broader view (abandoned by Thorndike, 1932) that both positive *and* negative emotions can be involved. We see the need for first developing (or making sure they are already developed) secondary reinforcers (conditioned stimuli) of both kinds, positive and negative. We see that punishment can be an effective controller of behavior by producing an inhibitory activity that lessens fear. We also recognize that something we may call punishment (say public "dishonor") may not actually be punishing to some people—some juvenile delinquents might enjoy having their names in the paper—and we come out with a definition, even though circular, of punishment: *Punishment is represented by any kind of stimulation ᷉ that results in withdrawal responses, avoidance responses, or inhibition of responses that have been initiated.* Thus, if a boy is spanked (or even yelled at) when his hand is extended toward the cookie jar, and if the hand is withdrawn cookieless, the boy has been punished. On the next occasion when the boy sees and feels his arm reaching for the jar, fear may be aroused. This fear will be reduced if further movement is inhibited or if the arm is withdrawn. Punishment is useful only if it generates fear. If it does do this, it works in teaching. Thorndike was wrong in his conclusions because he mistook *saying* "wrong" to college students in a chance situation as a punishment. We can be pretty sure none of his subjects was frightened.

Assuming that Mowrer is correct, we also come to an explanation for the common advice about punishing a malefactor in the act if the punishment is to be effective. The feedback stimuli from the response must be conditioned to the fear. In short, unless the malefactor at least begins to make the movements that will generate the feedback stimuli, he cannot be conditioned to be fearful and thereby inhibit the behavior. Thus the first practical rules to be drawn from Mowrer are:

Punishment can be effective in controlling behavior if it follows the behavior rapidly enough to allow for conditioning the feedback stimuli from the response to fear.

Similarly,

Reward must follow immediately upon a response to permit conditioning of feedback stimuli to the emotion of hope so that similar behavior can be fostered later.

Lecture, Reading, and Imitation Situations

The really important contribution of Mowrer's theory, however, comes when his views are applied to common teaching practices that for centuries have been followed without full awareness of what was being done —such common practices as telling someone or showing him (the demonstration) how to do something, emphasis upon *imitation* as a basic learning operation, and ordinary reading or listening to lectures. From the current kinds of criticism aimed at education, one would gather that no one ever learned anything in a lecture or from reading a book, and imitation has long been a dead horse in learning-theory circles. An examination of Mowrer's theory, however, gives fresh insight into these ancient practices and a new basis for evaluating them. There *are* values to these methods, even though they may not be the ones teachers previously imagined and even though teachers must establish certain conditions before the values can actually develop. We shall return to these methods later in other contexts and here only spell out the Mowrer implications.

1. The Lecture. What then, are the values of the lecture method if, according to Mowrer, we learn only to fear and to hope?

The lecture has been the long-established foundation of college education and, in less-formal character, of practically all education. Someone—the teacher—has been talking; the learner supposedly has been listening. If he is indeed listening, he will learn something. Even Mynah birds learn in this way. The amount that will be learned may be questioned, although there is probably no more efficient way to teach a great many people at one time. But there is another value to the lecture, which is frequently ignored as a value even if the listeners themselves provide the evidence for this value in remarks like "That was a great lecture!" or "What a lousy lecture —I wasted my time."

The value that should be recognized is, in my opinion, the real purpose of the lecture: It is an opportunity to condition the listening audience. The audience consists of people who are alive and as part of being alive, *emotionable,* to coin a word. They may be interested and excited, or dismally bored. They may be friendly toward a given content (kind of stimulus) or antagonistic, irritated, or ill disposed. The lecturer begins.

At this point, we must consider the lecturer as a stimulus object—he will be attractive or repellent in his own right. The personality of a teacher is of major importance. He must be able to arouse emotions. That is his job. He is the *US* for emotion. If he is flat and dull, the words that he uses (arithmetic words, grammar words, geography words) will become conditioned stimuli for boredom and apathy. If he is mean, sarcastic, irritable, his words will come to create emotional reactions of resentment, and the content words of the subject will become conditioned stimuli for such emotional reactions. The job of the teacher is to arouse emotional reactions of "feeling good" (hope) in connection with the content he is attempting to teach. Creating such positive feelings as responses to the content of a course is the job of the teacher. In effect, his purpose is to get the student to fall in love with the subject—just as a talking bird is said by Mowrer to fall in love with the sound of the human voice. If the teacher cannot do this, he is not a teacher, no matter what his job may be called. It is probable that only a few people occupying teaching posts actually are genuine teachers. The great majority probably succeed in killing interest in their subjects. In some cases they may not *completely* destroy such interests, and other people (parents or friends) repair the damage done by "teachers."

The successful teacher is one who finds his students reading books on his subject, taking more courses in the area, "majoring" in the field. The teacher does not "instruct." The student learns because he "feels good," saying (to himself or to others) the kinds of words about which he "felt good" when he heard them from the teacher. In summary, the teacher, through his appearance, actions, manners, "personality," or other characteristics, directly arouses (as an Unconditioned Stimulus) favorable (hope) or unfavorable (fear) reactions. The words he uses and the things he talks about become conditioned stimuli for these same reactions. These stimuli later guide and control the behavior of the student in other situations. He will, in a sense, seek to get more or less of such words, saying them to others or refraining from saying them, depending upon the conditioning undergone.

Of course, the lecturer must be efficient in his operations if he is to condition the learners effectively. His personality effects have already been noted. But personality is not the only important factor in conditioning learners. The lecturer must be aware of his role and must know what he is doing. It may be that some "great" teachers in educational history have been successful without knowing that they were actually engaged in an operation of charming their students. But such great teachers might have been even greater had they recognized their roles for what they were. They would then have had to answer a number of highly technical questions in their wooing of their charges. From these questions we can list at least the following: How many conditioned responses are to be developed in a given session—that is, how much can I expect the learners to learn in an hour or 20 minutes or whatever the time allotted? (What this question really asks is: Given a fixed amount of time per learning session, how many different conditioned stimuli for "hope" reactions can I effectively introduce?) How many repetitions (or near repetitions—generalizable stimuli) must be presented for each conditioning to become established? For how long do I want the conditioning to last—how long do I want the material to be "remembered"? How precisely must any "discrimination" be developed?

These questions and their answers are best left for later chapters. Here you need only recognize that what the lecturer is doing is conditioning his audience to feel "good" or "bad" about a given type and range of stimuli. The lecturer has the same problems as the laboratory conditioner. The stimulus must be received to be effective. This usually means that the stimulus must be *isolated* (ignoring the problem of attention, for the moment) and *identifiable* (not a complex array that cannot be specified). There must be an emotional reaction (feeling "good" or "bad") of at least some degree.

In the laboratory, the emotional response is normally controlled by manipulations of unconditioned stimuli—electric shock, food, and so on. In the classroom, teachers must rely on other stimuli—probably the learning situation itself. The learner comes to the lecture somewhat apprehensive, anxious, fearful (of being or remaining stupid). The lecturer, through his manipulations (humor, illustrations that tap the learner's past, assurances), begins to arouse in the positive learner some degree of hope in connection with the remarks or at least a lessening of the fearfulness (which in Mowrer's views amounts to the same thing). In one way or another, the lecturer keeps introducing secondary positive reinforcers along with his content material. This is probably the really effective operation. The teacher *must* reinforce in one way or another and keep the learner hopeful. He may do this by "leading" his audience to arrive at an obvious conclusion. He then may praise the listeners for having drawn this conclusion. If he uses such expressions as "It is obvious" or "As everyone knows," he should be sure that it is obvious to everyone listening. To describe something as "clear" when it is not clear will only lead to trouble. If the lecturer is skillful and does not increase anxiety by trying to do too much at any one time, he can succeed in creating a "favorable attitude toward the material"; the student is encouraged to pursue the matter further, to put down notes, to review these notes, to read more, discuss more. With each additional exposure, the student "learns" to continue to make certain kinds of remarks or perform certain exercises that make him "feel good." If these turn out to be the same kind of noises the lecturer made, we say the student has learned. If he does not make such noises, he has not learned.

A simple suggestion for amplifying the impact of a lecture is to provide the audience with a printed outline of the main points, the key issues, and easily forgotten facts like figures, dates, and references. Such outlines are sometimes called "throwaways" or "handouts"; and if they are poorly prepared, that is about what they amount to. If, in effect, they allow the audience to participate in the lecture by anticipating points or awaiting revelations, they can be invaluable. They can also show, if carefully prepared, a respect for the audience and a desire to be helpful. Such outlines can be eagerly sought and cherished from the first grade through graduate school and will add inches to the stature of the lecturer. This is of no small importance because his stature is the basic factor in the impact of the lecture.

2. *Reading*.[3] The only difference between learning through reading and learning through a lecture is the form of the stimuli involved. In reading, the learner becomes conditioned to printed words rather than

[3] The subject of teaching reading will be treated in chapter 13.

spoken ones. The same processes as learning from a lecture are involved. The author, if successful, is doing the same thing as the lecturer. As the student reads the first word, phrase, or sentence he feels "good" or "bad" as a function of his previous history with such stimuli. If the material is completely novel, in a foreign language, for example, there may be only a modest negative effect—certainly the reader is not likely to carry on. Similarly, if the material is too easy, the reader is likely to feel insulted and stop the effort. When the material is just sufficiently challenging and the reader can report that he "understands" or is "getting it," we assume that "hope" is operating to help continue the effort. When the material is difficult, we expect "fear" to be generated and call for various differences in behavior to emerge, including such responses as putting away the book, reading more slowly, or rereading. If additional external or extra pressures are introduced to keep the learner at the task, we can expect the reading to follow a complex pattern of hope, disappointment, fear, relief, and round about again. Eventually, if the reader learns, we can say he has been conditioned to make remarks that correspond to the content. That is what we mean by "learning." Frequently all the reader can say (as does the audience at a lecture) is "I enjoyed it," "It was great," or "I hated it"—all remarks that provide a kind of direct testimony in behalf of Mowrer's position.

The reader has, however, one great advantage over the listener at a lecture. He can read faster than the lecturer is likely to talk and, consequently, in the same amount of time he can go over the material more than once. He can go back and forth in the argument and check the mastery of the material. The listener hears the material only once.

But the advantages of reading may be misinterpreted because of the kind of test questions (usually "objective" details) that are often asked. The listener might be far more effectively conditioned (educated) by a really expert lecturer than by a written copy of the lecture. That is to say, a good lecturer may be responsible for attitude changes in the learner and emotional reactions toward the subject matter that cannot be tested for in objective, factual quizzes. By gesture, tone of voice, and expression, the lecturer can emphasize what must remain rather cold and lifeless in print. Students have been known to remark "I learned a lot in that course" even when they earned poor grades in tests. While such alleged values are difficult to measure objectively, they probably are the real core of the educational experience. The objective, factual material will soon be forgotten; the emotional reactions and attitudes probably will have a longer survival history. They can reinvigorate studying behavior later.

A poor lecturer, on the other hand, may condition the student negatively, whereas the written material may be quite inoffensive or even positive in emotional value. We must not ignore the fact that some teachers should not speak in public; others should not be allowed to write. There are good and bad lecturers and there are good and bad authors, and we can expect different results from both kinds.

3. Imitation and Demonstration. Psychologists have been discouraged in their studies of imitation by the fact that rats, cats, and dogs do not show themselves to be active imitators. But there is no question that human beings imitate, and the widely recognized imitativeness of monkeys should have suggested to psychologists that man, too, might possess this characteristic. What then is required or involved in imitation?

When we see that someone else is performing actions that appear to please him in a certain situation, we can readily appreciate such signs of pleasure on his part. Assuming reasonably similar behavioral backgrounds and acquired secondary reinforcers, we too can initiate actions in regard to the stimulus situation, and the closer our movements resemble the "copied" movements (really the feedback stimuli from the movements), the stronger the "hope" that is generated in us. The example of the writing model might be suitable. The "forger" begins to copy a signature or other writing. The more similar to the model the copy appears to be— that is, the closer the feedback stimuli from looking at the copy are to the feedback from looking at the model—the better the "forger" feels.

Such an analysis can be applied generally, regardless of the action involved—imitating a hairdo, mimicking an actor, ironing clothes, or planting roses. Consequently, after someone has demonstrated for us the method by which something is done, when we attempt to repeat these actions, previously conditioned emotional reactions are aroused and guide our movements. If the demonstrator was at all successful, he will have introduced or made use of the specific stimuli to which our emotions had been conditioned, and now, when these same stimuli occur as a consequence of our own activity, we are reinforced (emotional reactions are aroused that control our subsequent reactions).

Show and Tell: Learning by Imitation

The paragraphs above are a brief summary of Mowrer's conclusions about the role of imitation in learning. The importance of the general topic, however, calls for a somewhat more extended review, and the following comments are offered for the prospective teacher, who will have heard little but criticism of the function of imitation in teaching.

Imitation is probably the greatest single, and most widely practiced, operation in learning and in all human activity and, at the same time, one of the least understood or appreciated by learning psychologists. It provides an amusing illustration of the lengths to which theorists will go to protect a theory. It will be recalled that Thorndike had laid down the "dictum" that learning can take place only when a reward follows an act. This made it necessary for learners to act first and be rewarded later. But, it is clear, they had to *act*. Simply watching someone else was obviously not performing, and consequently nothing could be learned because there was nothing to reward. By sticking to the principle, Thorndike felt constrained to outlaw the concept of imitation as a learning mechanism and turned the direction of learning and educational research into a course it has unprofitably enjoyed ever since. Much of the orientation of learning by projects and discovery can be traced to this rejection of imitation by Thorndike.

That psychologists were willing to accept such arrant nonsense is a tribute to their dedication to theory if not to their objectivity. It is obvious to anyone that children are imitators almost from the cradle and that children's games are imitations of adult behavior. As children grow up, they take on the attitudes, religions, and politics of their parents, to say nothing of the mother tongue. The process of show and tell starts as soon as the child can be shown and told. The children learn their fairy tales and nursery rhymes, as well as grammar, by constant recitation, demonstrations, and admonitions by parents and siblings.

The case for learning by imitation hardly needs to be made for anyone but psychologists. After Thorndike's dictum, research on imitation ceased almost completely. Not until 1941 did Miller and Dollard bring up the subject in an effort to extend Hullian learning theory into the social scene. Miller and Dollard were still trapped in the reinforcement dogma and explained imitation as a matter of learning by being rewarded for responding to cues originating in the behavior of others. One still had to perform and be rewarded for it. In 1946 Thorndike, in one of his last psychological papers, attacked learning by demonstration with his original vehemence.

From 1941 on until 1960 the issue remained quiescent, and imitation was not taken seriously by learning psychologists. By 1960, rumblings began to be heard about the possible role of imitation. Mowrer's observation that talking birds learn to talk by imitating their masters led to his projection of this theory into the realm of human language learning. Mowrer had made room for learning via the senses, that is, through looking and listening. By this time many other researchers had entered the field, and in the 1960s imitation research enjoyed a belated renaissance. A great number of studies began to appear in the psychological literature. Some of these studies were stimulated by social problems and claims that increasing violence and crime could be traced to depictions of such activities on television screens. Perhaps the foremost investigator during the sixties has been Bandura, who with Walters (1963) published a small volume on *Social Learning and Personality Development.*

Bandura was the first to break completely with the old learning theory based on reinforcement. He set up experimental designs where a model (M) would do something, e.g., pick up a doll and put it on a table (or kick it) in the presence of some child observer (O). Later the child would enter the room, find the doll on the floor and be quite likely to pick it up and put it on the table (or kick it if that was observed earlier). With sufficient ingenuity it might be possible to suggest some reinforcing operation, but at least the experimenter does not engage in any. The child does not perform, nor is he rewarded. The model performs but is not, at least ostensibly, rewarded. Even if a model were rewarded the observer would not be, at least not directly for acting. Here we have a situation Bandura describes as one of "acquisition" (the initial observation period) and subsequent "performance."

In a review of Bandura's later work on imitation, Flanders (1968) prefers to call these phases or stages "knowledge" and "acceptance." Acceptance implies knowledge and is normally inferred from actual imitation. The observer, however, does not have to accept and might still have learned what the model did. He might not have the appropriate incentive for actual overt imitation.

The theoretical refinements in the area of imitation are still to be explored and evaluated. As far as teaching is concerned, it is enough to appreciate that the principle of imitation has at last been liberated. The teacher can feel secure that if a student is attentive and observes the behavior of a model, he can learn. Whether he will perform the observed behavior is another matter.

The great bulk of experiments on imitation, whether done with animals or children, involves simple motor responses of a discriminative type. Sometimes aggressive responses have been observed; occasionally benevolent behavior has been the "task." Rarely has anything relevant to a school performance been involved, yet the essence of imitation is a demonstration by the teacher (model or M) to the student observer (O). It has been noted that some model variables, such as the status of M and, in some cases, age or sex, may be important depending on the age and sex of O, but no great guiding principles have emerged from these attempts. It is important that M has control of "resources valuable to O", says Flanders, although this cannot be the case where O observes movies, cartoons, or television models which, according to Bandura, are as effective as live M's.

What is important for education is that children (and everyone else to a degree) will imitate at least some behavior and that, if the response involved is in the repertoire, the stimulating action of a model can be effective in the acquisition (knowledge) and acceptance (performance) of the behavior at a later time in the absence of the model.

Our foray into the field of imitation has not resulted in anything novel for teachers and instructors, who for centuries have been showing and telling learners how to do things. We can only admit the error of an earlier day psychology and recognize the facts always appreciated by parents and teachers, who have not been misled by learning psychology.

Perhaps our time has not been spent too idly. The importance of models on young children's learning behavior can now, perhaps, be appreciated more deeply. It is commonly acknowledged that parents and the home environment form the basic reaction patterns that the child brings to school with him. His language patterns and his reactions to books will consist strongly of mimicry. If the parents do not read or converse in sentences, if they use slang and other unusual modes of expression, if they are aggressive and excitable, we can expect the child to be molded by the models involved. To determine what can be expected, it might be well to look at the parents and their normal behavior patterns.

We cannot ignore the role of imitation in the teacher-pupil relationship either. Students frequently imitate their teachers, especially if they become teachers themselves. They identify with the teachers who were able to condition positive emotional reactions. Perhaps this is the meaning of identification. If the teacher, through his appearance or behavior, arouses positive feelings, then whatever he says and does will take on conditioned stimulus aspects and similarly arouse the same emotional responses. Students will then be found talking and gesturing like their favorite teachers. A negative response to a teacher will similarly result in negative responses to his speech, mannerisms, and even the content of the course and lead to avoidance behavior.

The basic lesson to be drawn from the new interest in imitation is that *students do learn by what is shown to them, by what they see, and that it is sufficient to be shown if one is to learn. It is not necessary that one actually performs.* This conclusion is predicated on the assumption that the observer can perform the required behavior. The paralyzed invalid cannot imitate a dance step, to be sure, but he can learn what he can do in the sense of knowing what is to be done.

Care must be exerted that the observer is observing what is to be learned and not something else. Similarly, the teacher must not ask for more than the memory span involved. One cannot imitate an entire poem after one hearing, but six or seven words at a time are not beyond the usual facility. Officials who administer oaths come to appreciate what can be imitated.

Learning Without Overt Action

When we underscore Mowrer's proposition that learning amounts to conditioning of emotional reactions and not to conditioning of muscular responses, we come to the important conclusion that all those theoretical writers and educators who have followed Thorndike and Dewey may have been wrong in their emphasis on *action,* on *doing,* as the basis of learning. Mowrer tells us that we do not have to *do* in order to learn. We can merely sit and look and listen, and learning will take place. Although education has proceeded on this basis for 2,500 years and many people have learned a tremendous amount, Thorndike, Dewey, Hull, Guthrie, and Skinner, all in the present century, have tried to convince us that sitting and listening and sitting and reading are wrong or ineffective. Now Mowrer gives us a modern endorsement of ancient practice. If he is correct, the others are wrong. To the extent that others have been successful in demonstrating some of their views, they may have been right for the wrong reasons.

Over the last few years some experiments have been reported that appear at first blush to be incredible and on the side of fantasy. In these experiments (see Richardson, 1969, p. 56f) subjects were first tested for skills like dart throwing, basketball foul-shooting, and high jumping. They were then asked to refrain from any physical practice but to sit quietly for five-minute periods daily for two weeks and *imagine* themselves performing at these exercises with some thought to improvement. In all three types of tasks significant improvement was attained with no actual performance and no reinforcement by anyone. These experiments have not been taken seriously by many psychologists, judging by the sparsity of references to them; yet, if they are substantially correct, they suggest that we have failed to exploit a potentially powerful technique for learning. The practical possibilities await development. In the meantime, without data, not much can be said in the way of suggestions for teachers. Further research may reveal flaws or other variables. At the present time, we are no better off then Meredith Willson's *Music Man* who, unable to teach music, urged his students to *think* the music.

While Mowrer's views, though supporting classical tradition, may be correct, teachers must be somewhat careful in evaluating what amounts to a radical revolution (even though some may call it a reactionary effort). Until teachers can be more fully convinced, applications of Mowrer's theory must be stated somewhat tentatively, even negatively.

1. **It is not necessarily true that learning requires overt responses from the learner, at least at the beginning of learning.**

2. **Learning can occur, to at least some degree, if not to a major degree, when one is merely sitting, looking, and listening.**

Here we need some amendments. One cannot learn to swim on dry land (although on dry land one may learn a lot *about* swimming that may facilitate the process). Physical skills, in general, do require active participation. The acquisition of information, however, need not call for gross overt activity.

3. **Learning involves prior emotional conditioning through reinforcement operations, so that the cues or stimuli that are to become releasers of emotional reactions can come to operate as secondary reinforcers.**

4. **It is not necessary to reward or "reinforce" a learner for some action. It is enough that he sees someone else reinforced for an action.**

Normally, when the learner now performs the same response, he, too, will be rewarded—*but* he has already learned before he performed.

5. **With an appropriate background of conditioning, a learner may on some occasion have a positive emotional reaction to some apparently "novel" stimulus or stimulus pattern.**

When this happens the learner *feels* "good," and he may say "Ah ha! I understand" or "Now I get it." Gestalt psychologists would call this reaction an "insight." It is not different in its nature from any other case of a positive emotional reaction to a stimulus. There is nothing strange, mentalistic, or insightful about it. A prior emotional conditioning has been released because of some adequate or sufficient aspect of the stimulus situation. We will return to the matter of insight later (p. 222).

CONCLUSION

With these applications of Mowrer's theory, presentation of the concepts of the major theorists in the area of learning psychology is concluded. While the preceding chapters did not attempt to examine the more controversial features of the theories, you must have been aware that none has won common approval. Indeed, it is rather more the opposite—all have earned much disapproval. Each theory has been destructively criticized and found wanting, insofar as a general theory of learning is concerned (W. K. Estes *et al*, 1954). But the work of each individual psychologist has not been without its reward for education, and I hope that I have succeeded in extracting something of value for the reader from each man considered here. Of course, there have been many other psychologists working in the field, many of whom have contributed to the area of learning. Some of these will be discussed later in appropriate contexts. The next chapter, however, will turn to the work of a man who is too broadly involved in psychological processes to be labeled a "learning" theorist yet has provided some important thoughts on the subject of learning.

Chapter Six

Early
and
Late
Learning

One of the most astonishing phenomena in the history of psychology was the readiness with which psychologists of all "stamps" accepted the ancient folklore of the "bent twig." Nearly every psychologist was willing, if not anxious, to endorse the proposition that the "early years" were the "formative years." No one ever really defined the early years, but everyone was willing to say that character and personality were formed early in the life of the individual and that after one, three, seven, or some other number of years the nature of the person was set and rather unchangeable. Correlated with this proposition was another that held that *environment* was chiefly responsible for the way in which personalities evolve and that early environment is the most significant feature in determining behavior.

THE INFLUENCE OF EARLY ENVIRONMENT

Despite the general endorsement of these propositions, there was little research to back them up. Psychologists simply made such assertions as a matter of faith. To the great credit of D. O. Hebb (1949), the Canadian psychologist, the renewed interest shown in the decade of the 1950s in this problem of early environmental experience and its subsequent effects was based on some real research. The reader, of course, must realize that long-term controlled studies of the influence of early environment are not likely to attract great enthusiasm from psychologists. Few will be found willing to wait 20 or 30 years to publish their results.[1] As the next best thing, psychologists resort to animals that mature rapidly, trying to assess effects on later behavior of controlled experiences in early life. Such animal studies generally show what psychologists apparently would like to believe: that early environmental experiences are significant determinants

[1] See J. W. Macfarlane (1963) for a study of personality changes over a period of 30 years. This study was not a controlled environment investigation, but the findings are of interest for educators.

of later adjustments. Only two studies need be cited here to indicate the general flavor of such research.

In one of the first studies of rapidly maturing animals, Austin Riesen (1947) reared some baby chimpanzees in total darkness until they were about a year and a half or two years old. When these chimps were brought "into the light" for the first time, behaviorally they proved to be completely blind. After a few weeks they began to make use of their eyes and eventually behaved like completely seeing creatures. With the dark-reared chimpanzees and various other control chimpanzees, Riesen was able to demonstrate that animals raised in darkness apparently must *learn to see*.

In another experiment (see W. R. Thompson and W. Heron, 1954), in Hebb's laboratory, Scottish terriers were raised in boxes that allowed a view only of the laboratory ceiling. The puppies saw nothing but the sides of the boxes and the ceiling for a year and a half. During this time they never saw a human or another living thing. When these puppies had grown to maturity, they were removed from this restricted environment and were compared with normally reared animals. In a sense, there was no comparison. The "restricted" dogs were more stupid, less aggressive, more "curious," and apparently unacquainted with pain. They would not retreat from flames held under their noses, would permit themselves to be pressed against hot radiators, would endure pin pricks, etc. Apparently these dogs had to *learn to sense pain,* have appropriate emotions, and eliminate a ubiquitous curiosity. Similar studies with rats showed similar negative consequences on subsequent behavior, although a number of these studies do not quite fit the psychologist's bias.

As a result of experiments such as have just been described, Hebb arrived at some provocative conclusions that, quite literally, changed the interpretations of behavior that psychologists had been presenting to the world up to about 1950. It would take us too far afield to describe Hebb's theoretical views in detail, and for our purposes it will suffice to summarize some key points that have bearing on practical education problems. The important contributions made by Hebb include his emphasis on the dynamic nature of neural activity and the differences in early and late learning. I will not spend too much time on Hebb's views about the nervous system as these are highly theoretical; the concept of early and late learning will take up most of the remainder of this chapter.

The Conceptual Nervous System

Hebb's real interests are physiological. He wants to translate or restate psychological principles in terms of physiological operations of the brain.

Because of the complexity of the brain and the relative paucity of our knowledge, Hebb felt obliged to speculate and invent a scheme of action for a nervous system that he thought paralleled the real operations of neural mechanisms. He called his scheme a "conceptual nervous system," but he tried to stay as close to physiological facts as he could.

1. The A/S Ratio. The first important point of concern to us is Hebb's description of the brain in terms of Association areas and Sensory areas. The former areas are parts of the brain that are not known to be involved in any specialized motor or sensory functions. For many years these really unknown areas have been assumed to function in the development of associations or "the higher mental processes." Whether or not these areas are actually involved in learning is not especially relevant for us. The important point is that in lower animals, such as rats, cats, and dogs, the sensory areas are much more prominent and occupy relatively more of the brain than they do in the higher primates and man. In short, the rat's brain, with its large olfactory lobes, is basically a sensory brain; it is extremely limited in potential for associations, and it makes of the rat a "sensory-bound" creature—that is, one that responds to every noise or flicker of light, every little olfactory change. The rat is so sensitive to external stimuli that it is relatively unable to inhibit reactions—it might be described as impulsive, stimulus-bound, a creature of its immediate environment.

The picture just drawn of the rat is the view that, prior to 1950, was more or less the working orientation of behavioristic psychologists about human beings. Man was considered a creature of his environment, a straw in the wind. Hebb argues that this view is a distortion of reality, that man, in contrast to rats, is far more complex in adaptation potential. His relatively larger association areas make it possible for learning and association factors to control behavior. While man may be sensitive to the same stimuli that activate rats, man's reactions will be less immediate and direct —they will be modified by experience and current as well as future circumstances and considerations.

According to Hebb then, the learning psychologies of the first half of this century that were based to such a large extent on studies of lower animals were inadequate psychologies. They might have been reasonably good interpretations of the behavior of sensory-bound creatures like rats but had little virtue for the complex learned behavior of human beings. These older psychologies had ignored the A/S ratio—that is, the ratio of Association to Sensory areas.

2. The Dynamics of Nervous Action. The next point stressed by Hebb is that the old psychologies thought of the nervous system as a static connecting system with no other function than to serve in the formation of associations or connections between the effects of external stimuli and motor activity. Hebb proceeded to call the attention of psychologists to the constant activity of the brain (as measured by electroencephalograms) and to the role of the reticular formation (an area of the brain just above the point where the brain begins to bulge out as an enlargement of the spinal cord). Recent neurophysiological discoveries have begun to reveal information about the functions of this area that was long known anatomically but that was ignored as far as function is concerned. It appears that this area (sometimes called "the arousal area") exercises important control over what stimuli ever get into the brain proper, in terms of effects, and what action is going to occur. Unless the reticular formation is itself active, the rest of the brain is relatively helpless to act. The importance of this area for behavior was unknown until the decade of the 1950s. The functioning of this area makes the old-fashioned picture of the brain as a connecting agency, pure and simple, distinctly inadequate.

3. Primitive or Early Learning. The conception of the brain as a more dynamic agency than previously believed was amplified by Hebb at the molecular level of cell firing. Hebb took advantage of other recent neurophysiological information about the way in which neurons react to develop a picture of learning. The reader should remember that much of this theorizing is largely speculative and not meant to be an exact and factual description of either the nervous system or learning. The important point, however, is that it is a known fact that if neurons are stimulated into firing there will be some persistence of this neural discharge for some time after external stimulation ceases. Hebb used this information to picture the formation of connections between numbers of neurons that would keep stimulating each other into discharging for a short period after the original stimulation. If the same (more or less) neurons were repeatedly fired by each other, they would tend to develop connections so that future self-stimulation—that is, one neuron by another—would be easier and more likely. What this amounts to is that any given stimulus would tend to discharge a particular group of neurons, and this group would be more and more effectively discharged with repetition. Such a group of neurons that would react to a particular stimulus Hebb called a "cell assembly."

In early life an organism would start out with a more-or-less unorganized brain. There would be no particular neural reaction to any particular stimulus. With repeated specific stimulation, certain cell assemblies would form and become more or less stable. Different stimuli would excite different assemblies; slowly the brain would become populated or organized with such assemblies. Some assemblies would include motor-neuron components and lead to some specific actions. If some assemblies were excited in succession by consecutive stimulations, the cell assemblies would themselves become organized into successive patterns or "phase sequences."

Most of the learning of a young animal would consist of such acquisitions of neural pattern connections, of cell assemblies and phase sequences, of simple stimulus-response connections. Such acquisition or learning would be slow and cumulative. There would be no meaning to such learning in any serious sense. On the human level, we could illustrate what Hebb is driving at by picturing such a situation as the following: A parent with an infant in his lap shows the baby a large letter "A." While showing the baby this letter the parent says "A." The baby, when and if it looks at the A, will have some neural pattern runoff which will persist for a while. If the baby looks again, the same or another neural pattern will run off. Eventually with enough looking, a cell assembly of a particular group of neurons will fire whenever the baby looks at A. Other visual assemblies will probably run off whenever the baby looks elsewhere, but persistent exposure to the A will arouse the cell assembly for A more and more reliably. Because the parent is saying "A," an auditory assembly will also form, in the same fashion. If the two assemblies are run off together repeatedly, they will come in time to arouse each other so that when the baby is shown the A, an auditory assembly will run off involving the same neurons that were active when the baby heard the parent pronounce the A. The firing of the auditory assembly would not be quite complete without an actual vocal stimulus, but it would be at least a partial reconstruction. It would amount to what we have been calling an image. Similarly, if the baby should hear the sound "A", a partial visual assembly, an "image" of A, would be activated. Hebb (1966) defined an image as "the occurrence of perceptual processes in the absence of stimulation that normally gives rise to the perception." The running off of the two cell assemblies would be a phase sequence in Hebb's terms. It would represent a primitive kind of learning and would be a function of simple repetition.

The example cited above should not suggest to the reader that the baby "hears" A when the A is shown. The reverse interpretation might be more appropriate, namely, that hearing means that a particular cell assembly has run off. All that was meant by this hypothetical example was that learning, according to Hebb, depends upon recurrent neural firing initiated by frequent repetitions of the same stimulus. It should be noted also that the child would not always see the A from the same viewpoint or in the same light nor would the parent's voice always be the same. Each variation would involve its own cell assemblies and this, in turn, suggests that even the simplest learning might be extremely involved and time-consuming. Because babies have nothing else to do except to look and listen, they can be learning a great deal in their cribs in the sense of forming countless cell assemblies.

The Meaning of Hebb's Theorizing

Whatever the eventual scientific fate of Hebb's speculations, the interpretation that we can draw for our own educational interests is quite clear (and may be correct even if Hebb turns out to be wrong). First, it is obvious that the early learning theorists had the wrong view of the nervous system as a simple connector. Such a simple connecting system was just what was needed to explain the behavior of simple stimulus-bound creatures like rats and to account for the kinds of learning such animals demonstrated, the learning of simple movements, such as turning right or left toward simple stimuli. Because animals were never used in experiments more than once, the kind of learning they exhibited could properly be called "early" or "primitive." It did not depend upon any earlier experience of any serious nature.

Now the outstanding feature of adult human learning is its relative rapidity, to say nothing of its complexity. How is it that an adult can remember a sentence that is stated only once whereas a child cannot do so? Hebb's answer is straightforward: The child is still busy learning the elements of the sentence; cell assemblies are still being formed for separate words. The adult has already learned all the essential elements and needs only to learn the sequence. Because adults are familiar (have the necessary cell assemblies already formed) with virtually all the elements they are called upon to use, the learning they do is of a far different nature than the slow, arduous learning of the child. An analogy to building a house might clarify the point. A contractor can quickly put a house together if all of the necessary materials (bricks, wood, glass, etc.) are on hand; he can work even more rapidly if walls have been prefabricated. A house may go up in days. The total time to produce the bricks, wood, and glass, however, should also be reckoned in the total achievement. The adult learner is like the contractor putting together available materials. The child is engaged in creating the materials.

The final point that needs to be spelled out from Hebb's views is that early learning may include certain kinds of associations (phase sequences) that may automatically recur and may hinder new kinds of associations on occasion as well as facilitate others. This is a point we can consider later when dealing with the transfer of training. For the present we must recognize that, given a large number of cell assemblies and a variety of experiences, it is possible for anyone at almost any time to have an assembly fired that might not normally be fired (for a host of physiological reasons). In effect, Hebb provides for the possibility that one can have an essentially new idea (a cell assembly that is run off out of its normal sequence) at almost any time. What this amounts to is that one cannot count on a fixed, mechanical, routine order of cell-assembly firings in complex, adult organisms to the same degree that one might in a rat or young infant. Such a state of affairs does not make education any easier, but it does make man more interesting and perhaps more dignified.

We can now turn to the problem of the teacher trying to apply the findings of the laboratory psychologist to the classroom. This problem was briefly explored in Chapter 1. Now we are in a better position to evaluate the psychologist's contributions and limitations. We can begin with the Hebbian suggestions that not only are people not rats, but adults are not children or infants.

The Learning of Children and Adults

The behavior of young humans—babies—is much more like that of lower animals than it is like that of adult humans. Human infants are just as much *sensory* creatures as are lower animals throughout their lives. Only gradually does the human infant expand its sense-bound behavior repertory and begin to respond rather freely to relatively minor changes in the environment. Where a bird, rat, rabbit, or baby reacts to every noise or shadow, an adult human ignores most of, if not all, the noises and shadows that surround him. Even the ringing of a telephone bell might invite no immediate reaction from a human adult. He does not immediately stop what he is doing and rush to the phone like a child or teenager. The differences between adults and children are obvious, especially to parents. Teachers may be somewhat less perceptive, especially teachers who have studied psychology and have tried to apply the lectures on learning to their own activities. Such lectures may be based on the behavior of sense-bound rats, not human adults.

It seems incredible that psychologists could have been as blind as they were to this difference between children and adults. Most psychological studies of learning have been conducted on college sophomores and white rats. Neither class of subjects is especially representative of anything else. The white rat might be closer to the human infant than the college sophomore is, but the learning of neither is comparable to that of a first-grader, nor is the laboratory learning of the college sophomore necessarily comparable to his library and study-room learning.

Psychologists probably should dispense with rat studies altogether as far as human learning is concerned, except for some extremely primitive kinds of conditioning as the very early ages. (The major contributions developed by the "rat psychologists" have already been reported in earlier chapters.) On the college-sophomore level, psychologists may only recently have come to some useful educational considerations. Most of this century's work with college-age subjects probably has little application to typical human learning. It stemmed from the original investigations of Ebbinghaus on rote memorization. As was said on page 17, Ebbinghaus, using nonsense syllables and himself as subject, introduced a great many methodological problems of some theoretical interest to psychologists. Little that he found has any bearing on what goes on in classrooms today, especially since rote memorization is no longer a standard operation. Even if it were, the kinds of principles that interested Ebbinghaus yielded precious little in the form of application, except to nonsense material learned by *adults* and not by children. Since adults do not ordinarily spend much time learning nonsense syllables, there is little reason to reconsider Ebbinghaus' findings. The important point to remember is that, even with nonsense syllables or other meaningless material, children do *not* learn like adults. Principles drawn from studies of one group do *not* apply to the other.

For one thing, children take much longer to learn the same amount of material that college students absorb in a few trials. It is necessary to go back to Hebb's cell-assembly hypothesis to clarify this statement. For very young children (as for most animals), learning at first is a matter of acquiring various sensory-motor associations on a more-or-less direct level. Such early or "primitive" learning, it will be recalled, is a long, hard, repetitive process. Over weeks and months, the human infant learns certain S-R connections through the repeated firing of specific neural circuits. But when such learning is virtually complete (say, by the age of six or seven), there is abundant room in the brain of a normal human for the neural circuits themselves to become associated with each other, so that any *S* can, hypothetically, result in any *R*. Put in other words, learning now is no longer a simple, uncomplicated matter of acquiring new *S-R* connections, because there is virtually no new *S* left—that is, no stimulus that has not already been equipped with some connections to some response. Of course there will be many new or novel *symbolic* stimuli, but even in these cases the learner will have acquired some kind of reaction to symbols as such (letters, words, numbers, mathematical expressions).

The learner's background now has to be taken into account. Some things will be easy for him to learn because he already has the neural connections. Other things will be difficult, because he has inadequate or even wrong connections aroused by stimuli the teacher is manipulating. Here we have the explanation for the fact that some children learn some things with ease and others with difficulty. Some things have already been learned, at least in part; other things may have improper neural reactions associated with them; still others may have virtually no neural foundation background and hence must start like all primitive learning "from scratch."

Enriched and Impoverished Environments

In support of his theoretical pursuits Hebb launched a variety of research programs calculated to provide supporting data. We have already seen reference to some of this research with dogs and chimpanzees raised in isolation and relatively empty environments. Hebb pursued this type of research with human adults, who would be asked to lie quietly on a bed in a dark room while earphones fed a gentle hum into their ears; arms and legs would be encased in cardboard tubes, leaving the subjects out of contact with the world. Very few subjects could stand the stress of such isolation, even though they were free to terminate their participation at any time. Those who did stay a few hours complained of hallucinations and uneasiness; when tested, they showed some disturbances of perception as well as a lowered problem-solving ability. It would, of course, be impossible to study human infants in such deprived environments. Where rats have been observed in impoverished environments (Forgus, 1954), they appear to show less problem-solving ability than rats raised in "enriched" environments. (For rats, an enriched environment includes considerable living space and various kinds of objects to crawl over and through, manipulate or play with.) In recent years some psychologists have been trying to assess the effect of over-stimulation (frequent and dazzling changes of colored lights and rapid and complex changes in sound patterns), but the data from such sensory overload are not yet pertinent for us. While the research results from animals are complicated and difficult to interpret, they generally confirm the psychologists' expectancies that growing up in an affluent environment with all sorts of stimulation from varied experiences will lead to a greater learning capacity.

Head Start

In recent years educators have been attempting to make up for deficiencies in the backgrounds of children who reside in what are deservedly called "deprived areas." Special programs have been developed to provide a background more similar to that of children coming from more affluent surroundings. Such programs have been criticized (see Jensen, 1969) as ineffective. The criticism might better have been that they "are too little and too late." In most cases the programs amounted to not much more than a speeded-up nursery school operation for pre-kindergarten children. Psychologists reviewing Jensen's findings (see Kagan, 1969) are inclined to agree with Kagan's remark: "The value of Head Start or similar remedial programs has not yet been adequately assessed. It is not reasonable to assume that compensatory education has failed merely because eight weeks of a Head Start program organized on a crash basis failed to produce stable increases in I.Q. score." There is little point to arguing about such programs. From what we have learned from Hebb it appears that such programs should begin at birth or shortly after and continue on into adolescence. A few such programs are underway, but the results will be some years in coming. One cannot expect much from short and sporadic remedial programs. To appoint pre-nursery or nursery school teachers to make up for the deficiencies of the first three or four years in slum children's lives is not even a half-measure.

The ideas discussed above were derived largely from Hebb. The reader is reminded that Hebb is a physiological psychologist and a theorist concerned with a hypothetical nervous system. Teachers, of course, can hardly be expected to become familiar with the workings of the nervous systems of their students. They must work in a framework of words and diagrams, at least in most of their daily effort. In the remainder of this chapter we shall deal more with words and teacherlike activities and have no further concern with neurons as such. The ideas that will be exploited, however, will still reflect Hebb's thinking. He was, after all, once a public school teacher himself.

SLOW AND FAST LEARNING

Much in the preceding paragraphs reads as though there are two kinds of learning. This may be so, but what is implied above is that there are *two kinds of learners:* those who are prepared (by early training) and those who are not. For the person with appropriate background, some new material can be learned in one trial; for the person without an appropriate background, learning may involve many trials, much repetition, and "practice." This statement can be illustrated by a summary of a recent study.

In 1957, Irwin Rock published a report that was somewhat sensational and aroused a flurry of excitement among psychologists. He had developed a rather unique technique to study "paired associate learning." In this operation, it will be recalled, a subject is shown a card with two items on it, say two nonsense syllables such as *gey-nur*. Then another card is shown, then another, and so on, depending on the experimenter's needs. Suppose a subject is shown eight such cards in succession with about three seconds[2] to view each card. He is then shown the cards again with only the left-hand side exposed, and it is up to him to recall the right-hand side and say it aloud. In the case of the sample he would see *gey-* and should say *"nur"* if he had learned it in the three-second period during which he had seen it before. Similarly with the other seven cards. Few subjects could recite all eight "responses" correctly after only one trial. Normally, the cards would be shuffled and shown again and again until all eight responses were given correctly (with college students this would take about eight trials). But what Rock did was unusual in the history of such experimentation. If the subject did not know some of the responses on the first trial, he withdrew those cards from the pack and replaced them with completely new cards. If none was known, there would be eight new cards to learn. If only one answer had been given correctly, there would be seven new cards, etc. Rock reasoned that if repetition is necessary for learning, a group of subjects learning under these conditions would have difficulty and would require many, many trials. In actual fact, his subjects learned eight cards in eight trials just as they would have learned the original eight if none had been withdrawn. Because of the arrangement, the subjects had only one chance or "trial" to study a given card. They had to learn it at that time or they would never see it again. Because the subjects did, in fact, learn eight cards in eight trials, Rock felt privileged to claim that learning took place in one trial and that repetition is unnecessary for learning to occur.

2 Rock actually allowed eight seconds per pair.

Such a conclusion about paired associate learning flies in the face of much research and at first glance seems revolutionary. But we must review Rock's procedure and reconsider the operation. If the subject did not know the answer, Rock threw out the card and replaced it. Because the subject then did learn these new cards in the same amount of time, we can only assume that some cards are easier to learn than others. For some subjects, of course, some cards are easier than they are for other subjects, but, in general, if one card is learned in one trial, as Rock says, and another is not, we must conclude that the former is easier. By this conclusion, we can only mean that the subject has already learned the card *before* he ever came to the laboratory. In Rock's experiment, the average college student of 1957 was well acquainted with the name of the motion picture star Mitzi Gaynor. If when he said *gey-nur* to himself, he set off previously acquired connections involving Miss Gaynor, he had the card under control. A student with a less fortunate history would have had to start from "scratch" and create the connection between *gey* and *nur*. Other students with other backgrounds might have found themselves saying *gey-grey-nur-nurse-grey nurse* or *nur-nun-grey-nun-nun-nunnery* (aha!) *gey-nur*.

The point I am making here is that when paired associate learning is involved, when past experience counts, the learning can (indeed must) take place in one trial—that is, the connection *is* available, if the proper neural circuits are stimulated. Sometimes the stimulation of appropriate circuits takes a little time. The more difficult the pair of associates (and by *difficult* I mean the less likely a suitable neural connection is to occur), the longer it will take before something occurs to the subject that will enable him to respond correctly. In the meantime, the experimenter, holding to a rigid time period, has thrown out the card. Note, then, that "trials" is a meaningless way of measuring paired associate learning. A trial really means a period of time long enough for a connection to occur. If the experimenter arbitrarily cuts this time, the subject cannot come up with the right answer.

Normally, of course, we do not try to learn (or teach) eight pairs of new material at any one time.[3] And again, normally, we have enough time to have the connections occur for most of what we want to learn, so that much of our adult experience involves learning in one trial and bears no resemblance to laboratory studies of batches of nonsense material.

[3] There are some occasions in academic learning when essentially "paired associates" *are* learned in groups, for example, foreign-language vocabularies, chemical symbols and formulas, geologic eras, states and their capitals.

To complete the discussion of early and late learning, we can compare the performances of children and college students with the same material. When first-grade children are used as subjects in a Rock type experiment, they do miserably (J. Powell, 1962). They cannot learn anywhere near an equal amount of material when new cards are substituted for old. They merely become confused. When given a small number (four) cards to learn, they sometimes learn in one trial but do this on the basis of immediate memory and repetition between trials and tests. If given familiar objects (pictures of pairs of things like wagons and kites) to learn, they too can learn some cards in one trial. Even college students cannot easily learn other kinds of material, pairs of numbers like 397-462, for example, with the Rock procedure. They have no available already-learned connections that could help in connecting the numbers.

That background, experience, or early learning makes a difference in later learning apparently is not open to question today. For later learning we make use of our past; our past *mediates* our present learning—that is, bridges the gap between Ss and Rs—and without such mediators we would be lost. Unfortunately, mediators will occur in all adult learning attempts, and there is little we can do to control their quality. They can mislead just as easily as they can lead, and sometimes we sit for hours thinking of wrong answers to even simple questions. It is this difficulty of controlling mediators that prevents us from always following a fixed course in thought, that enables us on occasion to have a new idea, and, in general, that keeps us from being predictable—which makes people more interesting.

PRACTICAL APPLICATIONS

Suggestions for practical application of what has been said about early and late learning may strike teachers as rather skimpy, if not sterile. When future research enables learning psychologists to develop procedures for making sure that the right experiences are in the backgrounds of the learners, and when they learn how this experience can be most effectively tapped, teachers will be in a position to help learners. Right now our capacities are limited.

One practical suggestion, however, is

Before attempting to teach anything, analyze the content or skill to find out what the components are. Then test for the components to be sure they are available. Don't teach a higher level operation without the lower level equipment or background.

While, admittedly, this sounds naïve and general, I can quickly make the point on a general level. During World War II, French and English boys came to the United States for aviation training. Somehow, they were generally considered as not quite prepared for many aspects of aviation, particularly along mechanical lines. They had not had the common experience of American boys of tinkering with automobiles and were, in these respects, slow learners.

The concept of early and late learning can be appreciated readily in connection with learning to play musical instruments. Some teachers like to assign melodies, "little tunes," to beginners to give them a sense of accomplishment. While this may benefit morale, it will not result in musical achievement. Basic to any real skill in music is a familiarity with scales, chords, intervals, rhythms, and tempos. These must be learned through systematic practice with so-called "exercises." When the components are mastered, the achievement operation is virtually completed. The properly trained musician can play any ordinary music. The melody-trained student will have to study it as a new experience.

In almost all areas of achievement we have the same pattern: certain basic operations must be acquired before the final performance can be effectively attained. Before you can read words, you must become acquainted with letters. This elementary proposition is not fully appreciated by all teachers of reading, some of whom, with their "look-and-say" methods, try to make readers overnight. They are making lookers or look-and-sayers, not readers. I do not make this point to support any special technique for reading instruction; rather I suggest that reading teachers have not really analyzed their job.[4] Most children learn to read in spite of the methods because eventually they master the fundamental skills by themselves. Some children do this at great time costs. Other children, coming from home backgrounds where the alphabet has been taught from various picturebooks, have already learned some of the fundamentals. They learn to read quickly, while the teachers despair over the slow learners who are then diagnosed as "not ready."

I will now summarize our considerations of the early and late approach to learning in a few general statements that can be taken to apply to all levels of human activity—to sensing, perceiving, feeling, thinking, problem-solving, motor skills, in fact to any level of behavior. To begin, the suggestions offered above can be subdivided into two more specific suggestions:

a. Analyze a skill or lesson into components and test for or train the components separately.

4 See R. Brown (1958). Also see Chapter 13.

This suggestion has a Guthrian flavor, but it stems just as strongly from Hebb. It is pleasing to have such agreement. As a practical example, teaching children about grammar involves endless confusion about the nature of the "subject" of a sentence because teachers commonly start out teaching about grammar by describing nouns and then equating nouns with subjects of sentences. If "subjects" are first described as "what the sentence is about," children should have no difficulties with various word forms used as subjects.

b. Where the components must be learned by "dull drill" and there is no alternative, then institute the dull drill.

Students can hardly be encouraged to act as if everything was fun and games. If the teacher has acquired the proper relationship with the students (remember Mowrer), the students will be willing to work. Children, for example, should be forced to memorize multiplication tables to a high level of efficiency before being asked to multiply. There is no alternative. Sugar-coating is a waste of time. It is probably advisable that the tables be learned up through 25×25 rather than stopping with 9×9 as is now customary.

A second suggestion deriving from the early and late learning division may not appear too practical on first consideration, but a whole philosophy of education rests on it. It is simply this:

c. Where feasible, train learners in the use of mediational devices.

Sometimes mediation devices can be simple, like jingles that enables a learner to retain a long list of elements. The alphabet patter song is an example. With other kinds of content, the teacher might need to use a labeling procedure. A student who has learned a B-minor scale and how to recognize it has a great advantage in playing a composition in B-minor over the student who is learning the same composition without knowing the scale features. Knowing the fundamentals of Communism and Capitalism will enable a student to evaluate a piece of propaganda from either side of the economic fence. The examples could be endless, and the procedures are, in fact, commonly endorsed but rarely practiced. In the art-teaching world, for example, many teachers supply the materials and, in effect, tell children to "go ahead and express" themselves instead of providing such basic techniques as color blending, pigment mixing, brush strokes, perspective, and shading. The child will have plenty of time to become an artist after he learns to use the equipment. The artist has to *know* that he has a problem in perspective before he can solve it! Instead of teaching art, some teachers ignore their obligations and rationalize by saying they do not want to influence the child's style or curb his creativity. What they are really saying is that they do not know how to teach art.

A third suggestion can bring this chapter to a close. It is perhaps the most demanding kind of advice one can give to teachers, although, like all advice, it is easy to give:

d. Where the background for adequate achievement is missing, supply the background before worrying about achievement.

When teachers feel pressure from administrators to bring their students up to local or national "norms," they may understandably feel inclined to ignore this suggestion. Yet it is a basic one. Its full implementation might call for many changes in educational practice, particularly for such operations as the "ungraded school." Frequently, teachers worry over underachievers and presume the basic difficulty is sheer orneriness or laziness—it may simply be in the lack of an appropriate background.

In some communities, with outside help, underprivileged children in low economic neighborhoods are provided with "new" experiences—they are given magazines, books, games, excursions, concert and theater experience; an effort is made to catch up with the normal routine experience of the middle-class child with his music, dancing, skating, and horsemanship lessons. Such attempts to enrich the environment of impoverished children amount to a belated effort to provide what should actually have been the "early learning" experience of children who are now asked to pursue a common course of studies in school.

In suburban communities and upper-income-level homes the routine physical luxuries may have been available to children from their birth. Here, the interests of parents may have diverted them from providing the kind of emotional early learning that might be effective in meeting the problems of adjusting to school requirements.

Whatever the lacks or the reasons for such lacks, teachers cannot expect students to make progress automatically when they present materials to students who do not have the proper foundation. Sometimes a higher-level operation may appear to be learnable without a thorough grounding in the fundamentals. It hardly needs pointing out that such superficial achievements can only result in future difficulties for the student and that cooperating in such ventures is unworthy of a teacher.

Chapter Seven

The
Problems
of
Action,
Attention,
and
Reinforcement

No proper teacher wants to be told *what* to do without also being told why he or she should do so. From what has been said in previous chapters, teachers should have acquired some appreciation of the logic and research that lie behind the views of the major learning theorists, although the emphasis in those chapters was on relatively abstract rather than practical approaches to the problems of education. These brief reviews of the work of the major learning psychologists, of necessity, could not bring out the degree of unity among these theorists on important issues. Consequently, the purpose of this and the following two chapters is to highlight the agreement among psychologists when dealing with matters that bear on the problems of teaching and on which they have done substantial research and serious thinking.

For the teacher, the key problems are (1) the problem of action or activity, (2) the problem of attention—that is, motivation, (3) the problem of reinforcement of learning, (4) the problem of forgetting and extinction, (5) the problem of transfer of training, and (6) the problem of understanding. In applying the principles of learning to these problems of education, Chapters 7, 8, and 9 will also consider related matters that will allow the reader to examine some of the work of psychologists who have not yet been mentioned. After the six teaching problems, teaching by machine, television teaching, and other current innovations will be evaluated in the final chapters.

ACTION

In American education, the emphasis today is probably on *doing,* on action or activity. Thorndike, Hull, and Skinner all based their entire systematic thinking on the proposition that without performance there is no learning. The emphasis on action is probably the result of their preoccupation with rewards—there is no way to reward anyone if he has not *done* anything. According to reward theorists, behavior must occur before it can be learned. From a philosophical rather than a psychological view, John Dewey, with his progressive education, likewise took the position that only activity has merit. For him, the job of the teacher was to see to it that every learner was busy. The "project" method of teaching is a direct outgrowth of this emphasis on activity. Among the theorists discussed earlier, only Tolman and Mowrer were willing to concede, and even to claim, that learning can take place without action. Tolman (1938) carefully distinguished between learning *and* performance and insisted that learning could occur if significates merely followed signs, even though the learner did not do anything observable. As we have seen, Mowrer, too, argued that the learner need not do anything except undergo some emotion in the presence of other stimuli for some kinds of learning to occur. Motor skills, of course, require action but only to provide feedback stimuli from the responses. Mowrer and Hebb, along with Tolman, did permit of the possibility of learning simply through seeing and hearing. And, as we have seen in the discussion of imitation, even motor responses in learners could be related to their observation of others who performed them (the demonstrators or models). The possibility of improvement in motor skills by practice through imagery was also suggested (see p. 135).

Research on Action and Learning

The efforts to establish the necessity of action in connection with learning have followed several lines, both positive and negative, and ranged from research designed to test whether one could learn anything while asleep to comparisons between discussion and lecture sections of college courses. We can begin a brief survey of such research by a quick look at learning-while-asleep studies.

1. Learning and Sleep. Those psychologists interested in proving that action is necessary for learning would be greatly disturbed if it could be shown that even a little learning could occur while the learners were asleep. They would not normally even think of investigations of this sort and would ignore the question entirely if it were not for various entrepreneurs who have advertised and sold (and still do) pillow speakers that a believer can set to recite lessons for him from a previously prepared tape recording, in the fond elusion that he will awaken with a head filled with knowledge. Newspapers like to feature stories of enterprising students who claim success with this method, but to date no satisfactory evidence has been produced that anyone can learn anything in this manner. When controlled experiments are performed (C. H. Simon and W. W. Emmons, 1955) where there is satisfactory evidence of sleep, findings have been that no learning takes place during the sleep periods.

2. Incidental Learning. A second negative research approach to the activity problem is exemplified by studies of incidental learning (see pp. 28–31). In these studies some subjects are deceived into believing that they are merely assisting the experimenter and that they present other subjects with material to learn. They might, for example, read material over and over to another subject who is supposed to learn. When the "official" subjects have learned, the assistants are tested. Older studies, under a kind of Thorndikian influence, usually failed to find any great amount of learning in the assistants. More recent studies, by Mechanic (1964) for example, indicate that so-called "incidental learners" can learn a great deal, depending upon the nature of their assignments. If what they are called upon to do involves some "orientation" (see p. 48) to the task and some "discriminatory" activity, they too learn almost, if not as well as, the standard subjects. The crucial variables appear to be the nature of the instructions and duties of the "incidental" subject.

Experiments with animals generally indicate that unless the animal is specifically forced to use some pathway, procedure, or piece of equipment (be active), little learning takes place. Thorndike (1946) once suggested that rats might be given rides through a maze and then tested for knowledge of the maze path. Such experiments have been performed (Bugelski, 1956), and generally it was found that the riders learned nothing (except, perhaps, that they had been taken for a ride). It is a common human experience for a person who does not drive a car but who is a regular passenger with another driver not to be very familiar with even frequently traveled routes.

Recently, the general negative findings in such research have been contradicted by P. C. Dodwell and D. S. Bessant (1960), who allowed the rats in their study to learn the pathway through a water maze by swimming from start to goal. Rats will swim quite effectively, and water mazes have been used quite frequently. What Dodwell and Bessant did, however, was to construct a small raft on which a rat passenger was pulled through the maze. When the rats were later forced to swim, the rats that had been given rides on the raft showed a significant improvement in their learning when their scores were compared with those of the rats in the control group that got no free rides first. These findings were somewhat astonishing in view of the previous negative history of this kind of research. Perhaps the important factor in the Dodwell and Bessant research was the raft. The rats may well have been somewhat upset by this strange means of travel that involved at least the risk of a wetting. There may have been some anxiety reduction with the journey's end, and the rats may have been more concerned over (or attentive to) environmental clues while riding the raft than when engaged in other kinds of "carrying-through" experiments. In other words, their learning in this study may have been more than "incidental."

Activity in Terms of "Tension"

Research that has sought positive proof for the activity principle has produced little direct evidence, although one favorite experiment (A. G. Bills and J. C. Stauffocher, 1937) is frequently cited. In this study, learners were asked to memorize material while squeezing handgrip dynamometers with a certain amount of pressure or tension. When they were thus "active," they learned better than when they were not so occupied. This evidence might support the conclusion that anyone should be a little tense when learning (as opposed to relaxed), but tension is not regarded as activity by those psychologists who insist that overt responses must be made. To call such findings evidence for the necessity of action in learning is masking the point. It is generally recognized that an erect posture, a hard chair, and a businesslike attitude are more conducive to learning than lying abed, but, again, these factors veer away from the point that no learning takes place without action in the sense of overt responding.

Learning Without Overt Action—Lectures versus Discussions

The real question is: Can anyone learn by sitting and listening (to teachers, storytellers, TV performers, lecturers, and the like)? Mowrer's position on this question was discussed at length (pp. 126–130), and it appears absurd to deny that people learn in this way. They may not be able to learn the kinds of things that call for specific sensory-motor adjustments (such as heart surgery or knitting), but they certainly can learn verbal material by listening—else many teachers have wasted much time in talking. No student is able to repeat verbatim the context of a prolonged and complex lecture after hearing it once. But to judge from this that nothing can be learned by sitting and listening is sheer nonsense. What we need, of course, is evidence about what kind of material is learned *better* by one procedure than by any other. If it turns out that nothing at all is learned better by some one procedure, in any circumstance or under any consideration, then that procedure for learning should be given up. Evidence for such a radical step simply is not available.

Teachers sometimes are told that the discussion method of teaching is more effective than the lecture method. Here the real questions are: What is to be learned? and What are the criteria—that is, how is the learning to be measured? Depending on the material, some things might be learned better (or more effectively) by one method or the other. A rather well-known attempt to demonstrate the virtues of discussion techniques was made by Kurt Lewin (1948) during World War II. He arranged a series of lectures for housewives on the values of inexpensive cuts of meats (visceral organs, etc.) and had other housewives participate in discussions on the same subject. Later it was found that the discussers continued to use the less-expensive meat cuts longer than did the lecture subjects. About all that we can judge from Lewin's results is that in a discussion people may commit themselves publicly to some position and find it difficult to withdraw. Lewin produced no evidence that the discussers learned more. In another study, a psychologist (V. Faw, 1949) conducted a lecture course and a discussion course on the same content. At the end of the course, the discussers had higher scores on an objective test than did the lecture hearers. An erroneous conclusion was promptly drawn as to the effectiveness of discussions. It should have been obvious to the researcher that he could not possibly cover the same material in the discussion class as in the lecture; there just wasn't time. To know the material better, or even as well, the discussers had to study their textbook outside class, and they may well have had to devote much extra time to the effort.

In a 1963 report, Stern reviewed a number of studies of directive (lecture) and non-directive (discussion) teaching efforts and concluded:

"In general, it would appear that the amount of cognitive gain is largely unaffected by the autocratic or democratic tendencies of the instructor. The majority of investigators who have attempted to measure differences in achievement report no particular advantage for either approach. . . ."

Much similar research has been conducted with quaint or amusing, but hardly worthwhile, results. Chapter 1 had an account of students who do not attend class at all (they merely register for a course, are told the name of the text and examination date) and do as well as students who, in formal classes, listen to distinguished lecturers cover the material. All manner of learning situations have been arranged—classes led by graduate students, discussion classes, no-teacher classes, or whatever occurred to the researchers—with similar results. No arrangement proves superior to any other when the criterion is performance on an objective test based on a textbook.

Unless the *time* of the learners is rigorously controlled, we simply have no way of knowing how much time actually is spent on the course in private study. A student with a good lecturer may spend no time at all outside class. The studying-by-himself student may have very tough going. To use an objective test based on a textbook is obviously meaningless in such research. What we need is to develop tests that will evaluate what has actually been learned in the several kinds of learning situations. The student with a fine lecturer as a teacher later may turn out to be an important achiever in that subject area. A poor lecturer may kill the student's interest. The possible values of the lecture have already been gone into and need not be repeated here. The whole argument may be simply a matter of criteria (values) and of measurement. When the wrong measurements are used, almost anything can be proved.

Recitation as an Active Form of Learning

During World War I, educational psychologists began to compare the effectiveness of various teaching techniques. A. I. Gates (1917), for example, was able to show that for meaningless material the student did better to spend more time trying actively to anticipate than simply reading materials over and over (see also G. Forlano, 1936). The student, of course, has to do some reading at first to become familiar with the material, but as soon as he has attained familiarity he should spend up to four fifths of his time in recitation. In the 1930s, H. F. Switzer (1939), in research pertaining to review for examinations, concluded it was far more efficient for the student to try to recite prospective answers than to reread pertinent materials, hoping that somehow something would "sink in." Recitation also benefits the learner in that he is actually practicing what he is later going to perform. Such practice can result in much time-saving during examinations, providing additional time for less-well-known material.

In more recent years, much research on the effectiveness of teaching techniques has followed the experimental pattern that now is known as "spaced versus massed learning." In most studies, it has been found that rests (see p. 85) between learning periods prove beneficial. Students should be advised to schedule periodic reviews at regular intervals rather than "cram" at the end of the term. Spaced learning is similar in effect to recitation. The benefit of periodic reviews (as well as recitation) is that they provide the learner with information about what he knows and what he does not know and needs to work on. Reading materials over and over without discrimination between what is well known and what is not is an obvious waste of time.

Optimal Stimulation

Discussion of the problem of action and learning would be incomplete without some mention of the concept of *Optimal Stimulation,* which recently has been publicized. Some psychologists (C. Leuba, 1955; D. O. Hebb, 1958) argue that, just as there may be too little, there also may be too much stimulation, tension, excitement, or interest to promote learning. In the hand-squeeze experiment, subjects would learn very poorly if they had to maintain a high level of tension. They would have to pay more attention to squeezing than to learning. Some place between sleep and excitement, they argue, there may be an "optimum" level of tension or stimulation that would result in the most efficient learning. Such a level might vary with the subject and the material being learned. But, again, we have no practical ways of discovering what the optimal level is for anyone. Some students cannot study unless they have absolute quiet in the area surrounding them. Others insist on blaring radios as a necessary accompaniment to their studies. It is not beyond reason that a certain amount of noise (stimulation) is beneficial for some students, and to insist that such students work in a quiet environment may actually result in making them less efficient.

In conclusion then, we can recognize that activity is helpful for some kinds of learning and of little moment for others. It is not a universal condition for learning. Sometimes, as with the tension and incidental-learning experiments, what we mean by "action" is that someone is "paying attention." There seems to be no solid reason why teachers should always insist on action—on projects, on participation, or on "creating" answers (as opposed to a true-false test)—in order for learning to occur. It all depends on what the student is learning. The best way to learn a story may be to sit and listen, as hundreds of generations of children might testify if we could bring them to the witness stand. Children who can read might "learn" the same story by reading it, but it is unlikely that they have learned exactly the same thing. In either case, there appears to be no other way to learn a story or other verbal content than by reading it or listening to an account. Neither procedure calls for much action of an overt kind, and both result in different learnings. One kind of test might show some advantage for one method of teaching over the other. Other tests might reverse such findings. Teachers might as well be wary about accepting conclusions based on tests that are not related to the educational goals involved.

Practical Suggestions about Active Learning

Our review of the investigations concerned with activity in learning can be summarized in five basic statements:

1. The degree of activity required for learning depends upon the kind of learning involved. Overt muscular exertion may be required for learning physical skills. You do not learn to swim or dance by reading about these arts. Some kinds of learning require only internal emotional responses. Remember the curare experiments (p. 43).

2. One does not learn by simply going through the motions. Guiding the student through a problem in fractions may prove quite immaterial in its effects. Much of what goes on in classrooms amounts to an "incidental learning" situation in that the students are not "trying" to learn— they may be complying with orders and enduring a situation.

3. Learning does require some degree of arousal, of being awake, under some tension. What the optimal degree of such tension may be is probably an individual matter. Mark Twain wrote in bed. Most students are probably more efficient learners if they are sitting up and leaning forward.

4. Some materials do not call for overt activity of any great degree. Listening and reading are effective methods for learning verbal materials. With some kinds of material and for some purposes (specific kinds of tests or performances), active recitation is more effective than silent rereading.

5. Students should practice or study in terms of the objectives to be met. A drama group about to put on a play had better plan on rehearsals— active, overt recitation on the stage. The director should call for "action" with the first reading. Imagine the kind of performance that might be given if the actors were told to "go home and read over your scripts until you think you know them."

ATTENTION

The importance of attention for learning has been appreciated for centuries. For psychologists, the concept of attention (or motivation) has proved troublesome, and for many years American psychologists tended to ignore the problem of attention, hoping perhaps that it would go away if it were not talked about. But teachers do talk about attention and know its value for learning. Today, more psychologists are willing to examine the problem and to look for ways and means by which attention can be more effectively harnessed to the teaching operation.

A Definition of Attention

The real problem here is that no one knows what attention is. Sometimes it is incorporated as a feature of a broader problem, namely that of motivation. Hull, it will be remembered (p. 72), held that learning could not occur without motivation; because learning cannot occur without attention some might think the two processes or states are the same. Similarly, some psychologists have flirted with the notion that attention is either the equivalent of, a component of, or a side-product of the orienting response (see p. 48). Many years ago an early American behaviorist, John F. Dashiell (1927), anticipated the Russian workers who include the increased muscular tonus as a feature of the orienting response by describing attention as "a tension." Dashiell, too, felt that learning would be more efficient with some additional activity of the muscular system.

We have already reviewed Hebb's concerns over the "arousal" system (p. 144) and recognized at that time that a teacher could do little directly about anyone's nervous system, even if the reticular activating system is a vital factor in attention, stimulus, and response processing, and perhaps, learning. Earlier reference to conditioning under curare, where muscles are paralyzed, must give us some pause in identifying attention with motor functions. About all we can say with legitimacy is that attention may be more of a result than a cause or a factor in learning. If it is a result, it might amount to a physical state (brought about by other factors, e.g., a noise, a painful stimulus, a bright light, or a change of stimulus background—we hear the ticking clock stop!) in which only relatively few stimuli have access to the nervous system at a given moment. Some psychologists, e.g., Hebb, argue that we can be attentive for only a moment as far as any one stimulus is concerned. In such a state, when only a few stimuli have dominance, the organism can be said to be affected by them, and something will happen to change the organism as a consequence of this activity of dominant stimuli. We like to think that we are in command, that we can attend or not, as we choose, to any part of our environment. It is likely that it is quite the other way around, that we are forced to attend or forced to turn away and respond to other environmental features by alterations in the stimulus complex that constantly surrounds us.

If we are acted upon for a sufficient amount of time by some stimulus patterns, associations will be formed among them. Here we have the old law of contiguity again, now modified by a time factor that determines whether or not we will learn.

Note that nothing, so far, has been said about any desires, wishes, or intentions of the learner. He is either attentive (attending) or not. His intentions (see p. 28) may have nothing to do with what he learns. If the teacher can impose some instruction or "set" on the learner while the dominant stimuli are impinging upon him, learning will take place. What I have said above amounts to this: Attention is a state (result) of the control of the organism by the operation (or manipulation by a teacher) of dominant stimuli, during which the stimuli involved can interact, affect each other, or be associated with each other in terms of their neural activities. The teacher's task is to know or discover the stimuli that can be manipulated to create such a state. Because of differences among individuals, there can be no specific suggestions. Television advertising producers are probably the most experienced in this field. Watch a few "commercials" and see how they try to catch and keep your attention.

Attention in the Laboratory

In the animal laboratory there is little point to talking about *attention* because of the subjective, mentalistic connotations of the term. Psychologists, therefore, have preferred to talk about *motives* or *drives* as a more-or-less parallel concept. When a psychologist of any orientation wants an animal to learn, he knows what his first step must be: make the animal hungry. He may not use the word *hunger*—Skinner does not; he "deprives" his animals, putting them on a feeding schedule whereby their weight is reduced by one third inside a week. If the now "lean and hungry" animal is placed in a learning situation, and if the reinforcer is food, the animal learns! What is the role of this hunger, this drive or motivation in learning, besides making food into a reinforcer? Obviously, hunger can have nothing to do with acquisition of correct responses in any direct manner. Its role is indirect even though essential. The safest interpretation anyone can offer is that hunger makes the animal *interested* in food (not in running mazes or performing other tricks designed by psychologists) and in *very little else*. In short, the hungry animal is not going to be interested in sleep, in such casual little discomforts as itches, in the opposite sex, or in any other less-important concern. It is becoming a one-track-minded little beast. Nothing that is unrelated to food will distract it or retain any stimulus value. It is becoming "hypnotized" in a sense, so that only a limited part of the world will operate as stimuli. It is this narrowing of the field of interest, the elimination of distractions (other stimuli with response-exciting potential), that facilitates the learning.

The reference to hypnosis is not at all out of order here. At the human level, Leuba (1940) has shown that subjects can be conditioned in one trial to respond to stimuli in specific ways when they have been hypnotized and all irrelevant stimulation has been suggested away. Thus, in an experiment involving a buzzer as a *CS* and a pinprick as a *US*, if a subject is hypnotized and is told that he hears nothing except the hypnotist's voice and a soft buzzer, that he is blind, that he can feel nothing except on the back of his left hand, conditioning can begin. The hypnotist sounds the buzzer and at the same time pricks the subject's left hand with a pin. The subject reacts vigorously and rubs the hand. After the subject has been restored to normal status by appropriate suggestions and if at some time when he is doing nothing in particular the hypnotist sounds the buzzer, the subject immediately will begin to rub his left hand. When asked why he is doing so, he is likely to respond with "I felt an itch" or "It seemed to hurt" or something similar. In such circumstances, conditioning is extremely rapid—one trial is enough.

Pavlov, in his work, did not hypnotize his animals. He advised that every effort be made to eliminate extraneous stimulation. His dogs were in one room, he in another, and no distracting stimuli were allowed if they could be eliminated. Many experimenters with animals have learned —the hard way—that learning has been hampered by their failures to control the environment. But with animals it is not always possible to tell just what stimuli are playing a role. In one of his experiments, Hebb (1938) discovered that certain stimuli that *he* thought were clear and evident were of no concern to his rats. He had arranged on a circular table, at 90-degree separations, three black cards and one larger white card. The large white card stood out sharply (to Hebb). Rats were supposed to run from a starting point to this white card where food could be found. When the table was rotated 90 degrees, the rats continued to run to where the white card *used to be*. They were responding, actually, to the light from a window some distance away. A frustrated experimenter elsewhere discovered that animals were being guided along a maze by sounds of water circulating in pipes in the floor, sounds the experimenter was unable to hear. In one of my own experiments a rat was being trained to jump a low hurdle when a light was turned on. On one occasion I closed the switch, the light did not go on, and the rat jumped. It had been conditioned to the sound of the switch, and the very obvious and bright light had little or nothing to do with the stimulus.

All these examples strongly suggest that learning (of one kind or another) may be going on, but it may not be the particular learning with which the teacher is concerned. To be sure that the learner is learning what we want him to learn, we must remove all irrelevant stimuli and make sure that he is responding to the relevant ones. This is what teachers mean by *attention*. The animal researcher attempts to do this by starving his subjects; the hypnotist, by suggestion. What, then, can the teacher do to attain the same state of "readiness" for learning in students? Can the teacher engage in some parallel operation and perhaps "starve" the learners in some way that will make them hungry for knowledge? We read about a "thirst for knowledge" often enough in biographical works. Perhaps more than a pun is involved here, and teachers must analyze the possibilities with care. But before this is done, the animal laboratory can provide further insight into the problem of attention.

Interest and Concentration

Why is it that the experimenter does not take a well-fed and satisfied animal and place it in a maze? Because the experimenter knows from experience that a well-fed animal *with nothing to do* will do just that—nothing. It will go to sleep. It will not engage in the kinds of activity that interest the experimenter. It will scratch itself, wash, poke around, and in general do nothing systematic. It is easily distracted. The experimenter cannot say more without lapsing into insecure anthropomorphizing. At the human level, where there is access to personal reports, the teacher may get remarks from the "inattentive" students that they are not "interested." Commonly enough, students refer to their lack of ability to "concentrate." Examination of such personal reports is pertinent here and worth the reader's time.

When a student says he "cannot concentrate," he should add "on this problem (or subject)." No normal human is likely actually to lack the ability to concentrate. Most children have no trouble at all concentrating on cartoons on television. Adolescents of both sexes have no difficulty in concentrating on the opposite sex. Boys can be extremely attentive to matters of physical form. Girls find it easy to concentrate on others' clothes, hair styles, and make-up. A girl college student can describe the clothing of male or female teachers in precise detail and recall little or nothing of the content of a class. There appears to be no weakness in any "powers of concentration"; the weakness is in the selection of material on which to concentrate.

An interesting little experiment performed on cats makes this point very nicely. The physiologist Hernández-Peón and his co-workers (1956), arranged to record signals from the brains of cats that indicated that a sound had been transmitted along the auditory nerve and had arrived, in terms of neural activity, at a certain neural locus. He was able to show that every time a little click was produced near the cat's ear, the neural record noted a specific change. At this point he placed before the cat a jar containing some live mice. The cat now became interested (absorbed?) in the mice. When the clicker was sounded at this time, the brain record showed no change. The cat *did not hear* a perfectly audible sound. It never got into the higher centers of the brain. A small child watching television similarly *does not hear* a normal call to dinner. It does not get into the child's brain. The student absorbed in his own daydreams (a personal kind of television show where everything is going along just fine) similarly does not hear the geography lesson or the (to the teacher) fascinating story of fractions.

The teacher should recognize now that whether a student is going to learn or not depends on whether or not the teacher has controlled the kind of stimulation that is going to enter the student's nervous system. Such control requires a knowledge of what stimuli are actually present and working. But, because of the pleasant and sometimes even profitable human capacity for daydreaming, a wide array of personally created stimuli about which teachers know nothing may also be present. A student can walk into a classroom, sit down, and keep busy with his private life until the dismissal bell, responding only to force, if at all, as far as the outside world is concerned. If this student does respond to the outside world, it may be to the teacher's glasses or wrinkles in his face or suit and not to the teacher's words or actions.

Attention and Set

Perhaps the clearest example of attention is encountered in the common human experience of listening to someone who is talking to us, but who is having some difficulty in expressing himself and seems to be searching for the appropriate words. Most of us find it difficult to wait, and we have some tendency to supply these words. When we supply a word and it is accepted, we have been attending, we have *expected* or anticipated the response. When students can anticipate the teacher's next word, they too are attending. If they cannot do so, the teacher might question the degree of attention—the students should be able or ready to offer some kind of word; the expression that might cover the situation, "Hanging on his every word," really includes the prospect of being able to supply the next one.

An example in a slightly different context might prove both clarifying and informative. At one time Luchins (1946) asked some college students to solve a series of problems that involved obtaining a specific amount of water from a supply source by using certain specified containers. Try the exercise for yourself:

In the table below you will find on the left a series of containers (A, B, C) to be used in getting the quantity on the right. Indicate, in the space on the right, how you would use the containers by listing the container you would fill first, next, and so on; indicating addition by + and subtraction by −. The first problem is solved for you as an illustration:

Table 3

	given jars		to get	Solution
A	B	C		
43	89	2	42	89—43—2—2
25	59	2	30	
32	69	3	31	
52	78	3	20	
43	93	4	42	
31	61	4	22	
17	37	3	14	
41	86	4	37	
47	68	4	51	
27	59	5	22	
13	35	3	16	

I cannot predict how you reacted to the problems, but most college students (Bugelski and Hutt, 1962) solve the first six problems quickly, they have trouble with Problems 7 and 8, handle 10 and 11 with comparative ease. Problems 7 and 8 are extremely easy; they can be solved simply by subtracting C from A, but even bright college students sometimes fail to see this and persist in trying to solve these problems as they did in the past. They have acquired a "set" that does them no good. They *expect* it to work, and the expectancy blinds them to alternatives. They are attending to the wrong features of the problems. Problem 9 is an "extinction" problem. It must be solved in a specific way (A + C). Even with this "lesson," students go on to 10 and 11 and frequently solve them in the B—A—2C method. Students have spent uncounted hours struggling with simple algebra or geometry problems for the same reasons: they become set on a particular pattern of reactions and go around in circles. Sets are like attitudes, biases, or prejudices. Frequently they help, often they hinder. In either case they predispose us to react to some stimuli in a particular way. It is this predisposition that teachers must learn to control.

The Self-fulfilling Prophecy

In recent years the role of expectancy or mental set has been extended to cover longer periods of time and more complex types of behavior. The most important educational application of this concept has been the attempt of Rosenthal (1967) to demonstrate that teachers' attitudes or expectancies can affect even the I.Q.s of primary school children. In Rosenthal's studies (*Pygmalion in the classroom*) teachers are falsely informed that certain children have test scores that indicate that they have high potential for academic work, that they will tend to "bloom" shortly. After a period of time all the children are retested and, according to Rosenthal, those that had been singled out or brought to the teachers' attention as "bloomers" actually demonstrated rather remarkable increases in I.Q. scores.

The interesting feature of these studies is that the teachers deny any special attempts to treat the children differently, and, in fact, claim not to recall which children had been labeled as "bloomers." Rosenthal and others, however, suspect that the teachers involved, having high expectancies of the selected children, tend to treat them with more respect in the sense that they show them that more is expected of them, and the children identify with this role of one of whom greater things are expected and begin to work harder to live up to it.

Rosenthal's study has been sharply criticized by Snow (1969) for inadequate controls, although some of the criticisms have been refuted by Rosenthal (1970). The actual facts in this study need not concern us as they concern only the I.Q. measures involved. Important is that Rosenthal has called our attention to the serious matter of teachers' attitudes toward the students as a potentially powerful influence on the behavior of both teachers and students. In discussing Mowrer's theory (Chapter 5), the personality of the teacher was described as of immediate concern for the development of students' attitudes toward the subject matter being taught. In view of the growing volume of data demonstrating the impact of expectancies on attitudes of both students and teachers, it behooves us to pay serious attention to this aspect of student-teacher relationships. We are probably justified in concluding that both teachers and students will perform to some degree as is expected of them.

In the classroom it seems clear that, if a teacher views a group as below par, retarded, incompetent, and otherwise inferior, or if the teacher regards a given lesson as unnecessary, inappropriate, or impossible, only negative results can be anticipated.

At most educational levels, even in college, teachers commonly teach more than one subject. If they cannot show the same degree of enthusiasm for each subject taught, we should not expect equal positive outcomes. It is unlikely that any teacher can really enjoy teaching all subjects equally. Consider the possible consequences if a teacher who has just relished a class in geography now reluctantly informs the class, "Well, it's too bad, but we have to turn to arithmetic now."

In some situations, as in slum schools, teachers may have attitudes that destroy any possible human relationships and make the teacher-student interaction a destructive operation on both sides. The many critical novels and evaluation of slum school teachers (Conant, 1961) suggest that there is precious little hope of carrying on an educational function when teachers regard the students as unworthy or impossible and vice versa. Clearly the selection of teachers for slum schools is a major and crucial problem. The usual approach is to send the newest applicants for teachers' positions to such posts, where the combination of inexperience and youth guarantees failure even without teacher bias.

Attention and Curiosity

To return to the problem of creating interest or motivation or attention in a student, of starving him for knowledge, we must consider the relationship between *attention* and *curiosity*. But before the concept of curiosity can be examined, a restriction must be made. It would be ideal if all students could be made equally curious about all subjects that they must study. At the grade-school level, this may seem a desirable goal for teachers; at the adult level, this goal becomes absurd. No mature adult can afford to be interested in everything. To be curious about nature and natural science, about people and social science, about the arts and the humanities, philosophy, athletics, and domestic science, politics and foreign affairs is to be scatterbrained and ineffectual. The last master of all trades was Leonardo da Vinci, and the last master of all knowledge was Sir Francis Bacon. In the twentieth century, the age of specialization, can anyone become a master of anything? Even in high school, a valedictorian with an unbelievably high average must, inevitably, find some subjects dull and must achieve the "mastery" at some kind of sacrifice—it may be on the recreational or social side of life or at the expense of a really superior achievement in some areas of stronger interest.

What has just been said sounds as though curiosity is taken for granted to be something admirable and desirable. We frequently act as if we are being complimentary to some youngster when we say "He's just full of curiosity," but how complimentary are we really? That depends on what curiosity is, and here psychologists have not been in complete agreement in their accounts or analyses. Their two most common explanations of the concept of curiosity are almost contradictory. One of these analyses is somewhat complimentary to people, the other rather less so. I will begin with the former.

1. Curiosity as a Positive Trait. The socially approved "complimentary" analysis holds that curiosity is some kind of native endowment, like intelligence, of which some people have more than do others. Some animals, such as monkeys, are "naturally" curious, while cats are presumed not to be (even if curiosity killed a cat). Evidence for this natural curiosity is found in the common experience of parents whose youngsters plague them with "why?" questions almost from the day their offspring begin to use language with any effectiveness. Whether a child's "why?" reflects any actual concern with the subject matter of the question is not easily proved. Such questions may be more of a game with the child and/or some technique that keeps the parents attentive rather than genuine curiosity. By the time the child has reached the nursery-school age, most such behavior is extinguished through lack of reinforcement. Few parents know all the answers, and eventually the child's "why?'s" come to be treated as a nuisance operation. If a child remains curious, it is because, somehow, he has a great deal of "natural" curiosity and it has persisted.

2. Curiosity as Disguised Anxiety. The psychologist's less-complimentary analysis of curiosity is quite different. Every child is naturally weak, inferior, incompetent, constantly in danger of getting hurt or into trouble, with consequent punishment. He has no control over his environment—in fact, quite the reverse is true—his environment controls him —and he is, for the most part, under one form of threat or another. Much of the environment is dangerous because the child is ignorant of means to control it. The child inevitably becomes somewhat fearful or anxious in connection with many stimuli or conditions, particularly whenever he is ignorant or incompetent. Ignorance and incompetence become, in a sense, conditioned stimuli for anxiety or fear. Under the influence of fear, the child will engage in one kind of behavior or another —he can shy away from the situation or engage in some form of action to solve the problem (some children never do learn to light a match even when they arrive at college—sometimes they pride themselves on being nonsmokers and therefore virtuous when one reason they do not smoke is that they quite literally cannot light a cigarette). Such individuals have met an anxiety-provoking situation by retreat—they have not developed curiosity. They have solved a problem by negation, by withdrawal. Because the problem was not a vital one, they were able to "get away with it." At the same time they have become incompetent in one area—lighting matches, in this instance.

In other anxiety-inciting situations children may attempt a more positive solution to a problem—they may try, with or without encouragement, to tie their shoes, open the cookie jar, tune in a television program, or even read a comic book by themselves when parents or older siblings refuse to cooperate. If their efforts are crowned by success they will learn to meet such anxiety situations with a direct attack. The feeling of ignorance may become the conditioned stimulus for approach behavior. When parents and teachers witness such behavior they call the child "curious."

Success in dealing with one form of fear stimulation may transfer to others, and felt ignorance can become a stimulus for positive achievement. This is only likely to happen under careful guidance by wise parents who take pains to insure that the child copes only with problems suitable for his level of competence. If children are not wisely guided, they may attempt an attack that brings the world down about their ears and subsequently may adopt retreat behavior in connection with ignorance. If they are encouraged to attempt too much, again failure will lead to inhibitory reactions. The frustrated, fearful child will learn to avoid areas or situations· that bring on more anxiety; the child who is reinforced for positive attacks will develop approaches that might bring about further successes. We call the first (the inhibited) child "stupid"; the second, "curious." Both are children in whom anxiety was aroused by ignorance and who developed different patterns of response to this ignorance.

3. The Normal Restriction of Curiosity. Whether the teacher chooses to go along with the "natural" or the "anxiety" analysis of curiosity, certain other facts are indisputable. In the early stages of development a child will tend to be curious about a great deal of his world, but his native endowments and his limited experience will not be adequate to cope with all the wide varieties of life's problems. He is bound to experience failures in some areas. Some children will begin to fail at sports and games, at interpersonal relations, at verbal or quantitative tasks, at manual or artistic operations. Gradually, they will begin to form discriminated response patterns and show "curiosity" only about baseball or stamps or English history, Greek mythology, or whatever. Their successes will be their guides. Such a development is inevitable, because no one can afford to be "curious" about everything. If, for example, a child attempts to master every potential problem that arises on his way to school, he will never arrive at his goal. If along the way the child examines every flower, shrub, tree, automobile, person, animal, street sign, and store front, he will only turn out to be the despair of his parents and teacher. In short, everyone must curtail curiosity and restrict it to limited areas. The man with too many avocations cannot afford a vocation.

Professions today have become specialized to a fine degree. When you need a tax lawyer you do not consult the specialist in criminal law nor do you ask the skillful obstetrician to treat you for a skin disease. Similarly, the teacher cannot expect students to be equally interested (curious) in all subjects. Ideally, each will be interested in some and not in others; some may be interested in none. Yet without interest there will be no attention and little learning in the time assigned or available. The practical question then arises: What do we do with the learner who has no interest in material that he must learn? Simply to change the program and reverse the condition—that is, to follow the lead of progressive educators and let the student's interests determine his selection of courses or activities—is to admit defeat and lead to the same kinds of weaknesses of educational curricula and practices we have some occasion to decry. What can be done by the teacher to create interest?

Practical Suggestions about Attention

While I would not like to rely on folklore, some of the old proverbs and maxims contain wisdom based on persistent human experience. Consider the ancient saws "Those who have, get" and "Nothing succeeds like suc-

> On the outside of each of the next two pages you will find a series of cartoons. Look at those on the left-hand page in order, from top to bottom, and name or label them as you go. Do the same for the cartoons on the right-hand page. When you have finished, show a friend one page or the other to discover his reactions.

cess." Skinner has used the latter to explain the results he has had with his teaching-machine activities (Chapter 10). He finds no reason to doubt that when a student begins to experience a series of successes in a teaching-machine operation, that student becomes motivated, becomes interested in working at more problems. Juvenile delinquents are reported to have become interested in mathematics through the simple expedient of leaving them alone in rooms with teaching machines containing mathematics programs. After some initial "fooling around," the juveniles began testing themselves, and, because the program was arranged so that success was virtually guaranteed on the first try, one young learner was heard to remark "Gee, I didn't know I was good at math."

Such an anecdote, of course, is not evidence that success arouses interest, but it suggests what a teacher can do to create interest, probably even more successfully with nondelinquents than with delinquents:

Arrange for the prospective learner to be successful at the activity that is to be learned.

It is because of a past history of failure (or, at least, of no successes) that students show no interest in the material. Such a history can only be combated by the teacher by building up an opposite new history. To control a history of success with groups of learners is not easy, and if the teacher cannot arrange to give individual attention, the battle may be permanently lost.

In the effort to achieve attention, teachers may find that there is some virtue to examples that show that some presently successful person at one time was just as ineffectual as the student concerned. It helps to know that Einstein once failed in a mathematics course. Nor are artificial inducements, such as prizes, to be frowned on. Some teachers want learners to learn because of the intrinsic values of the subject and sometimes carry their idealism or utopianism to extremes, insisting on some kind of virtue for virtue's sake. As far as learning is concerned, it makes no difference what the motivation is, just so long as the learning takes place. Once the learner has begun to learn, he may almost be trusted to find intrinsic rewards, but there is no harm in baiting the trap to catch a learner. Of the thousands of rats that have learned mazes, it is doubtful that any learned for the sake of learning or the joy of achievement.

The teacher who is attempting to solve the problem of attention must recognize that attention also refers to a "readiness" to react to stimuli yet to come. When the house lights in a theater are lowered, we expect the curtains to part. The hush that falls over the audience at the dimming of the lights indicates that the people in the audience have stopped talking and moving about, have settled down in suitable postures, are waiting for some new kind of stimulation, and are no longer concerned with former stimuli. They are "set" to watch the play. You can think of "sets" as equivalent to attention. Such "sets" come with practice, with experience, with success and reinforcement for such behavior in the past. Attention, or *set*, is a response. As such it is a reaction to stimulation, and a learnable reaction. The learning of such sets depends on reinforcement because the set is a preparation for a particular reaction of the type that will facilitate the reception or consumption of the reward involved. When children are repeatedly admonished by shouts of "pay attention here" or "attention" and no reward follows, extinction of the attention response will inevitably occur. Before we ask for attention we should be sure, generally at least, that what is about to come is going to be welcomed and that it has been welcomed in the past.

FIGURE 6. *The Development of a Mental Set*

Most people glancing at the cartoons on the left-hand page will describe the last as "an old man." People seeing only the cartoons on the right will very likely describe the bottom figure as "a rat" or "a mouse." In each case, the bottom figures are the same. We tend to see what we expect to see—and what we expect to see depends on prior experience (see Bugelski and Alampay, 1961).

When the prior history of success is missing, it still is possible to attain some attention indirectly. The successful teacher will already have established a suitable conditioning background in relation to himself as a stimulus in that he has been the source of prior satisfactions. If he now calls for attention, he is likely to get cooperation: this indirect operation for attention-getting is one reason why it is important for teachers to establish "rapport" with their classes, to be liked, to be considered or regarded as somehow related to satisfactions. Obviously such "popularity" can be carried too far, and an eventual facing up to the teacher role must come; but, in general, the teacher who is a source of satisfactions will be more effective than the one who scolds, threatens, and punishes. The former can use himself as a secondary reinforcer for attention behavior; the latter can expect to develop inhibitory, avoidance, and escape behavior.

In review, teachers can now appreciate the following appraisal of attention or motivation in connection with learning:

1. There is no such thing as a special gift or power of concentration. Everyone can concentrate and does so on matters that have previously brought satisfactions.

2. A history of successes can be equated with such satisfactions.

3. No one can afford to be interested in everything. There is not enough time to learn everything. Some kind of selection must be made. Where learners *must*, because of conditions beyond their control, learn material that has no interest for them, such interest can be developed by initiating a history of success. This may require starting at an extremely elementary level and may call for individual training.

4. There is nothing wrong with a teacher's supplying artificial incentives (prizes, money, gold stars, honor rolls, or whatever) as motivational devices so long as they can be attained! The learner may make his first efforts only for sordid reasons (such as money), but the satisfactions that come from success will eventually be adequate compensations. Even the highly admired learner who is "learning for learning's sake" is probably selfishly motivated and not especially deserving of the admiration.

5. The teacher, as a secondary reinforcer, can also function as a motivator if a preliminary history of satisfactions is associated with the teacher.

REINFORCEMENT

The concept of reinforcement has appeared over and over again in this textbook, although it was not always called by that name. Keller (Chapter 1) made use of it in his method of teaching telegraphy; almost every theorist in Chapters 2-6 included it among his principles in one way or another; and in Chapter 10 you will see how Skinner will try to show that reinforcement is vital to programmed learning. The teacher, however, may be more interested in reinforcement as a practical problem of education and not as a theoretical variable.

From what has just been said about the problems of action and attention (motivation), it should be already clear why some psychologists find reinforcement a necessary principle or operating procedure. There are two different points of view here that require spelling out. In the first place, even if one does not believe that rewards have anything to do with learning (in the sense of strengthening bonds or habits), it is convenient to use rewards for another reason. We have seen how some psychologists, such as Guthrie (p. 103), start out with the assumption that learning depends on action, that an organism must do something if it is to learn. But the doing must be in relation to some stimulus situation. Once the organism has performed the required response, the original stimuli must be removed or the organism might now do something else in the stimulus situation and thereby learn something that is not desired. One way of getting rid of the original stimuli is to present the learner with a reward, which now will capture his attention so that he will no longer respond to the original stimuli in some undesired way. Thus, rewards are used as distractors by those psychologists who insist on action as a first principle.

If the psychologist starts out with a basic assumption that rewards themselves are important as learning strengtheners, he automatically finds himself endorsing the action principle as well. As mentioned earlier, he can hardly go around reinforcing at random. The learner must do something before he can be rewarded.

With regard to the factor of attention (motivation), the situation is quite similar. If a psychologist believes that rewards have something to do with learning, he must likewise assume that motivation is important or else he will be unable to reward a learner. A reward, after all, must be something desirable. Without the desire, there can be no reward; consequently, the psychologist will start a learning session only with a "motivated" learner.

If the psychologist has no real use for rewards as theoretically important but starts out with a fundamental belief in motivation as basic to learning, he must see to it that the motivation is there, and he may introduce reward objects or stimuli (only now he calls them "incentives") to maintain the motivation or activate it. It might be a little difficult for the observer to decide whether a rat in a maze runs toward the goal for an incentive or whether he is rewarded for getting there. At the end of the maze there will be some food. Incentive or reward, it is still food. When we see that rats learn when food is present and do not learn when food is absent, we can at least conclude that food is important, whatever its theoretical role.

Reward and Punishment

Whatever the logic, all learning psychologists have found rewards to be useful in their training operations. The Thorndikian psychologists are most positive in their statements about the necessity of rewarding the learner. The Pavlovians either say nothing about rewards or admit that rewards have other functions, such as "confirming" expectancies (Tolman) or bringing learning situations to an end (Guthrie). Supporters in one camp or the other try to account for each other's findings in terms of theoretical approaches but, practically speaking, both schools of psychologists use rewards. It is interesting to remember, for example, that Pavlov used food as an unconditioned stimulus in most of his experiments. Hull (1943) carefully pointed out that food could also be a reward for hungry dogs. Pavlov's dogs were hungry.

When he sought to reconcile the divergent views about the nature of learning, Mowrer (1960a) adopted the Pavlovian approach and concluded that all learning, basically, was conditioning. But, far from abandoning the concept of reinforcement, he expanded it not only to include the positive or reward operation but also to reinstate punishment as a negative reinforcer. Mowrer also elaborated on Hull's interpretation of Pavlov's use of food as an unconditioned stimulus. For Mowrer, food was the unconditioned stimulation not for salivation (as Pavlov had it) but for the emotion of hope. Salivation was merely an incidental effect of the general positive emotional reaction. To parallel the positive reinforcement, Mowrer had negative reinforcement and described any painful stimuli as unconditioned stimuli for the emotional accompaniments of pain, namely fear. Mowrer went on to call one type of reinforcer "decremental" (hope) and the other, "incremental" (fear) and made them the basis of all learning. Leaving theoretical speculation out of account, we can say that Mowrer finds it necessary to use rewards if certain kinds of behavior are to be made to occur. Such behaviors will include what can be called "positive-approach" activities, in contrast to inhibitory or avoidance behaviors that will be controlled by negative or incremental reinforcers.

Partial Reinforcement. You will recall from the discussion of Skinner's work on schedules of reinforcement that behavior can be controlled with great effectiveness if the teacher doles out reinforcers according to some plan. It is not necessary to reward the student for every single performance of some desired response. The teacher cannot be haphazard or capricious in his function of reinforcement-dispensing. He must watch the learner carefully to be sure that the response probability is not weakening. The teacher need not become alarmed if occasionally he is unable or forgets to reinforce a student. The only real concern is to reinforce learners in the early stages of acquisition of some behavior. Once the behavior is fairly well established, the teacher can afford to space the reinforcements so that they occur frequently enough but without the appearance of regularity. The teacher should control the schedule, not the student.

The Empirical Law of Effect

Some thirty years ago, John McGeoch recognized that there was little likelihood that the disagreeing theorists would ever get together, as some colleagues fondly wished, but he pointed out that all used rewards in their practical work, regardless of their theoretical differences. This observation led him to frame what he called the *Empirical Law of Effect*. His words at that time (1942) incorporate more than teachers might wish to endorse, so I will paraphrase McGeoch's law simply as: *Rewards work*. In view of Mowrer's heavy emphasis on punishment and fear in the control of behavior (and the underlying learning), the restated law probably should be expanded: *Rewards work. Punishment works, too*. There can be little question that psychologists commonly employ punishments in their work with animals; likewise, there is little question that punishments get results. Once again the theorists don't agree. Supporters of Skinner insist that the use of punishment is effective only because the cessation of punishment is reinforcing. They speak of punishment as "aversive stimulation" and make the elimination of such stimulation the equivalent of a reinforcing operation.

Recognizing that rewards and punishments (even if the latter are called "aversive stimulation") both work does not solve the teacher's problem of reinforcement. Some psychologists, notably Skinner, argue that learning should, in general, be based on positive reinforcement and that aversive stimulation should be used as little as possible. In his novel *Walden II* (1948a), Skinner engineers some effective aversive stimulation when he wants to develop "frustration tolerance." In his regular work, his use of "deprivation," even though remedied by subsequent reinforcements, certainly raises the question of "aversive" conditions.

Skinner's strong preference for positive reinforcement is based, in part, on the side effects of punishment. If the teacher punishes the learner, the teacher will become a secondary aversive stimulus and his effectiveness will certainly be impaired. Other stimuli in the learning situation will also become aversive, and "avoidance" behavior that would eliminate such stimuli will be reinforced. Students will avoid contact with both teacher and subject matter.

In general, no psychologist advocates the use of punishment in the classroom. The day of the birch rod, hopefully, is passed. But for the teacher to identify punishment with physical force is far too limited. Many teachers still keep children after school, make extra assignments, compel children to "Write 500 times. . . ," and employ other similar punishments. Sometimes a child is required to read a book as punishment! Teachers often are personally abusive, scornful, sarcastic, and insulting. All such behavior can be expected to produce avoidance behavior in the learning situation. We can expect no good to come of it. Hebb once told, in a seminar, a story from his earlier days as an elementary-school principal that may be a good example of psychologically sophisticated practice. When he found children who were bored and unproductive in the classrooms, he sent them out to play; they were denied the privilege of attending classes and were not allowed to do any homework. The results, according to him, were most gratifying. The children began to beg for homework and for permission to stay in class.

The effectiveness of punishment for avoidance behavior itself is not to be denied. If it is desirable to teach avoidance behavior, then punishment may be the most effective means. But is this desirable? Instead of the question: "To punish or not to punish?" isn't the more appropriate question "What kind of behavior is desired?"

Because of the complex nature of human social life, no teacher can be expected to be always and completely positive or, at least, nonpunitive. To fail ever to show irritation, annoyance, or displeasure probably would stamp the teacher as abnormal. Students cannot be treated in a classroom as if the classroom were not a part of life. A teaching machine has been described as the perfect teacher because it never gets tired or cross, never scolds or punishes, and always rewards, but there is some question as to whether this feature of the teaching machine is really so praiseworthy.[1]

---

[1] H. Harlow and M. K. Harlow (1962) have reported their doubts about the virtue of completely acceptant "artificial mothers" as a result of studies of monkey behavior. When monkeys are brought up by real mothers, they are occasionally cuffed, knocked about, and otherwise chastised. Such monkeys grow up to be normal adult monkeys. When their infancy and childhood have been completely free of punishments, adult monkeys do not fare too well and may merit the label "neurotic."

One additional point about punishment should be made. Punishment frequently is discussed by well-meaning humanitarians and sentimentalists, who say that punishment cannot serve as a deterrent for others and therefore should be abandoned in the treatment of delinquents and criminals. They support their position with statistics that prove that crime does not increase when certain forms of punishment are abandoned. Such statistics probably are unassailable but the psychology involved is not. If you will recall the discussion of imitation (pp. 131–135), you will recognize that, in order to learn by imitation one must have prior experience (conditioning) with respect to the stimuli involved. To imitate some movement or action, a person must begin to "feel good" as he begins to see or feel himself performing the movement or action. In the case of learning by seeing someone else punished, the conditions are exactly the same. The child himself must have been punished (to some degree) in order for the cues involved to initiate the inhibitory fear. If a boy has not been in jail, hearing about someone else being sentenced to jail can have little or no effect on him. On a lesser scale, if a child has not been cuffed or whipped, such treatment administered to another will not result in effective fear conditioning to the cues or stimuli that led to the punished behavior. Punishment can serve as a deterrent for those who have the appropriate backgrounds, but such punishment must be intimately viewed in relation to the behavior that brought on the punishment. Delinquents and criminals usually have the backgrounds that enable them to learn from the punishment of others. Unfortunately, the criminal also attains positive reinforcement from his companions for delinquent behavior.

Finally, teachers do not always recognize that a failure to attain reinforcement may be strongly punitive. It is not just a neutral "nothing-happened" affair. According to Abraham Amsel (1958), lack of reinforcement is a frustrating state of affairs with consequences of its own. But cutting off of reinforcement is an extinction procedure, and the problem of extinction is dealt with in the next chapter.

Kinds of Rewards and Punishments

When learning psychologists talk about rewards and punishments or positive and negative reinforcers, they are usually referring to stimuli that are known, from experience, to result in approach or avoidance behavior. Such stimuli, for animals, might be food or shock. Other stimuli associated with these "primary" reinforcers can acquire the same relationships to approach and avoidance without any direct or primary consequence; these are known as secondary reinforcers. A dog can learn to salivate to a bell; he can also learn to run away when he hears one. Secondary reinforcers are used when primary reinforcers are too troublesome or awkward (see p. 32). Any stimulus that accompanies a primary reinforcer can acquire the reinforcer's function.

In the preceding discussions it has been made clear that in teaching humans, primary reinforcers are seldom used, perhaps only with very young children. As soon as children are old enough to attend school, they are not likely to encounter primary reinforcers; teachers are restricted to the use of secondary reinforcers only. On the positive side they use smiles, verbalisms like "good," "fine," etc. On the negative side they scowl or scoff and use other verbalisms too familiar to require citing.

The common use of "right" and "wrong" has been translated by learning psychologists into a secondary reinforcement function and given a label of its own, "Knowledge of Results," sometimes abbreviated KR. Thorndike popularized the concept of KR as a reinforcing operation, and it was adopted by Skinner in his programmed learning operation (p. 234). Thorndike assumed KR to be the ubiquitous reinforcer for learning skills or acquiring knowledge. Like other reinforcers, KR was supposed to work only if supplied immediately. We have seen (p. 65) that this is not clearly the case, although most learning theorists agree that reinforcers must be supplied within a matter of seconds if they are to be effective. Hull felt that after five seconds reinforcement effects fell off drastically and that it was relatively useless to reinforce after thirty seconds.

In most verbal learning experiments with nonsense material the learner is presumed to learn by KR effects because the correct answer is shown to him on each learning trial. The trouble with this assumption is that subjects can learn equally well without being shown that their responses are right or wrong (see Battig and Brackett, 1961). Similarly, if a long list of words is read to someone and he is instructed to try to remember the list, he is unable to say at anytime during the reading of the list whether he knows any of the words. When the list is finished, he cannot report that he knows any for sure *until he starts to report.* If the list is 20 words long, he might venture that he must know some of them, but he presumably cannot say which ones they are until they *occur* to him. Such demonstrations of free recall seem to suggest that Knowledge of Results plays but a modest role in learning at best. What KR does is to inform the teacher and the learner if he should continue to study or not.

Teachers sometimes misinterpret the preoccupation of learning psychologists with rewards to imply that grades, stars, and various forms of prizes given at intervals or at term ends are applications of reward psychology. Such prizes are undoubtedly cherished by the students who get them and also stimulate various negative emotions among those who do not; in either case they are probably irrelevant in the learning operation since the reinforcers we have been talking about are functional only if presented within seconds of other stimuli or responses. The problem of assessing the function of honor rolls, medals, statuettes, and Phi Beta Kappa keys is too complex to attempt here, and I will avoid it with the defense that such devices are irrelevant to learning. Their role in education and in society at large calls for a careful evaluation. I can only suggest that Hull's analysis of long-term goals in terms of immediately operating r_g's might be applicable. According to this analysis, wishing for a medal would amount to having r_g's functioning at the time of learning. In all probability, such r_g's would be interfering with the learning task itself and should be eliminated before the desired learning can occur.

Conclusions about Reinforcement

We can conclude, from this section on Reinforcement, that

1. Teachers must play an all-but-impossible role, determining when and how much to reward or to punish, while keeping in mind that failure to reward is punishing. The child with upraised hand who is ignored stops raising his hand—and perhaps stops caring about knowing the right answer. The teacher must control the reinforcement schedule to maintain the desired behavior.

2. When the teacher punishes in any manner or degree, the risk of being associated with the punishment is immediate and powerful. After an appropriate relationship has been built up, when the teacher has won the confidence and respect of the student, the risk of negative aftereffects is diminished, and calculated forms of punishment can be employed to foster a well-controlled anxiety that may result in greater student effort.

3. The reward psychology, so prevalent in modern writings, does not mean constant and concerned coddling of students. Even where the basic orientation of the teacher is to favor reinforcement, the teacher should remember that it is not always necessary to reinforce with the same quantity and quality of reward. As a student develops some mastery of a skill or content, any obvious and overt rewards are perceived as unnecessary "bribes." The mastery of material becomes its own reward.

4. Our review of the role of rewards and punishments suggests that they are both of fundamental importance in the process of education and in-

struction but not in learning itself. The teacher manipulates awards and punishments as stimuli. These stimuli function in complex ways as incentives, i.e., attention getters or, better, restrictors or controllers, or as unconditioned stimuli for various emotions, which can then be learned to other stimuli. They also, as Guthrie suggested, tend to terminate response sequences that they follow if they are introduced at such times. Rewards or punishments that are relatively distant in time from immediate activities are probably not effective unless they arouse r_g's of an emotional nature, which can support the more immediate activities in approach or avoidance operations.

Chapter Eight

The
Problem
of
Forgetting
and
Extinction

In education, the strangest and most interesting psychology problem is the teacher's paradoxical need to make the student remember some things and forget others. If the student is to learn, the teacher wants him to remember certain things at the same time that the teacher wants to extinguish in him the errors, the bad habits, the undesirable natural responses that interfere with effective learning.

The problem of forgetting is not usually appreciated as a complex aspect of the total picture of learning. Normally, the teacher regards forgetting as deplorable, negative, and inevitable. The student, too, looks on forgetting as his great enemy or danger, as some kind of mystic force that may assault him during a performance or test and leave him helpless. He is doubly tormented when, *after* the examination, he remembers something that just would not come to him at the crucial moment.

The problem of forgetting is one with the problem of learning. But before this unity can be appreciated, the various factors affecting or causing forgetting must be understood.

REMEMBERING AND RECALL

Forgetting is inevitable. The common experience of teachers and students is that, with the passage of time, previously mastered skills and knowledge fade or disappear. A foreign language learned in childhood cannot be spoken by the adult; as we grow older, the facts of history and the operations in geometry get lost in the haze of vague general identification as "history" and "geometry"; even a course taken last semester becomes a thing of the past and is expected to join the rest of our learned experience in some inaccessible limbo. Students may despair and ask: "Why should I bother learning in the first place if I am going to forget anyhow?"

The Efficiency of Relearning

The first answer to such a logical question may appear superficial, but actually it is the most meaningful. "Assuming that forgetting will occur, the basic reason for learning is so that we can *relearn.*" If any fact in psychology is a fact, it is that relearning some forgotten material can be accomplished in a *fraction* of the original learning time. While actual time fractions cannot be listed in a handbook for all the skills and contents or for all the kinds of learners, ages, times since learning, and so on, it is generally agreed that if anyone ever did know something, he can relearn it relatively quickly. The forgotten language can be "picked up" in far less time than it took to learn. The trigonometry that now seems completely strange "comes back like a song" if the student begins to relearn. In the learning laboratory poetry, nonsense materials, mazes, and many kinds of learned responses have been rapidly relearned after a period of "normal" or forced forgetting. Here we discover the great value of learning: *We can relearn quickly if we ever need to do so.*

But, suppose someone never needs to relearn! What value can any particular learning experience have if he will never need that specific information or skill? Again the answer is on the affirmative side: "Any learning results in a changed person." Once something has been learned, the learner is a different individual. He now will be affected differently by subsequent stimulation or experiences, even though he cannot recall the kinds of experiences that made him different. No one expects to remember a novel word for word, and few people remember a symphony note by note, but having had the experience of reading or listening will cause the person to react to the next novel or the next symphony (or even the same symphony on a second occasion) differently.

To put the matter more generally, the college-trained person is different from the noncollege-trained, even though the latter may know just as much as the former about a specific matter and even though the college-trained person has forgotten more than the other ever knew. The nature of the difference may be hard to define, but (as the next chapter will make clear) past experience can affect future performance even though this experience is not specifically remembered.

Recall of Learning

Does forgetting really occur? Admittedly much of what a person learns or experiences seems to disappear, at least as far as free recall is concerned. The fact that we cannot *recall* material does not prove that it is completely gone or that it had no effects on us. Psychologists frequently use other tests for retention besides recall. Relearning has already been mentioned, where the "savings score" (the difference in amount of time to relearn) testifies to the fact that something has been retained. Another test of retention is recognition. We can often recognize some forgotten material if someone else brings it up. Our recognition repertoire is enormous. We may have great difficulty in recalling names or buildings, locations of doorways, or what not and yet be perfectly capable of behaving adequately when the cues to which such responses were learned are present. For such a repertoire to be at the recall level would, in most cases, be of no great virtue, and to learn the whole repertoire to such a level would be extravagant of time, because it takes far less learning time to attain a recognition level than a recall level of most materials.

An interesting development in recall comes from brain-surgery work reported by Penfield and Rasmussen (1950). They found that, if the exposed brain of a conscious patient is stimulated with a mild electric charge, that patient frequently can produce long and detailed reports about previously experienced events that have been forgotten as far as recall is concerned. While it is obviously impossible for us similarly to stimulate our brains to bring out such total recall, it is important that we appreciate the implication of Penfield's and Rasmussen's findings: the learned material is there and can be brought out by some means. Psychoanalysis is one such means, and its practitioners have frequently managed to get patients to remember long-forgotten experiences. Their methods are not very efficient, to be sure, as far as ordinary recall needs are concerned. Few of us can afford to spend three years in free-association activities to recall some relatively trivial matter, but the implications of psychoanalysis, like those of Penfield and Rasmussen, are that nothing is ever forgotten in the sense of being completely gone. It should be noted that Penfield and Rasmussen were talking about people who recall relatively complete and minute details dealing with a fairly long period—and these events were experienced only *once*. Hence, from their experimental findings it could be argued that anything we ever hear, see, smell, or otherwise sense, *even once,* is permanently recorded in our brains and is there, to be revived if proper stimulation could only be applied.

Interference and Forgetting

John McGeoch (1942), for reasons to be explained shortly, concluded that, contrary to popular opinion, time has no direct bearing on forgetting. We forget, he argued, only when we learn something new that interferes in some way with our recall of the original learning. Of course, the more time that passes, the more opportunities there are for new learning to occur.

McGeoch engaged in considerable research on forgetting, using two groups of learners—an *experimental* group and a *control* group. Both groups would start out by learning the same material (experimenters called this *original learning* or *OL*), after which the experimental group would learn something else (*interpolated learning* or *IL*) while the control group merely stood by, doing as little as possible and presumably not learning anything. Then both groups would be tested for the original material. In chart form, his experimental design, which is known as a *Retroactive Inhibition* design, was

Group	Original learning	Interpolated learning	Test for OL
Experimental	yes	yes	yes
Control	yes	no	yes

Results of many experiments by McGeoch and others commonly show that the control group remembered perfectly (or nearly so) while the experimental group forgot some of the original material. Sometimes neither group forgot anything. If the experimental group forgot more than the control group, it appeared to be the result of having learned the interpolated material.

Slamecka (1969) has questioned the findings in many RI and PI (see p. 196) experiments on the grounds that the experimental subjects are asked to learn more than the control subjects in the same amount of total time and that, if the total time hypothesis (see p. 27) has merit, the results could be accounted for without an interference hypothesis.

Under the general name of *Retroactive Inhibition*,[1] McGeoch and other psychologists too numerous to mention have studied this problem of failure to recall original material from many angles. They examined the effect of different kinds of interpolated material, the degree of learning of both original and interpolated material, different species of learners, varying control procedures, and many other variables. Much work

---

[1] McGeoch preferred the term "Reproductive Interference" because he did not think that "inhibition" really meant anything definite whereas "interference" refers to some active process; furthermore, the interference was with the ability or process of reproduction or recall. The term "retroactive" implies something working backward, and this seemed an unlikely possibility.

has been done on time factors. Experimenters have studied the effect of introducing the interpolated material quickly after the original and the effect of introducing it just before the final test, and they have introduced it at various other time intervals. For example, the new material has been introduced a year after the original material and the test not given for a year after that. In most research problems, of course, the whole experiment is completed in an hour or so.

The general results of all this research suggest that such time factors are of no great importance and that new learning can interfere with the recall of old regardless of the time factors. What has been of even greater interest has been the finding that some materials interfere with recall more than do others and that, in general, the more similar the interpolated material is to the original, the more it will interfere. Note carefully that not *all* materials interfere—some can even help, depending on the type of final test—and a safe conclusion from the great body of research is: *If there is a failure of recall, it is probably owed to interference from new learning, but new learning does not necessarily mean that there will be a failure in recall.*

McGeoch's general approach was to treat learning as if it consisted of associations between S's and R's, so that some original learning could be labeled $S_1 \longrightarrow R_1$. If in the new learning the same (or similar) stimuli (remember the principle of generalization, p. 44) were associated with different responses, as, for example, $S_1 \longrightarrow R_2$, then on some future occasion when $S_1 \longrightarrow R_1$ was wanted, inevitably $S_1 \longrightarrow R_2$ would occur; R_1 would not occur because of interference. (It should be noted here parenthetically that whenever any of us is trying to recall something and say "My mind is a blank," we are not telling the truth. Our minds are never blank when we are attempting to recall. They are full of wrong answers!)

John Ceraso (1967), in a semi-popular article, described interference as "simply a name for the general difficulty that is experienced when searching for an item embedded among other things in memory storage." Ceraso argues, like McGeoch, that the items are there; they are not forgotten; only "the availability of items is lost." The problems of trying to recall something that does not come readily is like looking for a particular book in a second-hand bookstore where books are simply piled in haphazard stacks.

Unfortunately, there is no practical way for teachers to determine in advance whether some new learning will interfere with the old. There is just no real or meaningful measure of similarity. Some students (and teachers), after learning about *Retroactive Inhibition,* jump to the completely illogical conclusion: "I won't try to learn anything else; I'll save what I have." The fact has already been italicized that not all new learning interferes with recall of old; even if it did, we can quickly relearn. And there is one practical possibility for the teacher. If he suspects that something the students are learning is going to be interfered with, he can see to it that students *overlearn this new material* and make it less subject to interference. In such situations, a teacher who knows the program in advance and who is familiar with the kinds of responses that are forgotten can look for the possible similar stimulus factors and make sure that these are discriminated adequately before the competitive stimuli are introduced. If General Burgoyne is always being confused with General Braddock, the teacher can take the trouble clearly to isolate at least one of these men by overtraining the important associations.

Experimental results usually have shown less interference with well-learned material. Many students complain about forgetting when actually they never really learned the material in question very well. One reading of a textbook is rarely adequate for effective recall. Material that is learned poorly cannot be remembered well. Unfortunately, no one can spell out how well anything should be learned in order to be retained. The best advice a teacher can offer the "forgetful" student is: "Test yourself on several occasions to see if you remember." If he does not, then the student should realize that he obviously needs more practice or study. As successive and separated (in time) self-tests show that the material is being retained, he can begin to assume that he has learned well enough. This is the point of systematic, scheduled reviews in any subject area.

Proactive Inhibition

"The more you learn, the more you forget" might be a definition of *Retroactive Inhibition* (RI), but it also turns out, and more importantly, that the more that you *have* learned, the more you will forget of the new learnings you attempt. As we learn more and more, it becomes increasingly difficult to remember new material unless it fits in with a background of expertise and represents answers to questions we have been asking. This phenomenon is known as *Proactive Inhibition* (PI) and amounts to the statement that, if we have already learned something (*Original Learning,* OL) and now learn something new (*Interpolated Learning, IL*), we will not do as well on a test of the interpolated learning. In diagram form the experimental design for *Proactive Inhibition* research is:

Group	Original learning	Interpolated learning	Test for Interpolated learning
Experimental	yes	yes	yes
Control	no	yes	yes

When studies following the above paradigm are done, it is commonly found that the Experimental Group suffers; this is due to the fact that the members of the group have already learned something prior to the material on which they will have to be tested. The same factors that we found to affect *Retroactive Inhibition* appear to play a role in *Proactive Inhibition,* primarily the factor of similarity. If the two kinds of material are quite different, there will be no serious effects. The more the OL is like the IL, the greater the influence on retention.

Over the last thirty years studies have accumulated (see Underwood and Schultz, *Meaningfulness and verbal learning,* 1960) demonstrating that PI is a far more serious issue than RI. In fact, Underwood attributes as much as 90 percent of our forgetting to PI. Such a conclusion does not appear unreasonable; after all, we all have relatively extensive backgrounds of learning whenever we approach a new task. There is probably a great deal of potentially interfering material in our backgrounds compared with formerly learned material that is either an aid or related to new learnings we might undergo.

In one way PI suggests that education is somewhat self-defeating. The more we learn, the worse off we will be in learning still more. There are, of course, many saving graces. Much of what we learn is of only temporary value, and we can well afford to forget it as we go on into still newer material. More importantly, everything we do learn changes us in some way and, if of positive value, tends to help us. We also gain by learning how to learn (see p. 217) and by the practice effects that make us more efficient learners of the new material (even if we do not retain it as well).

What the teacher should appreciate from this discussion of retention is that there are reasons why students (and teachers) forget or fail to recall; it is not a matter of good memories or bad, there are no such things. There are fast learners and slow ones, to be sure, but even here it may be that the proper conditions for learning and recall have not been established.

Teachers might consider another proposition that would not be considered outrageous by McGeoch and many of his successors. Time, remember, is not supposed to be a factor in forgetting. What has been learned is not really gone—it has not faded away or vanished because of the passage of time. If something was learned, it is still stored in the learner. He may have great difficulty in recalling it because of interference from old or new learning; the practice of conducting speed or timed tests does not always permit adequate time to recall material. There may be some virtue to speed, and teachers should evaluate its importance, but there is also virtue in patience. Sometimes the better student is a bit slower in recall because he has learned too much rather than not enough.

Learning psychologists have not yet discovered applicable principles for study techniques that would aid recall. There are some signs that the deficiency will be remedied. Work like Tulving's (1962) (on "organized" recall) and the growing research in the field of imagery might prove helpful. We are learning that we can recall a great deal more than was ever suspected. Applications to the classroom will have to wait.

OTHER FACTORS IN FORGETTING

Besides interference, McGeoch listed two other factors as important in forgetting. These were the nature of the stimulus and the intent of the learner. The first of these is of major educational importance.

The Stimulus Factor

Guthrie, as you learned in Chapter 4, was insistent that learning amounted to connections between specific stimuli and specific movements or responses. McGeoch similarly argues for recognition of the importance of the stimuli in connection with which learning is taking place. If certain stimuli are important for a particular response, those stimuli and not some others must be present for the response to occur. If we learn that the name of the man with the fascinating bald head is Mr. Jones, we should not be surprised if we do not recall his name when we see him with a hat on.

McGeoch finds that learning is closely confined to specific stimuli. The teacher should be highly conscious of the fact that what goes on in the classroom under the stern gaze of George Washington in the portrait above the blackboard may not be remembered at home, on the street, or even in another classroom where Abraham Lincoln broods. McGeoch reports that children will do better on examinations when their own teacher serves as proctor than when a stranger serves; that they also will do better in their own classroom than in a strange one. The rule, while awkward and difficult to practice, is quite clear:

If the learner is expected to perform under varied conditions, he should be taught under varied conditions.

All too frequently, teachers ask the wrong questions (present the wrong stimuli) in testing their students because the students never learned the answers to the questions in the forms or terms the teacher is using in the test. Sometimes a teacher tries to be tricky and phrases test questions in equivocal or ambiguous terms. If the student fails to respond correctly, the teacher downgrades him as stupid, at least as incorrect. Yet that same student may possess the required information if the proper question were put to him; he has no chance to show his knowledge if the form of the question is unfamiliar. Teachers, of course, rationalize their use of the wrong form of questions as a matter of "understanding"—they do not want the student merely to answer the question as originally put. Somehow they expect some kind of mystical "understanding" to develop without their ever having taught the student this understanding (see pp. 220–222). Students should be trained to recognize the question as belonging to a class of questions that calls for the same answer. Without such training, the question can easily go unanswered. If a teacher wants a student to answer the "same" question when it is asked in different forms, the teacher must take the pains to teach the student that these different forms really are the same question.

McGeoch's findings about the nature of a stimulus can be applied to other learning situations. The child who practices the piano in private is going to have a difficult time at a public recital. It is no rare happening when a child flees the recital hall when faced with the problem of making a public appearance. Obviously such a child, all children, should be encouraged to practice before groups that are not too threatening. It also helps to practice on various pianos. The specificity of conditioning is sometimes so severe that the learner can perform adequately only in special circumstances. Some people cannot think without a pencil in hand. Others go through more or less elaborate rituals (superstition?) before they can begin to function. Learning becomes highly specialized to certain conditions, and if these conditions are not present, there may be a loss in performance. A child, asked at home what was learned in school that day, may report: "Nothing." This probably is not literally true, but his answer is as good as any; the question is too broad. Besides, the stimuli of school are lacking at home. The common habit of children throwing their "clothes" about at home although hanging their "wraps" neatly at school has already been mentioned. Similarly, the teacher who wants learning to be displayed in many circumstances must make an effort to teach in at least a few of these various circumstances in which the learning is applicable and not in only one. Boys who learn long division involving decimals by the use of baseball batting-averages problems will probably be able to compute batting averages and very little else if they are not given problems involving other kinds of data.

The Factor of Intent

McGeoch believed that the *intent to learn* at the time of original learning would affect retention. In some unspecified way, such intentions were supposed to affect the learning. The conclusion that intent to learn was somehow important fitted an age-old prejudice that is still prevalent. We have already seen (p. 28) that people learn whether they intend to or not so long as they *attend* to the appropriate stimuli. It is probably correct to conclude that, if stimuli are ignored or avoided in some way, learning will not occur. In the experiment cited on p. 30 (see Group III) it was demonstrated that, if we try to learn some material (by attending and imaging, in that case), we will do better than if we do not try. This is quite a different proposition, however, from simple intent.

McGeoch might have had in mind that we frequently make half-hearted attempts to learn, postponing real commitments to study until some later time; this is a particularly insidious practice in an affluent age. We own books, acquire magazines and journals, and after brief skimmings we set them aside for later serious attention. In the meantime more of the same come along, and we never return to the set-aside material. Even if we are somewhat interested in what we are reading, the easy access to materials provides an excuse for a rather casual effort—we can always come back. If books were rare and chained to library walls, we might make a stronger effort.

McGeoch did make an important point in connection with the discussion of intent. He cited an experiment by Lester (1932), who found that, if subjects were informed about the dangers of interference from subsequent learning, they would remember original learning more effectively. Unfortunately, Lester did not control for intervening practice. Her subjects were tested for original learning on the following day and could have rehearsed some of the material in the interval. The point is still well-taken, however. Most people are not aware of the interference potential of later learning for recall of earlier learning. In learning some new material, they may find that it is fairly easy and be content with a casual mastery. If they appreciated that some of the same stimuli, in new arrangements, could be encountered in the future in new contexts, they might not be so readily satisfied and would really examine the stimuli with a little more care. We have already discussed this possibility in connection with generalization and discrimination learning (p. 46), and a review of that discussion might suffice.

McGeoch's discussion of the factors in retention should remind us again that learning will take place under certain conditions (whether we want it or not) and, similarly, forgetting will occur under certain conditions, whether we want it to or not. Saying to yourself: "I must remember this" will be of little value unless you attend to, examine, and work over the material.

EXTINCTION

In treating forgetting we could hardly avoid the tacit assumption that forgetting is somehow undesirable. A moment's reflection, however, will suggest that perfect recall of all of our observations and activities would probably leave us continually boggled and staggering. There is a reverse side to the coin of forgetting, and there are times when it is necessary or important to forget. We must deliberately learn how to get rid of bad habits or undesirable responses and errors, learn how to effect the *extinction* of the sources of interference with effective learning (see pp. 51–52).

By now readers of this book should have recognized that education begins with a negative operation. If society accepted what any person does naturally in any situation, there would be no need for teachers. Society has decreed otherwise, and the natural response is rarely approved. (Even to sneeze is sometimes regarded as less than polite.) Natural responses, however, may come as the learner's first, powerful reaction to some stimuli, and before education can even begin such responses often have to be weakened or eliminated. Psychologists generally are agreed that any response which is to be learned exists, but, as discussion of the *Habit-family Hierarchy* pointed out (pp. 78–79), that response may be so low in strength of association with the stimuli involved that it is unlikely to occur. To make the desired response occur, the more natural responses in the hierarchy must be gotten rid of.

When the teacher is about to start some specific learning sequence, it is desirable for him to know how the learner reacts initially and to analyze the response pattern the learner exhibits. If this pattern contains elements that are likely to interfere with the desired final behavior, the teacher should begin by eliminating the interfering components. A good example is the golf instructor who sees his pupil behaving in ways that preclude a final effective form. He corrects the player's "stance"—the player may not actually know how to stand for the job at hand. In golf,

Drawing by Opie; © 1961 The New Yorker Magazine, Inc.

FIGURE 7. *The Power of Extinction*

the tendency to raise the head before the "follow through" will interfere with an efficient swing. The player must learn not to look up. He may be anxious to get started, but the instructor will not even permit him to have a ball to swing at until certain interfering responses have been eliminated.

The point is easily appreciated in connection with athletic skills, but extinction of interfering responses is equally pertinent to academic content courses. An incorrect orientation—wrong attitudes, poor study habits, misjudgments of the requirements of the course, fears of subject matter— all can prevent acquisition of knowledge and should be eliminated first.

Elimination of Undesired Behavior

But how does the teacher go about eliminating bad habits or wrong responses? How can anyone persuade someone else to "forget about" some more natural reaction? Essentially, this is the problem of extinction as first encountered in the work of Pavlov. Pavlov's approach to extinction was essentially negative: simply refrain from presenting the unconditioned stimulus (something that the teacher usually cannot do). Hull and Skinner, adapting Pavlov's view to their own procedures, advocate not supplying the usual reinforcers or rewards. Such an approach works effectively with animals, where the reward is known and is under the trainer's control, but with human beings in academic situations the teacher may not be able to withhold reinforcers because he may have no real control over them.

Where there is no control over reinforcers, the teacher possibly might resort to the *Beta Method,* or *Negative Practice,* devised by Knight Dunlap (1932). This method required the learner to *perform the undesired response* repeatedly, at the same time saying to himself: "This is wrong" or "This is not the way to do what is wanted." To illustrate: If a child misspells the word *Indian* by writing *Indain,* the teacher might resort to the ancient practice of having the student write *Indian* 50 times, and the chances are that the next day the child will write *Indain.* Dunlap would have the child write *I-n-d-a-i-n* 50 times, each time saying to himself "This is not the way to spell *Indian.*" Dunlap suggested that many habits can be broken by this *Negative Practice.* I once stopped smoking (for a time) by lighting one cigarette after another and so smoking a whole pack. After the first few cigarettes, I had no need to tell myself that the business of smoking was unpleasant; the poisonous consequences became very real by the tenth cigarette, and nausea almost prevented my completing the ridiculous experiment. I was cured of smoking; for three days I could not look at a cigarette. I don't recommend the procedure for anyone else who wishes to stop smoking, but it illustrates the point that *Negative Practice* can be effective.

Parents have often practiced this *Beta Method* (up to a point) when they try to get a baby to stop crying by refusing to pay attention. If the parents do not lose their determination before the baby stops, the method works. On the other hand, if the parents break down first, the baby learns that it must cry louder and longer to get results. Guthrie (1952) has suggested, similarly, that wild horses can be "broken" by tying blankets and saddles with weights on their backs so securely that the horse cannot shake them off or otherwise get rid of them. After the wild horses exhaust themselves, they become docile enough to permit a man to mount them.

In general, Dunlap's *Beta Method* for extinction of incorrect responses consists of conditioning a negative reaction (disgust, fatigue, or exhaustion) to the stimuli that formerly were followed by some "natural" response which usually worked out effectively. If the situation in the classroom provides an opportunity to employ the *Beta Method,* the teacher certainly should try it.

Counterconditioning and Punishment

Sometimes, of course, Dunlap's method would be difficult to introduce, and other methods must be considered. Two other possibilities for extinction of stimuli that interfere with learning are counterconditioning and punishment. Counterconditioning involves getting the learner to make the correct response instead of the incorrect and immediately reinforcing the correct response. To get the learner to make the correct response is not easy without some weakening of the original response. In the classroom, however, it is not too difficult for the teacher, by spoken directions, to get a student at least to say or do the desired thing. When the correct response has been reinforced a number of times, it might acquire sufficient strength to overcome the student's tendency to make the undesired response.

Punishment was discussed at length in the preceding chapter in connection with reinforcement. While punishment may be effective in creating avoidance behavior, the wise teacher will not attempt to get positive action in educational situations by punishment. We can only hope to suppress or inhibit undesirable behavior for some period of time (probably not permanently) by direct punishment for the response, when punishment is applied immediately in connection with the stimulus situation and while feedback stimuli from the response are still active. During the period of suppression teachers can try to reinforce any positive responses—that is, try to countercondition the learner.

Spontaneous Recovery

You will recall from the discussion of Pavlov's contributions that just because some organism has been subjected to an extinction procedure and no longer responds to a conditioned stimulus, this is no guarantee that it will never do so again. After a short rest (even 10 minutes) a former conditioned response may return. Normally, such returns are limited in response strength (amplitude, persistence), but Pavlov reports finding as much as a 50-percent return in response strength after a wait of several hours. The fact of spontaneous recovery should always be taken into account in evaluating the effectiveness of some habit-breaking routine or procedure. Continued tests should be introduced on later occasions to make sure that the behavior is no longer likely to occur. If it does occur, additional extinction sessions are called for. Four or five such sessions work nicely with rats. Humans may be more resistant!

Extinction, Forgetting, and Interference

Essentially, the process of extinction amounts to the replacement of one response by another. Pavlov concentrated on the disappearance of the conditioned response and did not concern himself with what else was happening. He had a negative view of the operation, just as the average person has of the forgetting process. Yet, forgetting is also a counter-conditioning or an interference process. There is a superficial difference in the operations that produce extinction in the animal laboratory and those that produce forgetting in the human learner. The laboratory worker obtains his results quickly by presenting the *CS* without the *US*, but the laboratory worker can also achieve rapid forgetting by requiring new responses to old (or similar) stimuli. The teacher does not work in an animal laboratory, and the normal human learner forgets because his daily world contains enough similar stimuli calling for different responses so that he finds himself forgetting, in a few days or months, depending on the frequency of contact with these similar stimuli. Usually, we assume that we forget because we *did not practice.* We do not notice how frequently we have to do something else to the original stimuli or stimuli that are somewhat similar.

PRACTICAL CONSEQUENCES AND SUGGESTIONS

This consideration of the problem of forgetting and extinction results in a number of conclusions for the teacher. Some may not prove practical for use with student learners, but all should provide the teacher with new reassurance.

1. No one ever forgets, probably, what he has really learned. **Before we talk about how much we have forgotten, we should ask ourselves how much have we learned and how well we learned it.** The better something is learned, the longer it will be remembered. There are no photographic memories, but teachers can teach some things to the point of overlearning. We remember the *Lord's Prayer* because it has been overlearned sufficiently.

2. **When learned material is forgotten to the point of no recall, it can still be tapped.** If recall or recognition fail, relearning, commonly, is extremely efficient. Teachers should encourage students to relearn material to bolster the students' own attitudes, which suffer from assumptions about weak and poor memories. Bolstering student attitudes is the basic reason for reviews and for advising students to review their work regularly. Reviews also inform students about what they know and do not know. This permits them to distribute their time more efficiently.

3. **Teachers should not pervert education by testing in forms or conditions that have not been taught.** Teachers should avoid trick questions and ask questions in connection with the conditions in which the material has been taught. If the teacher wants answers to trick questions, the students should be taught the tricks. Any student who manages to outwit the teacher's efforts to outwit him is not operating on the basis of what the teacher has taught. He has had to learn it some place else.

4. **Analyze the stimulus situation and consider the potential field of competing stimuli.** Psychologists are especially sensitive to the confusion among laymen with regard to such terms as "psychologist," "psychiatrist," "psychoanalyst," and even such terms as "physiologist" and "philosopher." Students frequently misspell each of these and sometimes never do learn the differences that presumably distinguish these professions. Similar difficulties prevail in all fields. An obvious example from the field of simple spelling might serve quite broadly if the reader takes it to heart. Suppose that children are being taught to spell words that happen to have homonyms, *vane, vain,* and *vein,* or *their, they're,* and *there.* Should there be any wonder if one or another substitute shows up on a spelling test or composition? These stimuli sound alike. Generalization can exert its

powerful effects. Other stimuli may look alike. The teacher might save a lot of erroneous learning by considering the material and stimuli to be presented in any given lesson and determining if there are possible sources of confusion that are likely to occur from prior learning or that may come up in the future.

5. **Eliminate competing responses as a first step.** Just as stimuli should be analyzed in advance, so should the possible responses that might occur. If erroneous responses are predictable (and the experienced teacher should have a fund of knowledge on this score), it is wiser to elicit and parade these responses as clearly undesirable in the new situation or context. If such responses are potent competitors for the new behavior desired, they should first be extinguished. If fear, for example, is preventing someone from learning how to swim, the fear must first be eliminated. Swimming coaches commonly start novices by proving to them that they are buoyant. They might start even more simply by demonstrating the buoyancy of hollow objects and ask their students why the objects float? The next step might be to ask the students questions about their bodies, lungs, etc. It is not being argued here that rational approaches will eliminate all fears, but they might at least get the learner into the water for a further demonstration.

6. **Take account of spontaneous recovery.** The teacher should not be discouraged by the reappearance of responses that were presumed to be eliminated by some extinction procedure. This should be expected. Repeated extinctions may be necessary. Patience is probably the most desirable virtue a teacher might possess.

7. **The road to success in learning is paved with good intentions.** By good intentions I mean that a student facing a learning assignment should say to himself: "I will forget this material, probably sooner than later, if I don't learn it now and well. I shall suffer from interfering materials that will come up later, and I must scrutinize this material to see what could possibly interfere with it." Obviously, reciting this formula has no merit in itself, but teachers must stress to students that there are dangers of forgetting if appropriate discriminations have not been made. If teachers can point out the kinds of cues that apply to this and only this material, the retention will be so much more enhanced.

The last suggestion is admittedly difficult to implement in practice, but students must not be allowed to assume that they forget things because they have poor memories or that they "just naturally forget." They forget for good reasons, chief of which is that they did not learn well, where "well" means a deliberate concern with potentially interfering stimuli.

Chapter Nine

The
Problem
of Transfer
of Training
and the
Problem of
Understanding

The last two of the key problems in education or instruction that have been selected for special treatment are those of transfer of training and of understanding. These are the crucial problems of education, since they involve the question of goals of education. The problem of transfer includes the general question of what is education for, why do we educate our children? Is it to prepare them for the future? If so, it must be demonstrated that what is being learned has some bearing on future behavior. The problem of understanding is intimately related to the same question. The perennial concern of teachers has been with getting students to "understand" so that general principles, learned in the past, can be applied to novel situations. The treatment of these two problems that follows may not delight established teachers; teachers in training may not be any more pleased. Psychologists are not too happy about the situation either.

TRANSFER OF TRAINING

The goals of parents and of some students, as was said in Chapter 1, may not be the same as those of educators. Classically and traditionally, education was supposed to be a preparation for life, and the student in his youth was supposed to learn the skills and knowledge that would be his guide and means of earning a livelihood for the rest of his life. Then along came the progressive educators who argued that children are alive in the present and should be regarded as living while learning, that the future is always changing and so it is impossible to prepare the students for the future. Old skills cannot transfer to new needs, and the goal of education cannot then be the preparation for life. The classical curriculum had rested heavily on mathematics, Latin and Greek, and similar "hard" subjects. These, progressive educators argued, have little or no application (or transfer) to modern, changing American life, and what should be taught, if anything, was "life adjustment."

The rationale for progressive education came from the early American *functional* psychology and from some investigations by E. L. Thorndike and R. S. Woodworth (1901) that demonstrated that students taking "hard" courses did not learn to "reason" any better than students taking less classical curricula. Students in both kinds of curricula were tested for reasoning ability before and after completing their respective courses, and no meaningful differences could be found. What the correct interpretation of such a finding may be has never been established. Nonetheless, the conclusions of Thorndike and Woodworth were taken as the license for opening the door to any kind of curriculum innovation and the general decline of selection of "hard" subjects by students.

While we have no evidence that studying Latin, Greek, and geometry results in better thinking (reasoning), we do have plenty of evidence that learning to solve problems results in greater problem-solving ability and that practice or experience in learning can and does increase efficiency of future learning. To take the Thorndike-Woodworth findings as an excuse for abandoning the teaching of "content" is, of course, asinine, but many educators did just that. The objective of schools and teachers has never been to train people how to think (and those courageous souls who have made this their objective have very little to show for their efforts). Rather, the objective of education has been to teach people *what to think and to provide the appropriate backgrounds for whatever thinking is going to be done.* My purpose here is not to propose curricula or to argue about the possibilities of preparing people for changes to come 50 years hence; obviously, with the geometrically expanding growth of science, no one can anticipate even next year's educational needs. My concern, instead, is to evaluate and appreciate the problem of transfer of training. Put in another form: What is the effect of any specific experience on some later specific experience? Any teacher should know by now that there is no universal answer to this question. Whether the effect of some specific experience will be positive, negative, or neutral depends on too many different conditions.

IDENTITY AND TRANSFER

One factor in the problem of forgetting is similarity of stimuli, and now in the problem of transfer of training similarity arises again to vex us. It was Thorndike (1932) who first emphasized that there will be no transfer of training unless there are identical elements in both the old and the new learning situations. Obviously, Thorndike did not mean complete identity, for in that case there would be no new situation—it would still be the old one. But parts of a new problem or situation can be the same as those met in some earlier circumstance. Then the student can be expected to react to the old familiar stimulus in his previous response pattern (correctly or incorrectly).

Thorndike did not spell out what he meant by "identity," and its meaning is open to some different interpretations. If we have learned to stand when we hear the "Star Spangled Banner," we may already know enough to stand in France when the "Marseillaise" is played. The two anthems are not identical, but both are *national anthems,* and in that respect they are identical. If a boy has learned to be polite to his grandmother, other old ladies may also elicit signs of politeness from him. Abstract features as well as concrete stimuli provide us with identities between many kinds of situations. One college course may be "identical" with another in that both use textbooks and have lectures, assignments, and examinations. We can expect that a successful adjustment to one course will carry over to another, at least to some degree. The motivation also may be reasonably identical, and the study habits, reactions to difficulties, and similar responses may well transfer. In an education situation, perhaps the most obvious "factor of identity" is the student's approach to his work. Is he a steady, regular, work-in-on-time pupil or does he postpone, procrastinate, and cram the night before examination? Does he regard every assignment as a potential pleasure or disaster? Whichever kind of student he is, his approach to a new subject is likely to be identical with his previous approach to earlier subjects.

If there is any virtue to having successfully mastered "hard" subjects, it is that future subjects do not seem so "hard," while a history of failure or barely passing will exert the opposite effect on attitudes toward future difficulties. If we now ask the question "Does it do any good to take Latin?" the answer surely must include recognition of how well the student did in Latin and what was learned *besides* Latin. A student may not have learned to reason, but if he did well, he may have learned much more of value for future studies involving prolonged application, translation, grammar, Roman history, and possibly many other things. Similarly, the boy who took a course in woodworking may also have learned a lot that transfers to some future situations he may encounter.

The conclusion is inescapable, then, no matter how "identity" is defined: *Past experience does count in the transfer of training and is of*

basic importance to future adjustments that involve identical elements.
Whether the effect of the past specific experience will be positive, negative, or neutral still needs to be considered.

Neutral Experience and Transfer

It is not easy to find a situation so novel that our past experience will
count neither for nor against us, where nothing in our pasts can help or
hinder. Perhaps jumping from an airplane with a parachute will do as
an example for most of us. Here is a novel situation where we must perform correctly on the first trial. If we don't, there will be no second trial.
Yet even in this imaginary situation, past experience involving heights or
danger might count toward or against our effectiveness. At a more practical level, a teacher might raise the question of the effect of learning some
kind of material, say a poem, on the learning of a list of numbers. Off-
hand, learning poetry and learning numbers seem quite separate and different kinds of learning operations, and teachers would not expect practice in one to affect the other. As a matter of fact, laboratory results have
shown that when subjects learn two separate lists of *unrelated* words, the
learning of one may have no effect on the learning of the other, neither
helping nor hurting the learning of the second or the recall of the first.
We can argue, then, that with some experiences, one has no effect on the
other. The difficulty, in a theoretical sense, is in deciding in advance
whether the two kinds of experiences are really neutral. The only conclusion here is, somewhat unhelpfully for the teacher, that: *Neutral experiences do not affect each other.*

Practice and Warm-up Effects

Even this conclusion is not very secure because of the unrecognized elements of identity in such learning factors as motivation, approach, and
technique. In almost all learning researches, a second learning session goes
better than the first, and a third still better. This is owed to the "practice
effect." The practice effect may also contain or hide a "warm-up effect"
that will help out the later learning assignment. People do become better
and better at learning successive assignments if these assignments are of
more or less the same form (say memorizing nonsense syllables) and if the
content does not contain interfering material. Once the learner becomes
fully practiced in the procedures, there is no further gain from practice.

Continuous practice, of course, will lead to fatigue and a loss of efficiency, but even with highly practiced subjects a warm-up effect will operate. Teachers should recognize the generality of the warm-up; it applies not only to baseball pitchers but to students learning spelling, arithmetic, writing, and probably to most other academic activities. It always helps to start out with a few easy activities and exercises. (College students will learn nonsense syllables better if they first warm up by naming colors that are presented one after another.)

Positive and Negative Transfer

The problem of assessing transfer of training is complicated in two ways: first, we must recognize that we are dealing with two problems, one of learning new material and of retaining old learnings; second, the effect of some current learning can be either positive or negative on the recall of older learning or on the acquisition and retention of future material. We have already met these difficulties in the review of *Retroactive* and *Proactive Inhibition*. What we did not discuss earlier is the effect of positive and negative transfer of former learning on the acquisition of current learning. Fortunately, as Osgood (1949) has pointed out, there appears to be an almost perfect, though negative, correlation between ease of acquisition of current learning and *Retroactive Inhibition*, i.e., if you learn new material easily you will probably forget some old material just as easily. The easy new learning may be due to the transfer of old responses to new stimuli. The new $(S_1) \rightarrow (R_2)$ patterns will then make it difficult for you to recall the old (R_1) responses to (S_1) stimuli. If you are having difficulty in learning new material (negative transfer), it is presumed that the old (R_1) responses cannot be readily attached to new (S_2) stimuli.

The above discussion opens another avenue of complication in the problem of transfer. You will recall that both RI and PI were considered functions of similarity of materials (p. 195 and p. 197). If we think of any learning materials as represented by S's and R's, we must now think of each of these as varying along a number of possible dimensions on a similarity continuum, i.e., present stimuli can be identical, very similar, similar, slightly similar, neutral, or different, e.g., opposite, to either past or future stimuli. In the same way, present responses can range from identical through neutral to opposite. The prospect of resolving the transfer possibilities under such conditions is virtually impossible, especially since we cannot even define similarity properly. Osgood (1949) attempted to

provide at least a rough perspective of what could happen both for retention of new, old, and future learning as a function of the similarity of old
or current stimuli and responses. Bugelski and Cadwallader (1956) tried
to provide data for at least some of the points on Osgood's transfer map.
For the immediate purpose it might be enough to point out that some
things seem fairly clear; neutral current learning does not have any systematic effects on the past or future. When new responses are highly similar to old ones, they are learned well if the stimuli are new or different. If
the stimuli are identical or highly similar, new (different) responses are
difficult to learn.

The findings just reported may not be too helpful to teachers, but they
underscore the responsibility of the teacher to analyze both the stimuli
(problems, questions) and the responses (answers, principles, formuli) that
the student is being asked to learn. Similarities and differences must be
detected and high-lighted if discriminations are to be made. The teacher
must take the necessary steps to point out that "this is like X but differs in
this way."

What the teacher can do about either positive or negative transfer of
training is limited. He cannot be aware of the entire training history of
the learner, nor is it always possible for him to determine what may be the
identical, similar, or neutral experiences. But, as was said in connection
with the concept of generalization (pp. 44–45), the teacher has opportunities to take advantage of some possible positive transfers in those subject courses that require highly similar responses to highly similar stimuli.
In spelling, for example, words that sound alike and are spelled alike
might be grouped in one exercise—*fight, fright, flight, light, might.* The
learner can take advantage of the *i-g-h-t* identity and learn a number of
words with little more effort than is involved in learning one. In mathematics, some rules apply to a variety of figures or forms, and these can be
learned together. Some argument can be made for the concept of teaching
a group of languages (Romance, Teutonic) at one time because of the
high degree of similarity among all the languages in the group and the
fact that differences among the languages follow some reasonably consistent rules. Some teachers may be appalled by the prospect of students
learning Italian, French, Spanish, and Portuguese at the same time, yet,
when there is a good reason for someone to learn these four languages, it
well may be that he will do better learning them together than one at a
time. (See *The Loom of Language,* Lancelot Hogben and Frederick Bodner, 1944.)

Learning How to Learn

Early in this chapter I stated that, while we have no evidence that study-ing Latin, Greek, and geometry results in better thinking, we do have evidence that learning to solve problems results in greater problem-solving ability. The availability of courses in Latin and Greek and any other of the "classical" studies is a matter of curriculum development, which only indirectly is a problem for the learning psychologist. But, lest the problem of transfer of training be distorted out of its real meaning, I would point out certain matters of interest to the teacher. Because there is no question about the reality of transfer is not to argue for the inclu-sion in the curriculum of "hard" subjects for their own sake. Latin does not train the student's mind, but *success* in Latin will foster or promote success in similar future endeavors *to the degree that identical elements are operating.* Failure in Latin similarly will foster failure in similar en-deavors. Likewise practice and success in stickball may lead to success in baseball (perhaps also in polo should the stickball player come upon affluent days). The best prediction of success is success.

This conclusion is perhaps best supported by the work of Harry Har-low (1949) of the University of Wisconsin on the problem of *learning how to learn.* In his research, Harlow trained monkeys to select one of two objects in order to receive a reward, a peanut or a raisin. The two objects differed in color, size, shape, texture, or material, and were randomly placed as to left or right. At first, the monkey faced with the task of select-ing the correct object, a red square, perhaps, or a blue circle, would have great difficulty and might need 16 trials to learn accurately which object to select. When the first learning was complete, Harlow changed the problem by using two new objects. Again the monkey would have trouble and require many trials. As each problem was mastered, new objects would be introduced, until after a year or so the monkey had solved some 300 problems of this type. By now Harlow was dealing with a very differ-ent monkey. For any two objects whatsoever, the monkey solved the prob-lem in one trial. If he made a mistake on the first trial, he never made the mistake again. If he was correct by chance, he stuck with his selection. As Harlow put it, the monkey had "learned how to learn." This college-trained monkey was an expert in a given realm of operations. He was not necessarily any better than before at other kinds of problems, but he was a little genius at picking the correct one of two objects. And the monkey could quickly transfer his training to such a related problem as the "reversal." In this situation, the object that had been correct on the first trial was incorrect on the second trial, and the trained monkey could handle such reversals in one trial too. It is not possible to spell out all the transfer elements in such situations, but the monkey certainly had learned what not to do in the situation and undoubtedly acquired a variety of sets, adjustments, and attention patterns that make for success in his two-object enterprises.

Harlow's work has been extended by Levinson and Reese (1967), to cover similar problems with children, college students, and the aged, with similar results. People, in general, do learn how to learn or at least benefit from prior experience. The more problems they solve, the better they get at it.

The concept of "learning to learn" has been supported by research with college students learning nonsense syllables. As long ago as 1937 it was observed by Ward that college students improved steadily in learning successive lists of nonsense materials. Improvement continued for as many as 15 lists. Ward thought of this as "cumulative positive transfer." More recently, Postman and Schwartz (1964) found that students would benefit from even one learning experience when this was followed by another, although the materials and procedures differed somewhat (e.g., learning pairs of adjectives after learning pairs of nonsense syllables). They concluded that interlist practice effects are partially dependent upon specific instrumental habits learned in the first learning task.

Such studies underscore the desirability of providing successful learning experiences for young learners in terms of useful study habits. There are no general rules for proper study habits, but the successful learner, of necessity, discovers what works for him and what does not. What probably happened with Harlow's monkeys and Postman's college students is that they found out what was ineffective and undependable; faulty approaches were eliminated or extinguished, and useful maneuvers were incorporated into a kind of general approach to the new problem. The important emphasis for the teacher is to be sure that the student actually learns the material assigned legitimately and does not resort to tricks, inappropriate outside help, or outright dishonesty. Such procedures are also easily learned.

The laboratory findings about "learning how to learn" have a broader implication for education that should be of concern to all teachers, one that must be evaluated with great care. At one time Guthrie (1944) argued that a man's personality could be evaluated or appreciated best from the knowledge of how he earned his living, i.e., from simply knowing his occupational label. We expect a banker, for example, to be neat, conservative, precise, orderly, cautious, etc. Similarly we have our anticipations of how a graduate of a military academy or medical school might react in various situations. If we know that someone is a college graduate, we already know a great deal about him prior to ever meeting him. Education molds a man in a way that makes him quite different from those who have not had the experience of meeting educational criteria. What happens in schools is important not for the details learned or the special knowledge one possesses but for the attitudes and procedures for coping with problems one acquires. The detailed information will be forgotten unless regularly rehearsed, the approaches to problem solving, because they are largely a matter of attitude or emotional conditioning, will not. The phenomenon of learning how to learn suggests that we do not go to school to learn facts but rather to learn how to learn more or other facts. This suggestion should not encourage teachers to underplay the importance of learning the facts in the first place.

The studies on learning how to learn suggest a general conclusion that might be useful to teachers: *Learners can learn how to learn.* They need only to learn something. To this an immediate precaution must be added: *They can also learn not to learn* if the teacher is lax. Recall here our earlier strictures against giving partial credit. Students learn about as much as it pays to learn.

Practical Implications

The discussion up to this point can be summarized briefly in a few practical assertions:

1. The effects of past experience can be positive, negative, or neutral. In a sense this is what has been said throughout this text, starting with Thorndike. Good student performance is not necessarily praise-worthy; poor performance, by the same token, does not deserve blame. This does not mean that the teacher should refrain from either, as both praise and blame can serve other purposes, as has been shown earlier. It does mean, however, that faulty performances must be considered in the light of previous experiences that hinder either acquisition or retention and that efforts should be made to counteract such prior experience through extinction or counterconditioning procedures. Admittedly, this is difficult and time-consuming.

2. Teachers might take advantage of identical elements in organizing materials and teach much more material, more or less at the same time,

where identical elements can be identified. In teaching comparative governments for example, a teacher might find it advisable to group the world's countries in terms of monarchies, constitutional monarchies, democracies, communist and socialist states, etc., and avoid a piecemeal approach. Care must be taken to discriminate any meaningful differences, of course. Modern geography texts do something of this nature in discussing large regions with similar terrain, economics, climate, and so on. It is easier to learn a label for a class than to learn the label for each member of the class separately at different times.

3. Teachers should deliberately institute warm-up activities with each new lesson or activity. In advanced classes there should be a short review of the last material covered. In more elementary settings, children could be given an opportunity to just scribble before settling down to serious writing practice. The cold, businesslike plunge into the work at hand will leave some of the learners behind.

4. Learning-how-to-learn calls for considerable practice with problems of a similar kind. There is no substitute for practice in this regard. Just how much practice is required for the host of educational tasks is not known. Each teacher must develop his own supply of work samples and find out by experience how much practice is needed. Success in handling one *kind* of problem is no guarantee of success in other kinds. There may be general gains from practice and success that do transfer from problem type to problem type, but specific skills have to be learned separately.

UNDERSTANDING

As was said earlier in this chapter, the teacher who has tried to train students *how* to think has struggled in vain. The objective of teaching is to train students what to think and to provide appropriate backgrounds for whatever thinking is going to be done. Similarly, many teachers have persistently raised the problem of understanding, holding that some place in the process of learning there must be room for what they variously describe as "getting the idea" or "principle" or "meaning" or "understanding." Yet none of the psychologists mentioned in this book ever seriously considered the problem of understanding. If he did not ignore it entirely, he implied that really there is no such problem. Since such a position is not likely to appeal to the teacher with an "understanding" problem in his classroom, more needs to be said as to why psychologists imply that learning is a mechanical process consisting of trial and error or Pavlovian conditioning.

One experiment that commonly is cited as revealing the virtues of teaching for meaning and principle as opposed to teaching rote memory was performed by G. Katona (1940). He gave two groups of subjects the same task: to learn to recite in correct sequence some number like

$$912161923263033374044475 1$$

One group was told to memorize as well as possible; the other was told to look for a principle on which the series of numerals was built. (The principle is not hard to discover—add 3 to the first number, 4 to this total, then 3 to that total, then 4, and so on.) As might be expected, the learning of the two groups was found to differ: the "principle" group learned more quickly and remembered much better than did the group that simply memorized. The conclusion was that learning by understanding is superior to dull drill.

But consider the experiment again. The drill group had to learn and remember 25 integers or units. The "principle" group did not even attempt this task; its members learned something completely different. They had to remember only one number, the first, and a verbal command or rule. Clearly they had much less to learn. To argue from such an experiment for the virtues of understanding is pointless. What if there had been no rule, if the numbers had been merely randomly arranged? Learning a rule or principle will not produce anything different from, in this case, memorizing the number. A rule is only a verbal statement that governs a class of facts. Rules are memorized like any other verbal material, and being able to cite them, or even apply them, does not mean that something unusual or nonmechanical has been learned.

When a student learns that *receive* is spelled with *e-i* and not *i-e* because of a rule about *"i* before *e* except after *c"* he now knows a bit of doggerel that permits him to spell *receive*. He has not been "enlightened" in any special way. The letter *c* has become a discriminating stimulus for the response *e* instead of *i* for a class of word spellings. Should the student of geometry learn the Pythagorian Theorem, he similarly memorizes a verbal statement that guides responses when right triangles are the discriminative stimuli. Uneducated carpenters have used the Pythagorean Theorem for centuries in terms of a 3-4-5 rule they follow in squaring a foundation. They know no more about *why* a 3-4-5 right triangle insures a square corner than does the student or the teacher of geometry.

Understanding and Misunderstanding

Of course, there is no disadvantage or harm in teaching rules or principles when such are available—it is obviously advantageous to organize facts into classes, especially if one need not worry over specific facts. But the argument is not at all about relative advantages; it is about the concept of understanding. Learning psychologists do not discuss understanding because they have no way of discriminating between understanding and misunderstanding. They are concerned only with right and wrong responses or answers. I used to give instructions to my students about certain operations they were to perform. Following the instructions, I usually asked: "Do you understand?" If no further questions were asked, I allowed the students to begin work. Frequently, it was apparent that my instructions were not being followed. Students would apologize and claim: "But that's what I understood you to say." Clearly "understanding" for them referred to some feeling of satisfaction and very little else. If they had no such feeling of satisfaction or if they had some doubt, uncertainty, or conflict, they would report not "understanding." Without such doubt, they would report "understanding," even if later they showed that they had "misunderstood." In brief, misunderstanding and understanding can occur with exactly the same feeling of assurance or knowledge. If the teacher asks a student if he has "the idea," he can say "yes" in either case. In the words of C. C. Pratt (1939), "a difference that makes no difference is no difference." There is no difference between understanding and misunderstanding in this sense.

"Meaning" and "Insight"

So much for the concept of understanding from the learning psychologists' point of view. But teachers still argue. The student must be made to see the *meanings* of facts. Today, psychologists are taking an increasing interest in exploring the various meanings of *meaning,* but their concerns are not close to those of teachers, and what they have to say is of little comfort to teachers.

We can examine some approaches taken by psychologists to the problem of the meaning of meaning. Such an examination might at least clarify the psychologists' positions. It might even prove of some help.

Among the world's most important delusions is the concept or idea of understanding. The goal of the teacher is frequently to get a student to understand something; a principle, or an idea. The teacher presumes or acts as if he has the idea, i.e., he understands something, and his function is to convey this idea to the students by telling or showing something on the blackboard or through some model or audio-visual device. Sometimes the procedures do not work well, and then teachers follow some procedure that is calculated to lead to "discovery" on the part of the student. That form of learning, in fact, has high status in educational circles. It has the incidental advantage that the teacher is freed from responsibility —if the student cannot discover the principle by himself he is at fault, stupid, slow, or otherwise deficient. Sometimes teachers even support their inactivity by relying on fatuous references to Gestalt psychology and cite the remarkable cases of Kohler's (1927) apes who allegedly solved problems by achieving some kind of internal illumination or "insight."

The operation of insight has never been explained in a satisfactory manner. The cartoonist who shows an electric light bulb over the head of one of his characters who suddenly gets an idea is about as scientific as anything else written on the subject. What the expression refers to is that we frequently hear people say, "I get it" or, "Ah ha, now I've got it," when they have been confronted with a problem that was not immediately resolved by appropriate action. What we usually fail to notice is that often enough those who say, "I got it," do not really have it. They have merely announced another blunder. With successive trials and repetitions of "I got it," they may eventually stumble upon a correct answer or solution. The attendant satisfaction may make them think that some mysterious enlightenment occurred in them and arranged all of the elements in some happy pattern.

The ape experiments of Kohler have been criticized effectively by Mowrer (1960b). Pavlov, too, found his apes not especially gifted with insight and dismissed the concept as a fiction. We cannot dismiss the fact that people say, "Ah ha, I've got it," but we can reserve judgment about the occurrence of any special manifestation of some agency called Insight, as it appears an unnecessary and irrelevant impediment to educational practice.

Many psychologists have struggled with the concept of meaning without too much success. Perhaps, like the philosophers who too have worked on the "meaning of meaning," they have been looking for something that does not exist, at least not in the sense that teachers and ordinary citizens and parents use the term. That usage has been described by Malinowski (1938) as the "bucket" theory of meaning. What it amounts to is that someone believes he has a "meaning," and he wishes to convey this meaning to someone else. He then incorporates this meaning into words, which he writes or tells someone, and the "bucket" of words carries the meaning from one person to another. The problem of meaning becomes identified with the problem of communication. Judging by the frequent reports about failures to communicate, the theory is not a very satisfactory one.

Two psychologists who disagreed with each other about the nature of meaning, and who are probably both correct to a degree, are Noble (1952) and Osgood (1952). Noble tried to suggest that we could approach the meaning of meaning by counting the number of words people could recite in a minute as responses to some stimulus word. This count would give a measure of "meaningfulness" or m. Thus, the meaning of dog for me could be: cat, horse, fire, shoe, skin, fur, smell, chase, car, can, garbage, animal, wet, climb, jump, bark, swim, poodle, hair. In one minute I wrote down 19 words initiated by "dog." Dog, therefore, for me, has an m of 19. Other words would have more or less. Some would have virtually none. Osgood pooh-poohed this theory because, he would point out, one of my responses was cat, another horse, and *clearly* neither of these can be conceived of as part of the meaning of dog. But Noble would argue that he is not trying to describe a concept of dog but only what a dog, in effect, means to me, or, really, the "meaningfulness" of a dog. Noble might have said that such a count measures my reaction, or a part of my reaction, to dogs, and he would be closer to Osgood's own view, which is that a meaning is some reaction of a person to a stimulus. Osgood tried to measure such reactions by asking people to mark scales defined by pairs of adjectives like good-bad, strong-weak, fast-slow, etc. Such scale markings could be measured and analyzed in terms of what Osgood called the "Semantic Differential." Osgood found that people in general could indicate quite reliably how they reacted on essentially three axes (sets of scales), which could be described as an activity scale, a power scale, and an evaluative scale. Most of the reaction could be accounted for as an evaluative or emotional reaction of acceptance or rejection, positive or negative. According to Osgood, most of the meaning of any stimulus word is an emotional reaction of the individual "having" the meaning. Osgood translated the reaction anyone might have to a given word as some kind of unspecified internal response or "representational response" (the *meaning* response or r_m). Such a response, like any other, would generate stimuli or s_m that might lead to overt responses. The general proposition of Osgood could be symbolized by ($r_m \longrightarrow s_m$). A meaning, for Osgood, is this internal $r_m \longrightarrow s_m$ operation, process, or mechanism. The resemblance to Hull's r_g is more than coincidental, as Osgood ascribes his derivation of $r_m \longrightarrow s_m$ to Hull.

Mowrer (1960) accepted the basic position of Osgood and emphasized the personal, individual, reactive aspect of meaning. Meanings are not, then, something to convey, explain, or communicate. They are reactions that are aroused in an individual and depend on *his* experience, not that of the teacher or arouser. Now we can "understand" the failure of communication. There is nothing to communicate.

Both Osgood and Mowrer recognized that there is a sensory component to meanings. Such a sensory component will be aroused directly if there is a present stimulus, e.g., an apple, or via *imagery* if there is no physical stimulus present. The image, you will recall, was regarded by Mowrer as a conditioned sensation or perception. Such sensori-perceptual processes can be considered to be physiological reactions with no necessary mentalistic implications.

Thus for Mowrer, if not fully for Osgood, a meaning is the emotional-imagery reaction aroused in anyone by stimulation. It should be clear by now that a teacher cannot provide meanings—the student is going to react in terms of the meanings dictated by his own experience. To control the meanings, the teacher must control the experience of the student. It should be equally obvious that the meaning experienced by one person may be quite a different one from that of another. The name of a candidate for political office can arouse different meanings in members of opposing political parties. Some people see black when white is intended.

While the above account may contribute to an "explanation" of meaning, it does not help teachers much except in a negative way. It may be possible, however, to take some educational advantage from such negative propositions. To do so requires an excursion into the nature of imagery.

The image represents our past experience, and the survival of past experience is the significant power that enables us to take advantage of learning. Without imagery there would be no learning, no memory, no thinking, no behavior at all that represented anything beyond a primitive reaction to a present stimulus.

The hiatus in experimental work on imagery in the thirties, forties, and fifties left us without much to go on in the area of imagery, but more recently some experimenters (Paivio, 1969; Bower, 1969; Reese, 1965) have reopened the subject and have demonstrated at least the relatively primitive findings that imagery facilitates learning. Paivio has been especially active in this field. He has developed a measure (i) that represents a rating of the image strength of a word. He has repeatedly demonstrated that words that are high in imagery are learned far more effectively than words low in this rating. Moreover, Paivio has compared the learning of words measured in terms of Noble's (m) and his own measure (i) and found that the (i) measure is consistently superior. Actually the two measures correlate highly, and what (*m*) measures may really be imagery content. Paivio (1970) is not averse to the suggestion that meaning, itself, consists mostly of the imagery generated by a given stimulus. In some ingenious studies of sentences (measured in terms of (i) strength) he has suggested that the meaning of a sentence consists basically of the imagery aroused. (See Chapter 13 where this suggestion is considered at greater length.)

To illustrate the operation of imagery, consider its use in a study by the author (Bugelski, 1968b). College students were asked to memorize the names of ten common objects in numerical order and were tested at random after a single reading of the list. The usual recall is about 46 percent of the ten words. They were then instructed to learn the old nursery school jingle of one-bun, two-shoe, three-tree, four-door, five-hive, six-sticks, seven-heaven, eight-gate, nine-wine, and ten-hen. After this was well learned, they were instructed to learn another list of ten words in numerical order, but this time they were to imagine the first thing in a bun, the second in some relation to a shoe, and so on. Random testing now demonstrated virtually perfect recall for everyone. Furthermore, they could keep on learning successive lists without any trouble. (Such imagery association accounts for most of the memory experts' successful demonstrations.)

The fact that people can learn to recite ten (or any number, really) words in order with the use of imagery is of no great importance in itself. Important is, first, that the process of association involved takes time (it has been shown that about seven seconds are required, on the average, to form a suitable association with the jingle words), and second, it is also important that the subject participates actively, that is, he selects his own image from the stream of imagery that occurs to him. He cannot easily remember somebody else's images if these are supplied for him. Perhaps this has some bearing on the old adage about "put it in your own words." The active participation referred to above really "means" what we otherwise speak of as paying attention; this we can now recognize as a matter of, paradoxically, "letting ourselves go" as far as the learning process is concerned until a suitable response occurs to us. How we determine such suitability is not known, but it seems to be a definite operation as subjects reject and select from the inevitable train of imagery.

What happens in an exercise such as the one just described is the same as occurs in any thinking or day-dreaming. The experimental format requires that the imagery dwelled upon fit the stimulus situation. In daydreaming there is no external control over what imagery gives rise to the next.

In the present context, teaching amounts to controlling the imagery of the learner (which amounts to controlling his attention). To a great degree this is impossible if the imagery background of the learner is scanty or inappropriate. For this reason pictures, movies, or models are of great importance if one is to control the thought processes of a learner. It is also important that the learner have had sufficient and appropriate prior experience if he is to think correctly or realistically. The average American has a head full of nonsense about cowboys and Indians, for example, that makes it almost impossible for him to learn about the real West of the nineteenth century. His imagery is replete with gun-fights and saloons, dancing girls, and intelligent horses. In this connection it becomes important to create effective and detailed experiences for children in their early years so that the necessary equipment for appropriate thinking and learning will be available when required.

From the discussion above we can draw the conclusions that data seem to force upon us. Two such conclusions we will meet again and again. It takes time to learn anything. During that time we will automatically experience a succession of images and select those that somehow provide satisfaction or "closure." We do not know what the latter amounts to, but it happens. Whether our satisfactions or closures terminate with a correct or incorrect answer is not for us to say—that is a function of the real world. Our meanings are strictly our own. They do not necessarily correspond to the truth.

A last word on "insight" might not be amiss in the light of the above discussion. To attempt to teach insight is impossible, even by definition. Insights either occur or do not occur. Some teachers have been misled by those who regard insight as some kind of higher-level intellectual operation into virtually abandoning teaching and waiting for insight to occur. They may demonstrate some process or proof and ask: "Do you get it now?" After a while any student will report that he "gets" it in order to relieve the teacher's anxiety. Unfortunately, none of us will ever know what "getting it" means other than, if Mowrer is correct, feeling better about the stimuli and the overt responses we are making to them.

PRACTICAL CONCLUSIONS ABOUT UNDERSTANDING AND PRINCIPLES

1. Learning can take place whether or not a student "understands." Understanding does not contribute anything but a feeling of satisfaction which can be enjoyed even if the student "misunderstands."

2. Even if understanding were desirable as an aim of teachers, there is no technique for teaching understanding or "insight"—these are reactions that either come or do not come.

3. To assume that understanding is taught by presenting "principles"

is to confuse the issue. Principles must be recognized for what they are: verbal statements that summarize a collection of facts. Such statements are learned in the same way that any other statements, even foolish ones, are learned. A short verbal statement or formula that can be taught as a response to specific stimuli may well be an efficient tool. Where there are principles, teachers should obviously present, illustrate, and exploit principles. The student must be taught to recognize and discriminate the stimuli that fit the formula or principle. To expect these to come about naturally or automatically may be dangerous.

4. When there are no principles (organizing statements) and when dull facts are to be learned, there is no alternative to learning the hard way. Rote learning must be learned by rote. There is no other way.

5. There may be some virtue to allowing students to try to develop principles by themselves instead of telling them directly. Wherein the virtue lies cannot be said. Perhaps it is in the effort or time involved, in the rejection of confusing and incorrect statements of hypotheses. In short, the student who found the principle by himself had to do a lot of work. The instructor might have made this work a little easier by guiding the acceptance and rejection of hypotheses. Appropriate instruction might easily exceed the presumed advantages of "digging it out for himself."

Chapter Ten

Programmed
Learning

Since about 1955 the educational world has been increasingly exposed to speeches, publications, and salesmanship dealing with teaching machines, automated learning, and the general operation of "programing."[1] The average teacher could only view the new prospects with mixed feelings. On the one hand, he saw his job either disappearing or changing into that of a clerk or mechanic; on the other hand, he felt obliged to listen to any message that promised to make an impossible job a little more possible. The rapid expansion of the field of automated learning has been bewildering to teachers as they listened now to the description of one machine or program and now to another. Should the teacher adopt the Harvard model with its "operant-conditioning" orientation or is there some better approach—the programmed textbook, programmed workbook, multiple choice programs, *pre*-texts, or what? Adding to the confusion, the aura of "modern psychology" has hung over the scene with the implication that psychology has had something to do with automated learning. No teacher defies modern psychology with equanimity, but to accept without questioning the implication of some statements that automated learning has behind it the "authority" of "modern psychology" is sheepish behavior and no way to arrive at a proper basis for evaluating teaching machines, programmed learning, or anything else.

At the outset, one thing must be made clear. Some psychologists, probably most psychologists, are capable, intelligent, and astute men. Faced with a problem calling for "common sense," they are as likely to arrive at a solution as are any other professional men. Should the problem be one of improving some aspect of learning, they might hit upon ideas and approaches that have merit, not because they are psychologists but because they are capable, intelligent, and astute. Chances are, however, that any good they might achieve will be popularly credited to their knowl-

1 Professional programmers have adopted this spelling of programming with one "m" and use it as a kind of group identification.

edge of psychology when this may have nothing to do with the matter. But—and this fact must be appreciated—psychologists, perhaps more than other scientists, are strongly inclined toward statistical manipulations and evaluations, toward running controlled experiments, toward an "operational" orientation and getting objective records, all mixed with considerable skepticism. It is these skills or attitudes that are likely to help psychologists develop more careful progress in solving problems *involving people* than might the training and work of chemists, biologists, or geographers who do not work so closely with human elements.

We start out, then, by recognizing that the psychologists (but not necessarily as psychologists) are largely responsible for the current flurry of excitement about teaching machines.[2] It was, in fact, Skinner who began the whole modern movement. Skinner (1954, 1958) credits Sidney L. Pressey with introducing a teaching machine back in the 1930s, but this is more modesty than truth on Skinner's part. Pressey introduced a *testing* machine that, incidentally, was found to appear to improve learning. Pressey, however, offered no theory and took no action. Skinner, from his long preoccupation with the control of behavior, offered both—although he claims that learning psychology is not ready for a theory, that he deals only with empirical laws. Other psychologists generally agree that Skinner's laws at least come close to a theory of learning.

THE WORK OF SKINNER

Skinner started with a strong desire to help out in the educational crisis that began in the United States in the 1950s (a shortage of competent teachers) and a conviction that the successes he had attained in the control of rat and pigeon behavior revealed the basic principles that underlie successful teaching.

Because Skinner had automated the training of his animal subjects in his laboratory to a remarkable degree, he was inclined to believe that much of the training of humans could also be automated successfully. Such automation was not meant to *displace* teachers. Automation would only *replace* some of their functions, freeing teachers for other kinds of tasks, permitting them more latitude to experiment, and allowing them to be more creative in their basic role as educators.

2 Readers interested in the history of teaching machines, varieties of devices employed, and comparative studies of machine vs. traditional techniques of teaching should consult Leonard Stolorow (1961), A. A. Lumsdaine and Robert Glaser (1960), W. A. Deterline (1962), and Wilbur Schramm (1962).

In order to automate some, if not all, of the functions of a teacher, two preliminary needs must be met: (1) The functions of a teacher must be analyzed carefully to determine exactly what the machine must do. And (2) there must be available information about the principles of behavior to translate into machine operations. On the first need, Skinner has never been very precise. He has not spelled out the detail functions of a teacher except by implication. It is reasonable to infer from the various innovations he developed that Skinner considered the functions of a teacher to be the following: (1) The teacher must provide for and control the necessary motivation of learners. (2) The teacher must present a carefully arranged sequence of stimuli that cover the learning task from start to finish; in deciding upon what these stimuli are, the teacher should begin with the final product or end results, so to say, the last response, and work out the sequence, step by step, backward to the beginning. (3) The teacher must control the presentation of reinforcements that will presumably make the behavior more likely on a future occasion. Underlying all three of these functions is the assumption that the teacher's task is to see to it that the learner initiates all response activity, that the learner *creates* the responses (or answers) by his own activity.

On the second need Skinner felt that sufficient information was available about the principles that govern learning to justify an attempt at automating the teaching process. And furthermore, he felt that techniques for translating these principles into operations that could be performed by a machine were sufficiently well understood. These principles have already been presented in detail (see pp. 87–98). Some of the principles described in the earlier discussion are not pertinent to automated teaching in any direct way. For example, Skinner does not make any systematic application of his extremely important work on scheduling of reinforcements. It will help, however, to review the Skinner approach to learning briefly and restate some of the attitudes that underlie the practical work.

Skinner's Principles

In the brief review to follow, six of the major and most pertinent of Skinner's generalizations will be included. When put to work in the form of some mechanical agency, they represent the traits or features of a teaching machine.

1. Operant Conditioning. Most important human behavior consists of *emitted* responses. These responses are presumed to be part of the basic equipment and will occur sooner or later during the life of the organism.

It is not necessary to know the specific stimuli that precede such responses. It is enough to know that they will occur with some frequency (the "operant rate"). Learning amounts to a change in the operant rate (raising or lowering). Such changes are brought about by reinforcement or failure of reinforcement of such responses when they occur.

2. Reinforcement. When an organism emits some response, the trainer can introduce some new stimulus that either does or does not change the operant rate. If it does change the rate, it is called a *reinforcer;* otherwise it is presumed to be ineffective, a *non*reinforcer. While this definition appears to be, and *is,* circular, it can be readily demonstrated that food provided for hungry animals is reinforcing. A wide variety of stimuli can be classed as reinforcers under certain conditions, usually conditions of deprivation. Thus, warmth can reinforce a cold creature, and vice versa; sex partners can reinforce animals that have been isolated for some time; and removal of a painful stimulus can reinforce an organism that is suffering. On the human level, praise, gifts, money, and privileges of various kinds can serve as reinforcers. The most easily applicable reinforcer is simply knowledge of results (KR). When a human learner (even a child) emits a response, and this response is then shown to be correct, this knowledge of results is found to reinforce with sufficient potency to obviate any other "rewards."

3. Immediacy of Reinforcement. A reinforcing stimulus must be presented very shortly after a response is emitted. Otherwise, the learner may emit some other response that, if followed by a reinforcer, will be learned in place of the desired response. Experimental findings quite generally confirm that a "correct" response should be reinforced within five seconds or there will be no benefit.

4. Discriminated Stimuli (S^D). Sometimes, probably most often, it is desired that the learner emit a certain response at certain times or under certain conditions and not others. This can be arranged by reinforcing the desired responses only when a certain stimulus is present. We do not normally want people to salute at random; only when the flag passes by. We therefore would reinforce saluting only when the flag was passing and not otherwise. Similarly, we do not reinforce people for saying "Please pass the salt" by supplying salt unless we are at the table and salt is available. The special conditions or stimuli that must be present in order for reinforcement to be provided are called *Discriminated Stimuli* or S^D.

5. Extinction. If a response has been reinforced and has a high operant rate, it can be reduced in frequency back to its operant level by failure
to reinforce such responses. The response then gradually drops in frequency until it is no longer considered important, meaningful, or learned.

6. Shaping. Much learned behavior consists of complex sequences or
chains of simple components. The sequence is not likely to occur as a
single operant. Thus, we do not expect a child in kindergarten to write
his name when he has not even learned the alphabet. The necessary
procedure consists of knowing the final sequence that is desired and indi-
vidually reinforcing each step in the sequence, starting with the very first
component, whatever that is. Then, in stages, the next step is required, in
sequence; the two steps are reinforced as a unit (the first step is no longer
reinforced separately); next, the third step must occur before reinforcement is granted; and so on until the entire sequence runs off appropriately, and reinforcement is attained shortly after the last step.

Skinner's Teaching Machine

With these principles of learning in mind, Skinner built his first teaching
machine in 1953. Although many improved models are now available,
what is in use today is basically the same as his first machine. Skinner's
machine shows the learner a question in printed form, the question appearing in a little window or "frame"[3] in a box before which the learner
is seated. Next to this window, another window exposes a plain section
of paper on which the learner writes an answer. As soon as he has committed himself (emitted or "composed" an answer), the learner is able to
release the lever that carries his answer under a third window where he
can then read both the question and correct answer and compare his
own answer with the correct one. If the two answers are the same, the
learner tries the next question and repeats the operation of checking. If
the student's answer is not correct, he can set the machine to show this
question again after the entire set has been tried. Question by question,
the learner continues until he has arrived at a predefined goal, which for
purposes here can be called "having answered all the questions in the
assignment."

And how does this machine embody Skinner's principles? Skinner

---

[3] The word *frame,* derived from this window in the teaching machine, has been adopted
by program constructors for any individual or unit question in a learning program, automated or otherwise.

would say that because the learner must emit (compose) the answer (not merely recognize it out of a choice of two or four), *operant conditioning* is present. Because the emission of the answer is controlled by the question, we have a *discriminated-stimulus* situation. The learner does not emit answers at random—they are the kinds of answers that are desired under this and only this stimulus situation. If the answer is correct, the learner has *reinforcement* and *immediacy of reinforcement;* he knows he is right; he has immediate knowledge of results. Wrong answers presumably become *extinct* because of failure of reinforcement. Finally, the sequence of the questions results in the *shaping* of the learner. Questions are so phrased that the learner starts out with a simple answer to a simple question. Almost anyone qualified to be working at the machine can answer the first question. In the context of question and answer, the next question also appears easy and is likely to be correctly answered. Thus, step by step, the learner is led, controlled, or reinforced into more and more complex behaviors until, when he finishes the entire sequence, he has achieved a goal that can be loosely described as "knowing a lesson."

Advantages of Teaching Machines

A machine or apparatus, of course, is not essential to learning. Teachers who are familiar with modern innovations also know that a machine is not essential for programmed learning; the question asked by Skinner's teaching machine can be asked orally, if anyone wishes to work that way; they can be put on cards or on tape; or they can be included in programmed textbooks, such as J. C. Blumenthal *English 2600* (1960) and J. G. Holland and B. F. Skinner *The Analysis of Behavior* (1961), with questions on one page and answers on the next page and not immediately available until the learner has at least read the question. The gadgets[4] so glowingly described in the literature or by promoters are only of incidental help for *controlling* behavior. But a teaching machine of the Skinner type does have certain practical advantages, even if these have no real bearing on learning.

1. A machine controls cheating. The student cannot advance to the next question without attempting an answer to the one at hand. He can, of course, ignore the answering and just jog the machine around for a complete trial, but this will be noted by the behavior controller. The

---

[4] While I believe Skinner should be credited with the invention of the teaching machine, many other people have developed devices that serve some teaching purpose. At this time I am describing Skinner's type of device.

problem of controlling cheating has preoccupied many teaching-machine manufacturers but need not concern us.

2. In special cases, with children who cannot read or with adult illiterates (at least in the language of the machine), a machine can present a lesson so arranged that the learner merely pushes buttons or other gadgets to match picture answers to picture questions.

3. A machine can be equipped to keep track automatically of the errors that are made, so that common errors later can be spotted easily by the controller for program revision. (This is not an exclusive advantage of the machine but of all programs and will be commented on again later in the chapter.)

4. A machine insures attention. Because no progress can be made until and unless a question is answered, the student is forced to look at the question. The student need not look at the question until he chooses to— he can work slowly or rapidly or just sit around and daydream as long as he desires. Sooner or later, however, if he is to complete the assignment, he must look at the questions comprising the program. In other methods of study a student need not listen, need not look at texts or other forms of presentation of material, or can browse around as he pleases, paying attention occasionally. The machine requires specific attention to each step. I will return to this point later.

5. Perhaps the most commonly cited advantage is the individualized instruction the machine provides. Individuals can work at their own speeds. Individual work at machines is in marked contrast to the usual class operation where the teacher may be ahead or behind any individual in his effort to teach the "average" student. This self-pacing feature of machine instruction is so strongly promoted that it too deserves more extensive discussion at a later point in this chapter (see p. 254).

6. Skinner points out that, at least at the early stages, a mechanical gadget may have some inherent motivational features. In Chapter 7 I mentioned the anecdote about juvenile delinquents being attracted to a teaching machine and getting sufficiently involved to attempt answering questions about mathematics. It may be that children, especially, are stimulated into activity by gadgets that permit pushing and pulling buttons and levers. Skinner suggests that such originally irrelevant or external motivation may be replaced by more intrinsic interests as success follows activity.

7. Another advantage claimed for teaching machines was pointed out earlier in connection with the aversive behavior of some human teachers. Machines do not scold or punish. Whether or not this is a genuine virtue

may depend upon what behavior is being taught. While the machine may not punish or repel, it may also be limited in its capacity to inspire or win affection, which, it has been suggested above (pp. 125–126), may be of primary importance for teaching. As you will see later, a common finding with machine teaching is the large complaint of boredom.

Disadvantages of Teaching Machines

The disadvantages of teaching machines are not fundamentally psychological in nature if we overlook the reported boredom of users. Rather the difficulties that arise are those inherent in any new mechanical innovation on a commercial basis. Far too many manufacturers (some publishers fearing competition from books) began production of their own special devices. Each had its own individual characteristics incorporated for local reasons or special purposes. When programs were developed by these manufacturers, they would be so printed or arranged as to fit one and only one machine. In effect, this meant that a user of several programs might have to purchase several different types of machine.

The solution to problems arising from a multiplicity of types is, of course, standardization. At present, there appears to be no indication that any one model will become the standard in the field. As a matter of fact, it is probably too early in the development of this type of operation for any fixing of standards and, if present problems in the matter of supplying programs for machines are not solved, there will be no real problem about the nature of the gadgetry.

THE PROGRAM

At the present time, it has come to be recognized and openly admitted that the problems associated with the construction of machines are secondary, if not minor. The real problem is with what goes into the machines. What goes into the machines is a "program." Programs consist of a series of questions (sometimes prefaced by short paragraphs of information, diagrams, and, in some kinds of programs, explanations of why a wrong answer was constructed or chosen). As a series of questions a program must have a beginning, a development, and an end. The construction of programs has turned out to be an extremely exacting and expensive task. In general, the difficulty starts at the very beginning. One has to decide what is the first question to ask, and this is rarely an easy decision. Each question after that must follow systematically, if not logically, from the answer to the first question. The best way to find out about programs is to look at one. The remainder of this section will present a sample program for inspection, and the reader is urged to try it out. The reader is also advised that, since this is only a sample, it is necessarily brief.

A Sample Program

The program that follows illustrates well the essential techniques of programmed learning. Although Dr. Evans prepared this program for use in a different format, the format here in no way detracts from its value as an illustration of a modern program. All the reader need do here is to place a sheet of paper or a bookmark over the answers and not look at any answer until he has attempted to "compose" the answer called for. This sample program was based on Skinner's learning principles, although, not all modern programmers follow Skinner.

Squaring Two-digit Numbers Ending in 5[5]

1. To SQUARE a number, multiply it by itself. EXAMPLE: To square 3, multiply 3 times 3. The answer is 9. Also: To square 6, multiply 6 times 6. The answer is ___.   36
2. The square of 8 is: 8 times 8, or 64. The square of 5 is: 5 times 5, or ___.   25
3. The square of 7 is 49. The square of 3 is ___.   9
4. The square of 4 is ___.   16
5. When you count, the number that comes next after a number is called the FOLLOWER of that number. The follower of 4 is 5. The follower of 6 is 7. The follower of 8 is ___.   9
6. The follower of 9 is 10. The follower of 2 is ___.   3
7. The follower of 6 is ___.   7
8. A number and its follower can be multiplied together. Multiplying 7 and its follower gives: 7 times 8, or 56. Multiplying 5 and its follower gives: 5 times 6, or ___.   30
9. Multiplying 1 and its follower gives: 1 times 2, or 2. Multiplying 2 and its follower gives: 2 times ___, or ___.   3
                                                                                 6
10. Multiplying 4 and its follower gives: ___ times ___, or ___.   4
                                                                                 5
                                                                                 20
11. You are going to learn an easy way to square two-digit numbers which end in 5. 35 is an example of a two-digit number which ends in ___.   5

[5] This sample program is a course written by James L. Evans, Ph.D., published by Teaching Machines, Inc. (1960), and distributed by Teaching Materials Corporation, a Division of Grolier, Inc. Permission to include this course was generously extended by Dr. Evans.

12. To square a two-digit number ending in 5, first find the left digit.
In 45, the left digit is 4. In 75, the left digit is ___.   7
13. In 85, the left digit is ___.   8
14. Next, multiply the left digit times its follower. EXAMPLE: for 65, multiply the left digit, 6, times its follower, 7, and get 42. Also: for 25,
multiply 2 times ___, and get ___.   3
                                                                             6
15. For 35, multiply___times,___, and get___.   3
                                                                             4
                                                                             12
16. After multiplying the left digit by its follower, write down the result:
For 65, write down 42. For 45, write down 20. For 25, write down ___.   6
17. After writing down the result of multiplying the left digit times its
follower, write 25 after it. Example: for 35, write 12, and then write
25 to get 1225. Also: for 45, write 20 and then write ___ to get 2025.   25
18. For 25, write: 625. For 65, write ___.   4225
19. When you write the result of multiplying the left digit times its follower, and then write 25 after it, you have squared the number ending in 5. EXAMPLE: The square of 85 is 7225. Also: the square of 25
is ___.   625
20. The square of 35 is 1225. The square of 95 is ___.   9025
21. The square of 55 is ___.   3025
22. The square of 85 is ___.   7225
23. The square of 75 is ___.   5625
24. The square of 45 is ___.   2025
25. The square of 15 is ___.   225

The Evans' example is an excellent illustration of five of the operating practices of programming that are generally approved by programming experts:

1. There is no time limit. Every learner can proceed at his own rate (this is sometimes referred to as "self-pacing").

2. The student is called upon to formulate, produce, "compose," or "create" the answer and to write it down. Programmers consider that this practice involves *activity*. Activity, remember, is considered a virtue by some psychologists.

3. Reinforcement is immediate. As soon as the learner writes down his answer he can confirm it by glancing to the supplied answer.

4. Learning proceeds in small steps. Not only are the steps in the program small, but they incorporate considerable repetition, review, and self-testing.

5. The answers called for provide a record. Such records can be checked to determine whether or not any specific item is too difficult or unnecessary.

While programmers are concerned about other practical aspects of programming, these five are probably sufficient for the reader of this book.

What are the reader's reactions to this sample program? Probably no single reader can say very much that is meaningful in an *evaluative* way until he has considered the matter further.

Any reader old enough to be reading this book is likely to be annoyed at being asked to multiply 3 × 3. Evans' sample program is not designed for college-trained people. College students may not know without having it pointed out to them that two-digit numbers ending in 5 can be squared by multiplying the first digit by the next number in the ordinal series and tacking 25 on to the result. They can be *told* this, however, in one sentence, and then work out the problem perfectly. They do not need the seemingly elaborate program Evans designed to learn to do this squaring, and, immediately, the question arises: For whom *is* the program designed?

In this instance we cannot be sure; Dr. Evans is merely illustrating the programming technique. But the question is pertinent to programs in general. The prospective student must be ready to study the material that is programmed, and he should be able to answer the first question. That is why first questions are always answerable. To fail at this point would abort the learning. The first question is designed to be answered to encourage the student to go on. Future questions build on successful answers to the early ones. The early questions provide practice and security. Each new bit of information or material is introduced gradually and checked repeatedly. Note how, in the Evans' illustration, the concept of "follower" is introduced and reviewed, checked, and double-checked. But because this is meant only as an *illustration* of programming, we cannot be sure that it really is necessary to do all this reviewing and checking. In an actual educational effort, a teacher would have to find out just how often it is necessary or desirable to repeat items, review, and otherwise test the material. The sample does show, however, that it is clearly possible to find out if any item is necessary. All a teacher has to do is to give the program to a sample of students and omit questionable items. If the students do as well with the shorter program, omission is justified. If they do not learn so well, then the items must be retained, changed, or amplified.

The Evans' sample program illustrates another feature of programming. Skinner has strong opinions that there is no virtue in errors. Learners should be so controlled that they always or almost always do the right thing. Errors only delay arrival at the goal. Each question should test or try the student to some degree. He should have a good chance of coming up with the right answer, but not a perfect probability (Skinner has suggested a 95-percent chance—that is, 5 out of every 100 students, but not always the same 5, should miss an item). The concession is made because errors are of value not to the student but to the programmer. He knows that the questions are not too easy if there is some chance of their being missed. But the teacher should realize that the danger of this programming policy is that the learner will go too slow. The college-trained reader probably missed none of the questions in the Evans' program. This might make it a poor program for him; it may not have been sufficiently challenging.

THE "PSYCHOLOGY" IN PROGRAMMING

The basic proposition on which programming is built is that teaching can be carried on more effectively when such a program as the Evans one is used instead of traditional procedures. Psychologists, as was said, were responsible for the excitement over teaching machines. Skinner based the functioning of his teaching machine on his views of learning, but what about the learning theories advanced by the other psychologists discussed in this book? If other programmers disagree with Skinner, are they basing their programs on other learning psychology?

Operant Conditioning

Is it true that the learner working through a program must "create" or compose an answer and go through some overt activity, such as writing out the answer in order to learn effectively? Notice that Skinner and his followers have translated their emphasis on the "emission" of responses into an emphasis on having a human learner make up answers to questions. This emphasis on composing answers is carried over to the point where they do not approve of such operations as marking answers "true" or "false" or checking items in multiple-choice lists. Other workers in the field of automated learning are not so committed to the activity principle and, as you will see, make up programs that do call for checking multiple-choice selections.

To prove that actual composition and writing out of answers is important we would have to have a control group going through a program in which no writing is required. In the Holland and Skinner (1961) text, no writing is actually required even though some teachers might suggest it or even demand written exercise sheets. The fact is that, to date, we have no good evidence that writing out answers is important. There are some studies (J. A. Barlow, 1961; L. S. Goldstein and L. G. Gotkin, 1962; and M. Alter and R. E. Silverman, 1962) that show no differences between groups that write and groups that only read. Of course, the latter groups can be considered as behaving covertly, but if this is to be the argument, then there is no argument because people have been engaged in such covert behavior ever since books have been read. Actually it is probably not even necessary to read! In one study (A. Roe, 1960), where a programmed *lecture* was given to a group of students, these students learned as well as a group that wrote out answers and a group that merely read the program. No one method was better than any other. The lecture took the least amount of time, and, on that basis, could be considered the most efficient teaching technique. If learners neither write nor read, then what of *action* as a principle? It can be claimed, of course, that *listening* is behavior, and with this all of us now can surely agree, but that is not the kind of behavior about which the teaching-machine advocates have been talking. (*See also* Meyer, S., 1960.)

The individual pacing feature is generally accepted as the really big advantage of programmed learning. Yet, even this feature lacks complete support. The lecture presentation referred to above was not self-paced by the students. In a study by Carpenter and Greenhill (1963), presentations of programmed material on film strips and video tapes did not suffer when compared to individual control over the presentation steps.

In reality, what comes out of such studies is that in order to learn a student must be presented with material. He must see it or hear it, he must, in short, attend to it. What else he does appears not to be too important. There is no real proof that he must be asked to compose or create answers. But seeing and listening imply that the student is paying attention to the material (and hopefully, very little else). In short, the advantage of the teaching machine with young people or with the easily distractable person is that it controls attention. Where attention can be attained in some other way, there is no need for a machine. Any procedure that contributes to the control of attention will be an aid to learning. To find that teaching machines are of value for controlling attention is not an empty finding. Few other techniques or devices have worked so efficiently. In the past only a few students could be expected to be serious attenders because of personal interests. Now it is possible to command interest, or at least attention, from everyone forced to use a machine. The machine achieves this end by the simple expedient of not permitting a student to advance without attending. He can no longer allow a lesson to pass over his head while he feigns attention. It must pass through his head. Pretense, cheating, conniving, cannot get him ahead. The machine cannot be bribed or worked on for sympathy. Yet despite this virtue of requiring attention, we find little support for the principle of activity.

Immediate Reinforcement

Most of the psychologists this book has considered endorse a principle of immediate reinforcement in learning. While some prominent leaders (Guthrie, Watson, Pavlov, Tolman) did not recognize reinforcement (rewards) as vital, they show some tendency to go along with McGeoch's *Empirical Law of Effect,* which, it will be recalled, was a general (nontheoretical) statement to the effect that rewards seem to work, whether or not we understand the underlying mechanisms. The reinforcement psychologists made their position virtually unassailable with the introduction of the secondary-reward principle, which allowed them to call anything a secondary reinforcer if it had been associated with a primary reinforcer. We have seen how Thorndike had anticipated the Hull and Skinner theoretical developments when he used the words *right* and *wrong* in early experiments; he considered these words as rewards and punishments. Out of his use of these words arose the practice of referring to "knowledge of results," or *KR,* as secondary reinforcement. Knowledge of results was adopted by the teaching-machine developers as a perfectly satisfactory reinforcer. As soon as the student working at the machine had written down an answer, he could be told what the correct answer should be. In this way he had immediate reinforcement.

The use of knowledge of results as a reinforcer makes it impossible for us or anyone else to determine whether the teaching machine really represents an application of a psychological principle. While the machine does have the feature of indicating the correct answer, I must point out two important reservations.

First, knowledge of results is not a unique property of teaching by machine. In any non-laboratory learning situation it is almost impossible to keep the human learner from knowing how well he is doing. In the laboratory, of course, it is possible to assign somewhat rarefied kinds of tasks to subjects. They can be asked to shoot at targets and not be allowed to see these targets. It should not be surprising if they do not learn to hit the "gold." They can be asked to guess at meanings of Turkish words in a long series of several hundred, and again no one should be surprised if they do not learn. Or, as Thorndike was so fond of doing, they can be required to "draw a four-inch line" with their eyes blindfolded. Again, we should not be surprised if they do not learn when Thorndike refused to tell them how well they were doing. Such tasks, however, have no parallels in ordinary life. A student reading a text is constantly aware of whether the material is making sense or not. As he continues to read, he is always being reinforced by the correct anticipations of the oncoming words. A comprehensible book is a self-reinforcer. A child asked to spell a word in the classroom need not be told anything by the teacher about his success; all he needs is to have the teacher ask the next student another word to know he is right; should the teacher repeat his word to the next student, he knows he was wrong. In short, as Mowrer (1960a) pointed out, knowledge of results is ubiquitous in human learning situations; in one form or another, it can hardly be avoided. The precise method of providing correct answers by the teaching machine in programmed learning, then, is not a novelty in education. In many ways it is a hindrance to the student who knows he is right and would like to get on with the lesson, especially where the items in the machine have been too easy for him (Susan Markle, 1963).

Second, the fact that the machine provides *immediate* reinforcement is, again, of no special advantage. The emphasis on immediacy may well be distorted. The student may know he is right even before he checks the machine's authority. He may thus receive some additional confirmation, but we have no evidence that such confirmation is essential for learning. The studies cited on page 243 demonstrated that equal progress could be made without benefit of reinforcement in the machine sense. It is difficult to separate out the immediacy factor even when the official reinforcer is delayed. Markle (1963) was able to obtain adequate and comparable learning from students who were informed about their performance 24 hours later. The human learner can, of course, quickly revive a problem or question and the reinforcer after 24 hours actually can be thought of as immediate at that time. We have already mentioned the finding of the Bilodeaus (1959) who showed that subjects working in the Thorndike line-drawing situation could learn, even though 20 seconds passed before they were informed about their performance. But even here we can suspect that some kind of aftereffect of the response was retained and present when the information was given.

The incorporation of immediate knowledge of results in programmed learning, then, is not the application of a psychologically established principle so much as it is the inclusion of a normal, quite ordinary operation in any situation where the learner is put to work. To keep information about his progress from him would be ludicrous, if this were done deliberately and the learner had no other recourse. To provide such information, immediately or after some delay, is not of special virtue to programmed teaching. It is the routine feature of ordinary learning. The emphasis on reinforcement made by programmed learning advocates may have some salutary effects on those teachers who persist in bewildering students by calling for answers in situations where the students have no way of finding out whether they are correct, but aside from this (hopefully rare) situation, it is more a matter of common sense than psychology to provide answers to questions after giving students a chance to proffer answers of their own.

In conclusion, the case of the programmers for the virtue of immediate reinforcement has not been clearly proved, and, in the nature of the case, it is quite unlikely that any proof can be presented that will be acceptable to a broad spectrum of psychological thinkers.

Shaping

The Evans sample program is an effective illustration of Skinner's principle of shaping, as was pointed out earlier. Step by step the student is led to the final goal. The fact that this is so does not mean, however, that the psychologist has demonstrated a principle of learning. In its normal laboratory usage, the concept of shaping refers to some specific and *sequential act* (see pp. 32–33). For example, a dog can be trained to lie down and roll over by a shaping process. Before he can roll over, the dog must lie down. This the dog often does on his own, and the experimenter can quite easily get control over this, either by waiting for the dog to lie down (which Skinner might do) or by pushing the dog down as any boy might do who wanted to teach his best friend a trick. The next step is to get the dog to roll over and not to get up again until he has rolled over. To do this the boy would hold a bit of meat over the dog's head and slowly rotate the meat as the dog's head follows it, meanwhile applying a gentle pressure to the body to help out. In the completed act, the dog would then go through each shaped stage *in succession.*

This is not what is done in a program of learning such as was illustrated in the Evans sample. Here we find a learner at the end of the program doing something he may never have done before, to be sure, but he does not go through the entire sequence of steps or movements laid down in the program in performing the last operations. He is now a different person. He has been *shaped,* to be sure, but the analogy with the laboratory has been lost in the process. What is called *shaping* in the laboratory is not shaping in programmed learning. Here shaping means that one has carefully built up a series of steps that lead to a specified goal, but this goal behavior can be performed without going through the original steps on each new occasion. In learning to decode telegraph messages, for example, the trainee at first has to acquire a whole series of separate response patterns and combinations. He may start with some simple letters like *E* and *S*, then *A* and *N*. Later, as a skilled operator, he no longer goes through the separate stages of decoding single letters; he receives whole messages and phrases with only a modicum of attention. The dog still has to lie down, rotate his head, and flip his body in the same old sequence.

Shaping, in programming, means then something quite different from what it means in the laboratory. It is still valuable and meaningful to learning, but its function is that of forcing a learner down a special path or molding a final product by a sequence of steps that are first carefully determined as the most logical or most efficient steps by which the goal can be reached. In general, and in a sense paralleling a laboratory performance—but only in a sense—the teacher examines the desired final performance or outcome, which perhaps is the ability to do square roots. The teacher notes what abilities, aptitudes, or skills are required to produce the answer and works backward from this analysis. In this hypothetical example, the student cannot do square roots without a knowledge of decimals, without an appreciation of multiplication, division, and subtraction. Addition is not required except as one conceives as addition the operation of introducing pairs of zero's after a decimal point. If all these skills can be presupposed, then a program for extracting square roots can be pieced together by working backward from the final operations (rounding off) to the first: drawing the radical sign. In short, knowing what is wanted may suggest various alternate ways of achieving the goal, and "shaping" amounts to selecting one of these alternates that, hopefully, consists of a "logical" set of operations where one step leads more or less inevitably, neatly, or effectively to the next. What I have been describing as "shaping," others might call logic or common sense. In teaching anyone anything, even tying a knot, the teacher has to begin some place, and this beginning should not be randomly selected. It should lead up to a next step, which, again, should not be random but should bear directly upon a third step and so on.

A Socratic Example

As long ago as the days of Socrates this principle of logical sequences was appreciated by teachers. The Socratic method is famous for its logical progress from simple beginnings to more complex outcomes. In Socrates'

TWO KINDS OF PROGRAMS[6]

Socratic Method	*Programed Adaptation*
1. "Here we have a square of four feet, have we not?"	1. Each side of this square, ABCD, is 2 feet long. Then the size of the square is _____ square feet.
2. "And here we add another square equal to it?"	2. Here we add another square, DCFE, equal to it in _____.
3. "And here a third, equal to either of them?"	3. And here a third square, CHGF, _____ in size to each of the others.
4. "Now shall we fill up this vacant space in the corner?"	4. Now we can fill up the space in the corner by adding another _____ of _____ size.
5. "So here we must have four equal spaces?"	5. All four squares, ABCD, CDEF, CHGF, BIHC, are _____.
6. "How many times larger is this whole space than this other?"	6. How many times larger is this whole space, AEGI, than the square ABCD? _____.
7. "And does this line (BD) drawn from corner to corner, cut in two each of these spaces?"	7. The lines BD, DF, FH, HB, drawn from corner to corner in each of the squares, cuts each square in _____.
8a. "And have we here four equal lines containing this space (BDFH)?"	8. The four lines containing the space BDFH are of _____ length.
8b. "Now consider how large this space is?" (Response: "I do not understand.")	
9. "Has not each of the inside lines cut off half of each of these four spaces?"	9. ABCD is a square, since its four sides are of equal length. Since the four sides of BDFH are equal, it too is a _____.

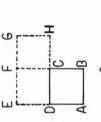

10. "And how many spaces of that size are there in this part?"

11. "And how many in this?"

12. "And four is how many times two?"

13. "And how many feet is this space?"

14. "From what line do we get this figure?"

15. "From the line drawn cornerwise across the four-foot figure?"

16. "The professors call it the diagonal: so if the diagonal is its name, then according to you, Meno's boy, the double space is the square of the diagonal." (Response: "Yes, certainly it is, Socrates.")

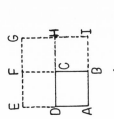

4

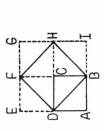

5

10. Has each of the inside lines (BD, DF, FH, HB) cut off half of each of the squares? (yes/no) _____.

11. How many spaces of that size (for example, DCB) are there in ABCD? _____.

12. How many of these spaces (for example, DCB) in BDFH? _____.

13. Four is how many times two? _____.

14. Since there are four of these spaces (e.g., DCB) in the square BDFH and two of the spaces in square ABCD, then BDFH is _____ as large as ABCD.

15. If our original square ABCD contained 4 sq. ft., then how many sq. ft. does this square BDFH contain? _____

16. From the line (BD) drawn cornerwise across our original 4-ft. figure (ABCD), a square can be drawn which is _____ as large as the original square.

17. Such a line as BD is called the *diagonal*. To double the size of a square, you may draw a square from the _____.

18. From what line in square ABCD can a square be drawn which will be double the size of ABCD? _____.

20. To double the size of a square, _____.

6 Supplied through the courtesy of Dr. Ira Cohen. The frames on the right have been revised since the publication of his original version (Cohen, 1962).

days there were no learning theorists, but his work often has been cited by programmers as examples of what they are about. In the *Meno* of Plato, for example, Socrates attempts to establish the notion of "innate ideas." He undertakes to prove that a slave boy with no education already possesses rather complex mathematical ideas as part of his inborn reasoning capacity. It is interesting to watch Socrates at work and to compare his operation with what a modern programmer would do with the same problem. Dr. Ira Cohen (1962) has prepared just such a comparison, which appears on pages 248–249. In what follows, I will refer to the separate steps as frames. The reader is invited first to "go through" the program as presented by Socrates and then to compare it with the modern program as revised by Dr. Cohen. Scholars generally assume that Socrates drew figures in the sand while he was talking, and Dr. Cohen has supplied such figures, which the reader should examine in the order called for.

If the reader worked through the Socratic program, he may or may not have arrived at Socrates' goal with full satisfaction. When university students were asked to follow along with Socrates, only 17 out of 32 were able to state the theorem with which Socrates ended his lesson. Let me note here that we have no proof that the slave boy was any brighter than modern college students. He was not asked to state the theorem—*only to agree to it;* This he could do, just to please the teacher. This is very different from what modern programmers want from their subjects. There is no proof, then, that the Socratic program has any merit, only presumption. Because Dr. Cohen has given his modern-dress version to many students, he has been able to check their answers and discover where the program was faulty. He found that, in general, Socrates had presented a reasonably good version of a proper modern program. Some of his steps were a little too large and needed additional help; some of his steps were not in the best order. By revising Socrates' program, Dr. Cohen was able to get 27 out of 33 college students to state the theorem involved when they had completed his program, a marked improvement over the results mentioned above.

AN ASSESSMENT OF PROGRAMMED LEARNING

On pages 233–235 I listed six Skinnerian principles derived from laboratory observations. You have now seen four of them (operant behavior, reinforcement, immediacy of reinforcement, and shaping) translated into the construction of programs to be used for teaching with or without the aid of mechanical gadgets.[7] The other two principles (extinction and discriminated stimuli) were barely touched on because they were so obvious or commonsenselike that they hardly need discussion. Just to be sure that the reader has not overlooked them, however, I point out that extinction is involved whenever the learner makes an error (receives no reinforcement) and has to return to missed items in a program. Discriminated stimuli are, of course, the entire content of the program—they are the questions that require specific answers.

In the preceding discussion of the principles I have indicated that the translation has not always been precise or accurate. In fact, I questioned whether any "psychology" had been applied or whether "psychology" was necessary. The reader might have gotten the impression that the effectiveness of programming was being questioned. It is time to correct any such impression and attempt an evaluation of the art of programming. There can hardly be any question about the value of programming where programming is possible, just as there can hardly be any question of the value of some features of machine learning (such advantages were spelled out on page 236). The Cohen revision of the Socrates program points up many of the virtues of programmed learning. It can serve as a ready reference.

Cohen's work demonstrates one immediate advantage of the modern programmer's operations. When records of errors are kept, it is possible to make changes in suitable places in the program to prevent these errors in future editions and to strengthen the appropriate behavior. In short, the basic advance in teaching in 2500 years may have been the development of *evaluative* methods. Here teachers may see the advantages of working with groups and of keeping exact records so that present and future comparisons can be made. But the real contribution to teaching was still that of Socrates. He taught us that a *logical presentation of material can be effective.*

This "logical presentation of material" is really what programmers try to arrange. Where material lends itself to logical presentation, programming can be effective. This means that, if material is not susceptible to such arrangement, it cannot be programmed effectively. Unless one cares to argue for some special branch or theory, the subject matter of history, for example, does not lend itself to easy programming. On the other hand,

---

[7] In the subsequent discussion whenever I refer to teaching machines the reader should keep in mind that a machine is of no value without a program. I will treat them as more or less synonymous.

mathematics and especially geometry, which in many ways is a deductive operation, can be programmed relatively easily and with success. Similarly, aspects of both physics and grammar lend themselves to shaping operations.

The reader has noted that Dr. Cohen reported gains in efficiency in teaching *after* he revised Socrates' program. Perhaps the thought has already occurred that we are back again to the question "For whom is the program designed?" To get better results, Dr. Cohen added items, restated items, and rearranged items, but when he tested the revised version, 6 of 33 students still could not state the theorem. Presumably, further revision could have reduced this number of failures. With more and more work, more and more success could have been anticipated. Programs for poor students might call for an amount of work that would be prohibitive. According to Markle (1963), programmers are caught in a dilemma: they try to work out programs for "average" students and then have great difficulty finding average students. A program worked out on one group does not work out too well on another. This means revision. The next group may call for more and more revision, until, frequently, the programmer finds he is working with the "least common denominator"—the poorest student. At this stage the program contains so many small, really "tiny" steps that the brighter student is insulted or bored. The apparent advantage of being able to revise loses its attractiveness as the chore of preparing new frames grows.

Further, when programmers urge that teachers spend more time programming their efforts, they seem to forget what they fully appreciate; namely, that a competent job of shaping up even a single lesson can be very time-consuming and that an already overburdened teacher is in no position to do what normally calls for a team of experts. The fact that teachers are urged to program their own lessons suggests again that there is little *psychological* science behind the operation. When rules for guiding programmers (Markle *et al*, 1961) are provided, they sound more like common sense than psychology. We cannot be too sure that the more psychological hints are especially effective. Professional programmers are constantly revising their views on the advisability of this or that method or procedure. They debate the size of the steps, the need for preventing boredom, the appropriate amount of "prompting," the location of blanks in the frame, and so on. With each new attempt more problems arise. What appears to be a simple "frame" often calls for 30 or more minutes of work. This frame later may be found to be inadequate or in the wrong place. To ask classroom teachers to become programmers borders on the ridiculous. They simply do not have such time at their disposal.

The Cohen program followed the Skinner technique of controlling progress, limiting the student to small errorless steps insofar as possible. But not all programmers agree with Skinner that students should never make errors. They follow instead the advice of Guthrie (1952) to the effect that learners should be trained to recognize the cues or stimuli that are followed by failure or accident and discriminate these from the ones that lead to successful responses. The "branching" technique of Crowder, to be discussed next, is based on the expectation that students will make errors and should be told why they do so. Skinner can argue, of course, that he can also teach the appropriate discriminations, but to do so he has to introduce many more items of a negative nature than he has so far done in his programs. In such items, discrimination is being taught by reinforcement, not by extinction. Such a procedure is at least superficially a violation of Skinner's own advice about how discriminations should be taught. Whether or not students should be permitted to make errors is a question that cannot be answered until the programmers discover the most effective procedures.

The procedure advocated by N. A. Crowder[8] (1960) mentioned above does concern itself with the problem of errors. Crowder objects to the so-called "vertical" programs of the Skinner type that follow the path of the small-step arrangement, one step leading to the next until the goal is reached. Crowder offers what he calls a "horizontal" or "branching" method. In this method the learner is presented with frames consisting of multiple-choice questions.. The student selects an answer out of a number of tempting alternatives. If he is correct, he moves on. If he has chosen an incorrect answer, he is directed to some other frame (or page of a book) and shown why he was wrong. He is then instructed to return to the original item and try again. Sometimes in both kinds of programs, students who are able to answer certain items correctly are instructed to skip over a number of following items and thus speed up the progress. If they cannot respond correctly, they must return to the earlier stage and move ahead by the smaller-step routine. The advocates of the several approaches are not likely to decide that only one method is correct. We can expect continued controversy and new methods.

8 The Skinner approach to programming has been followed by the great majority of programmers. One estimate has been as high as 95 percent. For this reason I have concentrated on this approach rather than numerous other innovations that might qualify as either machines or programs.

Earlier in this chapter, I mentioned one of the most commonly cited advantages of the teaching machine or of programming: that it provides for individualized instruction. The machine has been compared to a private tutor with the underlying assumption that individual tutorial instruction is the best of all possible kinds. The machine was to be a replacement for Mark Hopkins. There is no question, of course, that, as far as learning is concerned, it is the individual who learns and that one teacher or more per student would be a more effective way of teaching some skills and facts than the common practice of one teacher attempting to teach 30 or more students at a time. We will not worry about the problems of slow and fast learners, segregated classes, and the various arguments that have surrounded the problem of individual differences in student populations. What must be pointed out, however, as was done by Markle (1963), is that the way the teaching machine operates does not really solve the problem of efficient individual instruction. Individuals remain individuals. Some are bright and some are slow. Programmers regularly discover that programs do not fit all individuals. To teach individuals might call for individual programs. The analogy between the machine and the tutor breaks down at the very first step in a program. The human tutor can adjust his program as he goes along. The machine program runs into constant difficulties. There is no "average" student. Each requires different amounts of practice; each has his own size of step; each has his own boredom threshold. The best that can be said for this aspect of programmed learning is that it might be an aid, in some instances a very great aid, to teaching. It has not solved all the problems of learning.

Now that we have looked at the teaching machine and the programming operation, it is clear that such innovations can be of some advantage in the classroom when properly introduced and properly used. We cannot expect a large number of effectively evaluated programs for some time. There are, of course, hundreds of programs now available; many of these are apparently quite good for teaching certain operations in industry and in the Armed Forces. Most of them are relatively brief and cover only segments of traditionally classified subjects. If the current interest continues, we can, of course, expect more and more. The teacher's task may be somewhat eased; certainly it will be somewhat changed.

The teacher may possibly have more time to participate in new programming and in evaluating old programs. There may be more time to work with individuals or special programs or in the expansion of horizons, discussions with students who know something. Programs may be used to help retarded or slow learners, isolated students in rural areas, prisoners, sailors at sea, or to provide special experiences for the advanced learners. On the other hand, programs may prove boring (as has been reported of some) and call for more of the teacher's efforts toward inspiring and motivating learning.

Some Words of Caution

On the whole, the concept of programmed learning is good and positive. After all, it is only an attempt to be logical about teaching, to start with first things first, and to end up at the goal, which is presumably defined. There can be no serious objections to the concept. It does appear, however, that the task of bringing into programmed form the ordinary array of courses through which students pass on their way from kindergarten to graduate school is formidable. To create even one really successful program calls for an almost prohibitive amount of work. To produce unsuccessful programs calls for little or no effort at all.

Manufacturers of new products sometimes use the phrase: "In the present state of the art" to explain weaknesses of their product. Frequently they go ahead and sell the product anyhow. "In the present state of the art" of programming we find the same attempt to sell programs to educational institutions or systems. Teachers are invited to examine displays of machines and programs, and sometimes they are urged to try them out in their classrooms. In view of what has been said above, a teacher might well take time for second thoughts about introducing any specific program in an effort to improve the instructional effort. Among these second thoughts might be the following:

1. Does the seller of the program and/or new method or technique state precisely the content area or skill it purports to cover? Sometimes sellers of such materials tend to use broad course labels, such as "Chemistry" and "Biology," where, actually, the program covers only a limited amount of material. Perhaps only those aspects or topics that are amenable to programming are included. In other words, the learning goals to be met and the costs or savings of time, work, and money should be spelled out. The goals and costs then can be compared with the teacher's present operations before a decision is made.

2. Does the program contain a statement of the nature of the population for whom it is intended? Programs can be and are designed for different levels of preparation. Prerequisites, if any, must be listed. If the program presumes to begin at the beginning of a subject, it may prove boring, repetitive, and wasteful to the advanced student; if it is an excel-

lent program for high-level students, it will be too difficult for low-level classes. In general, the teacher should consider the introduction of a program in terms of a total curriculum pattern. Does a program lead to more programs or do students work at programs only occasionally? At present, the effects of switching on student attitudes have not been evaluated.

3. Has the program been adequately evaluated over some reasonably extended period, preferably with several groups of students? Sometimes teachers have no way of knowing whether experimental groups have exhibited consistent superiority over "control" or traditionally taught groups. Sometimes only one experimental study has been conducted to test the value of a program in the field. It is meaningless to argue from one experience. A group that has been treated as an experimental population and knows this may have been influenced by the Hawthorne Effect,[9] and the teacher needs to be given full information if only one experiment was conducted. Even when a program has been extensively tested, a would-be user needs to be cautious. The introducer of a teaching program can be presumed to have worked as hard as he could to develop cooperative attitudes and enthusiasm for his program, and it takes time for the effects of suggestion and novelty to wear off. Before a fair test of a program can be expected, its method must have become as routine as any other method. It is also possible that the program experimenter has obtained a negative Hawthorne Effect. Students may not have trusted the new method, regarding it with suspicion or otherwise being adversely affected, and this could have led them to supplement the experimental study with additional studies (homework, reviews, consultations, and discussions). Students who put in more time *in toto* can be expected to learn more, and if this were

[9] The term comes from studies made by R. J. Roethlisberger and W. J. Dickson (1939) at Western Electric's plant in Hawthorne, N. J., where girl employees were studied under different work conditions. The girls were given to understand that their employment was quite secure and that nothing was going to happen that in any way would jeopardize their status. They were further given to understand that they were partners in a scientific effort and that their cooperation was being sought as individuals, not as mere employees. It appeared that the girls began to feel themselves to be important and unique. Their morale and motivation were high. When the experimenters began to make changes in the working environment, the work productivity of the girls began to rise. It soon became evident that the actual environmental changes had nothing to do with the productivity because the direction of the changes did not appear to matter. If the work areas were better lighted, production rose; if the areas were darkened, production rose. With every change the girls worked harder and more effectively than before. Simply knowing that something new was being tried (and with themselves as the centers of attention) appeared to have strong effect on the girls' attitudes and motivation. E. L. Solomon (1949) showed that a similar effect could occur in a teaching situation. In connection with the introduction of a new method of spelling, he found that simply giving a preliminary test prior to introducing the new procedure had an effect on the subsequent spelling learning.

the case, the program being tested should not be credited for the presumably good results.

Conclusion

Programmed learning will eventually find its place. That place has not yet been defined. Programming will not be the answer to all problems. It is not a panacea. It is not even new. It is what every teacher has been trying to do from the beginning of teaching, but it now has a new class of technologists working on the problem and they may prove helpful. It is obviously nothing to fear. It is, really, something to evaluate, but the evaluation should not become an extra burden on the teacher. It should remain the salesman's problem.

Since the first edition of this text appeared, interest in programming has fallen off among learning psychologists. They have turned to new problems, and with justification. They had already laid out the basic plan for programming, and it was now up to others to implement that program if it was desired. Some psychologists have continued to operate as consultants to various firms and educational systems, and we can continue to look forward to some progress. Programming, however, is such an expensive and time-consuming operation that, while most promising in principle, it is difficult to introduce in school settings. The probability of a growth in interest in teaching *machines* does not appear strong. Instead we see more and more program-type paper-back texts appearing, which individual students obtain for a self-help effort either before or during a course. College instructors commonly assign such texts as auxiliary activities with some success. The great value of the programmed learning movement has been to stimulate teachers to prepare their courses in more logical sequences and to assess their own efforts in terms of more meaningful schedules of operation.

Chapter Eleven

Technological
Aids
to
Education

The educational world has been slow to take advantage of technological advances that could make some of its work more effective. Perhaps this reluctance stems from a "cultural lag" or possibly from a kind of defensiveness against invasion from other fields. The mechanical skills of some teachers appear to be limited to handling a piece of chalk on the blackboard, and such people face with dismay the problem of threading a film projector; certainly others feel threatened by any kind of apparent competition, in particular the teaching machine. Whatever the causes of their reluctance, teachers, it would seem, should welcome any technique or device that might improve the efficiency of learning. The processes of education are unlikely to change radically during any one teacher's lifetime, and to oppose technological improvement because of vague fears of being "taken over" is to fail to recognize the inherent conservatism of education.

The hesitation demonstrated by teachers toward innovations in technique and tools is, of course, not likely to be lessened by the enthusiasm of promoters. The eager salesman of these innovations is apt to be carried away with enthusiasm and to promise more than can be delivered. And far too often it is the businessman and the politician, not the educator, who sees in some new technique or tool, such as television, the answer to the school budget, with one "great" teacher teaching the entire school population.

This is not the place to raise concerns about the economic and political impacts of technological advances on education. The only concern of this chapter is to examine the instructional advantages and/or disadvantages of such advances and to raise for the reader the psychologically important questions that should be answered before any new device is introduced in the teaching operation. The basic question then becomes: Can students be taught more effectively with some new tool than without it? As has been true for so many other questions that this book has posed, the answer must be "Yes," "No," or "Maybe" depending on the answers to other questions that inevitably arise.

AUDIO-VISUAL AIDS

The term *audio-visual aid* has by now become identified with various classroom devices involving the use of sound or pictures or both. Usually, a teacher arranges with the school's audio-visual department to bring into the classroom a motion-picture or slide projector, phonograph, or mechanical model for the teacher to use as a part of his teaching effort. As yet, not all classrooms are equipped with projection booths, built-in turntables for record players, or even motor-driven screens mounted above the blackboards. Nor do all classrooms have television sets. In many schools the entire student body must report to an auditorium to witness some important event or program presented on television.

The restriction of the term *audio-visual* to the efforts of some non-teaching department or personnel is, of course, a gross error. The entire teaching effort is itself an audio-visual operation (unless we are dealing with the deaf and blind). The teacher is an audio-visual aid of the first order—everything the teacher does with students is "audio" and "visual"—and anything that will advance the effectiveness of the teacher's operations should, *ipso facto,* be used whenever and wherever possible.

As far as the learning psychologists discussed in this book are concerned, learning is a matter of arranging for certain stimuli to be followed by certain responses. Now the time has come for readers of this book to recognize that education can best be looked at as a special kind of communication, as a process whereby a teacher presents primarily visual and auditory stimuli and a student comes to react to these stimuli in a manner acceptable to or dictated by society. Whether the stimuli are the occasions for the responses or whether the responses are associated with or evoked by the stimuli, whether rewards are necessary or even useful need be of no concern here; these matters have been examined at some length in previous chapters.

In the special kind of communication that is education, the teacher in presenting auditory and visual stimuli is limited to voice and gesture unless otherwise supplemented. Even Socrates and Archimedes could not accept such limitations and drew diagrams in the sand for their students. The modern teacher, however, is not restricted to such temporary supplements as sand drawings and commonly makes use of more permanent illustrations, either on a blackboard or through the medium of print. The need for illustration is inherent in the teaching process; illustration not only supplies a missing object or scene, but it also eliminates the need for a continuous effort to recall what has been said before. It is this dual function of illustration that clarifies the old cliché: a picture is worth a thousand words. Pictures have the additional advantage of being susceptible to enlargement, thereby magnifying the capacity of the human eye— as is done by telescope or microscope, two of our oldest "visual aids." When pictures are presented as natural-color photographs, when they move realistically, when they are accompanied by appropriate sounds, as in motion pictures and television, their usefulness as aids is multiplied greatly. If the question is: Can students be taught more effectively with audio-visual tools?, the answer is Yes, depending on which pictures and/or sound are used and when.

Because no one can anticipate all future developments in audio-visual aids and because of the wide variety of such items now in active use, discussion here is limited to some samples of a somewhat controversial nature. But the controversies should help to highlight matters of psychology that may influence the teacher's decisions on what aids to use and when. "Flash" cards, overhead projectors, models, workbooks, and slides can be presumed to have obvious merits (and limitations) as audio-visual aids, and the following section will concentrate only on motion pictures and television.

MOTION PICTURES AND TELEVISION

The discussion that follows assumes that the world of education will not quietly surrender to Hollywood and the television industry and that the teacher will still be found in the classroom using these tools when they are appropriate. There is no more danger that teachers will be eliminated by motion picture or television machines than by the teaching machine; from the viewpoint of teacher replacement, they have made little or no impact on education. The movies have been with us since *The Great Train Robbery* without replacing a single teacher. Radio broadcasting replaced no teacher; neither did the addition of sound to movies in the 1920s; and television can be anticipated to take its place and do likewise.

Advantages and Disadvantages

The great difference between television and motion pictures is the simultaneity feature of the former, which can provide an immediate view of an event at some distant place. The inauguration of a president, a press conference with some dignitaries, the launching of a spaceship, a baseball game—these can be witnessed on television by the entire world (with the development of satellite broadcasting) at the time they are occurring. Of course, all such events can be photographed by motion-picture cameras and seen later. The question then is whether simultaneity has any advantage over delay. For educational purposes it is doubtful that it does. Most of what we learn represents the work or thought of people who lived long ago, and the virtue of witnessing some event as it occurs, being present actually or vicariously, can be doubted.

Perhaps the more important advantage of television's simultaneity is the possibility of two-way communication between some distant teacher and students present in a classroom elsewhere. This has been attempted in various television courses, but its weaknesses are obvious when we think of the problem of the teacher answering simultaneous questions jamming into a switchboard. Without the two-way communication feature, television teaching appears to have no virtues that motion-picture films cannot duplicate. As a matter of practical fact, most television courses without the two-way communication feature are taped in advance and hence are nothing more than movies.

When television material is on tape (and in black and white), a motion picture in color in large-scale projection would appear to have obvious advantages over small-screen television presentation. Of course, the brilliance of television pictures permits their use in lighted classrooms, which makes note-taking more convenient for students. Movies must be shown in a darkened theater, which lends itself also to skylarking by students if the film is not powerful enough to absorb their energies.

Television lessons are commonly shown only once. It is of course possible, with tapes, to repeat them either whole or in part (instant replay), and they also share with motion pictures the possibilities for using stopped scenes, slow-motion, zoom lenses, etc. In short, the advantages and disadvantages are not weighted in one direction. Television and motion pictures each possess certain advantages over the other under certain conditions, but taped television would seem to be no different from a movie.

Effectiveness for Teaching

What the teacher is more interested in is whether or not television and motion pictures can be used to instruct. The answer is easy: If a "live" lecturer or demonstrator can teach, so can a photographed one. The teacher on film or tape can talk as well as the one in the classroom, perhaps better. He can demonstrate more effectively, because, in a sense, it is possible for him to take the students with him to a foreign country, the bottom of the ocean, a surgery, or a launching pad. He can use equipment that would be prohibitively expensive for any single class or school. His one weakness is that he cannot see his students and cannot judge (to the extent that this is possible for the live teacher) whether he has the class "with" him or not. He cannot ask the class if some point should be repeated or illustrated further. The filmed teacher cannot see that some students are not paying attention. In fact, he might be talking to an empty classroom.

Supporters of television instruction can point to many studies that showed no differences in achievement between groups taught by television and those following traditional methods. Shramm (1962) reviewed over 190 such comparisons. Of 100 studies in higher education 84 showed no differences. Similarly, Erickson and Chausow (1960) found no achievement differences. Such studies, like those of programmed learning or lecture vs. discussion groups, are difficult to evaluate. Achievements on objective tests may not be the appropriate measure. No one knows what the students did on their own. When college instructors use tests based on textbooks, students frequently manage to do reasonably well without ever attending class.

At the college level, some teachers are no different from television teachers in that they present carefully prepared lectures (as far as time is concerned), permit no questions, and pay no heed to expressions of boredom or signs of inattention. They can be effective or ineffective, as we have already found in the discussion of lectures (pp. 126–129). If a television teacher does no more than talk, he might be the equivalent of some lecturers such as those described. Because the medium lends itself to the use of photographs of many kinds of scenes or materials, however, the television teacher tends to make greater use of such illustrative material. In fact, he tends to go "off camera" as much as possible. The classroom teacher is always "on camera" and to that extent may be less interesting and effective.

This brings us to the crucial concern of teachers regarding photographic teaching. Some psychologists (Thorndike, Hull, Skinner, Guthrie) strongly urged that learning occurs only when some action is performed by the learner, that learning involves some new or creative action on the part of the student. These psychologists would regard talking to students or showing them scenes as only part of the instructional process. Even those psychologists (Tolman, Mowrer) who found that at least some kinds of learning can occur when a person only witnesses passing events would agree that, sooner or later, the learner must try for himself; he must test or otherwise go through some actions. If a boy is to learn to toss a basketball through a hoop, he must toss basketballs in the general direction of hoops. He cannot content himself with watching a basketball game on television. If he is to learn to spell, he must emit letters one at a time and observe whether the consequences lead to the appropriate emotional reactions that were previously conditioned in him. In short, photographic teaching concerns itself primarily with the stimulus side of the behavior story. Learning psychologists want to see an equivalent interest in the response side.

The conclusion is unavoidable that photographic teaching (like any lecture) can only be an adjunct, an aid to learning. Unless such teaching is supplemented by additional work, practice, questions and discussions, homework, reading assignments, papers or other productions, the teachings will be incomplete and superficial. There is no substitute for practice, repetition, and active experience. Even the most "memorable" television "spectaculars" are not "memorable." They quickly fade and cannot be restored. While one-trial learning is possible with some kinds of materials, the educational process as a whole cannot depend upon single presentations of audio-visual material. Watching a film once, like listening to a record once, does not result in the permanent appreciation of what was presented. As a matter of fact, just because a person looks at a film or listens to a record does not mean that he saw and/or heard everything on the film or record. (Viewers of home movies can readily testify to having overlooked some item in a film in the previous 30 showings.) Even the most effective programmer cannot be sure that the important items in a lesson will serve their stimulus function.

Use as Teaching Aids

The conclusion that television and movies can only be aids to education is not particularly helpful to the teacher if left as such. If they are aids, they must be used as aids—that is, used where and when they are helpful. This is the real significance of the nature of programming in the sense of lesson-planning. The teacher must have a program, as detailed as possible, not necessarily in terms of minutes and hours but in terms of steps to be taken from the beginning of a course down to the last operation. Where the intervening steps are broken down into separate lessons, each lesson must be separately programmed. At each step the teacher must ask himself how the objective can best be met. Where film illustrations are required the teacher can then select from film libraries those films that meet the needs. Because most films present more than the teacher is likely to be interested in, the films can be "cut" and spliced and shown where the content happens to be the best available way of presenting the desired stimulus material. There is no reason why students should look at lists of credits, listen to fanfares, and otherwise waste their time. Two minutes of a 50-minute film might be all that is necessary for a given goal to be met. In short, the use of any audio-visual material must be carefully planned and not used as an excuse to stop teaching for a while.

The trouble is, of course, that teachers cannot own films to cut up as desired; nor do they have the time to edit and splice films into small sequences to be projected at a particular moment when it could be useful. It would be very useful to have a projector set to go at a moment's notice and run off a few feet of film. The next desired sequence might not be needed for a week. The logistics for such teacher-control of audio-visual aids are probably prohibitive.

The teacher also must retain control over scheduling programs and not permit outside authorities to schedule television shows, from aircraft or otherwise, for specified times. The teacher and the students might not be ready for the television presentation. If they are not ready, there is no point to watching. To coordinate classroom plans with broadcasters' interests may well be awkward if not impossible. It should remain the teacher's prerogative to turn on the set and expect the program to come in when desired. If the opposite is allowed to happen, the teacher becomes the aid.

A word should be said about a less-expensive form of teaching at a distance. There have been some attempts to teach by telephone: so-called "telelectures" are delivered by a prominent lecturer over a telephone hook-up. At the school end, the auditory presentation can be amplified so that a whole school can listen. Microphones can be used to ask the speaker questions. One lecturer, Moses Hadas[1], Columbia University classicist, who delivered such a telelecture remarked that the idea is not as good as "a flesh-and-blood teacher, even a bad one." There may be some educational value for students in hearing the actual voices of eminent figures in various fields. Celebrated actors are probably much better at reading poetry and Shakespeare than are classroom teachers. If such readings or lectures are taped or otherwise recorded, they can probably be used effectively in education, if not as actual instructional material, then as motivational devices. But even with such materials the teacher should be in

[1] *Time,* July 19, 1963.

charge and should select the material—some authorities are not very effective in recorded media and may prove of more motivational harm than good.

The paragraphs above have emphasized that aids are aids and not teachers. There are no substitutes for teachers. In small and isolated communities, where teachers may not be available to provide appropriate instruction in some subjects that students might wish to study, there is every reason to use whatever aids are available to help the student learn by himself. There is no question, of course, that almost anything can be learned without formal tutoring—after all, the teachers had to learn somehow, and at one time there were no teachers. Correspondence courses have enjoyed a long history of success with highly motivated students. The Armed Forces have arranged many highly effective correspondence courses for servicemen in isolated outposts. *In every case*—as I have tried to demonstrate throughout this book—*it is the student who learns*. The teacher's role is one of presenting materials (hopefully in terms of some meaningful program), motivating the student (by conditioning him to like the material), and reinforcing him (keeping him aware of how well he is doing). If these functions are fulfilled by the student himself, there is no need for a teacher. It is because these functions cannot be readily handled by the majority of people that we need the teachers.

LANGUAGE-TEACHING TAPES

In the United States the teaching of foreign languages is undergoing a revolution at the present time. For generations, the procedure for teaching languages consisted of the study of grammar, vocabulary in terms of isolated words, and translation. Teachers varied in their interests and their goals; some were concerned with pronunciation, others with literature, still others with philology. From 1910 to 1948 there was a steady decrease in the number of students taking foreign language courses, but since then the trend has been reversed, especially with regard to modern foreign languages. About 1949 some new procedures were introduced in the teaching of languages largely as a result of military experience. The new procedures have been incorporated into what has come to be called the "Language Laboratory." I hasten to point out that this label of *laboratory* is a misnomer, unless by it one is referring to a workroom. The language laboratory actually is a means whereby students are given individual practice in listening to and speaking a foreign language. It is credited with a marked "improvement" in the teaching of foreign languages, and it deserves some consideration here as an example of technology applied to education.

The Army Language School

As it nears the end of its analysis of the psychology of teaching, this text returns to the "human-engineering" movement that was considered in Chapter 1. As now widely practiced, the teaching of foreign languages is an appropriate illustration of the application of human-engineering principles to an educational purpose. Teachers, of course, will appreciate that the application was not deliberate, that it came about as a result of pressure for more people with a special skill than could be procured by selection. Just before the United States entered World War II, the Army was faced with a need for far more people competent in the use of foreign languages than were available. The need had to be met in a hurry. There was no time to wait for the colleges to produce the skilled people needed; in fact, the colleges could not have produced such people with the methods then in vogue. To handle the problem, the Army started its own language school, a school that was unique in many respects but especially in one: the school administrators knew what they wanted. Not only did the authorities know what they wanted, they were also determined to get it, regardless of how many educational practices and traditions fell by the way.

The Army Language School[2] established procedures that can be stated in terms of the human-engineering practices described in Chapter 1: goals, criteria, job analysis, and determination of variables—not that such practices were consciously followed in all respects; there was too little time. The goals were determined by military needs: men who could understand and speak a foreign language. The criterion, somewhat idealistically, was: to pass for a native of the country whose language was being learned. The job analysis was hardly adequate; it recognized that native speakers do not speak like grammar books, that they use slang, colloquialisms, that there are various dialects, that various liberties are taken by native speakers, and that military men need specialized vocabularies. The job analysis also recognized that reading was a required skill but that writing was less likely to be needed. (To learn to write Chinese or Japanese characters would require more than the six months or year the Army was able to devote to language instruction.) The determination of variables was even less ade-

2 See A. Friendly, Jr. (1963), for a description of the Army Language School.

quate. It was recognized that only native speakers could be used as instructors; that native speakers speak rapidly, with confidence and without hesitation; that they are not necessarily familiar with their own grammar; that they learned their language as children by the process of listening to it and speaking it; and that the process of acquiring the native tongue involved a practice period of five years to speak like a five-year-old, ten years to speak like a ten-year-old, and twenty years to speak like a soldier. The Army's problem was how to collapse some twenty or more years of practice into six months. It was recognized that some of the practice enjoyed by a native consisted of hearing speech on the radio, records, in the movies, and through singing. All such aids and activities were incorporated as tools along with the native-speaker instructor.

The major task facing the instructors was how to compress a large amount of practice into a relatively short time. The program adopted called for six hours of daily classroom activity of listening and talking, in classes limited to eight students, three hours of daily homework, and supervised recreation where only the foreign language was spoken. Counting only the study time of nine hours per day for about 150 days, some 1350 hours were spent in learning how to speak a foreign tongue. The average college student with three class hours per week in a 15-week semester devoted to learning grammar, reading some "literature," and learning something about the "culture" of the country could hardly enter into a conversation with a graduate of an Army school.

The Aural-Oral Method

In the Army Language School, some of the daily class time was spent in listening to tape recordings made by various native speakers—children, women, people from different parts of a country. In addition to listening, the students tried to mimic what they were hearing on the tapes in order to develop appropriate control over accents and pronunciation. The tapes consisted of certain key sentences repeated over and over again, covering a wide variety of phrases that might crop up in routine conversations. It was assumed that hearing the sentences would bring about automatically a familiarity with the language structure so that suitable tense, mood, case, gender, and adjective endings would occur to the learner in future different contexts. Because the learning involved both listening and speaking, it was termed an aural-oral method.

It was this use of tapes that changed the techniques of language instruction in our schools today. Tape-recording is one of the technological advances that education has put to its own uses, although the success of this new method of teaching a foreign language is a controversial subject. Scherer and Wertheimer (1964), for example, find the audiolingual methods do produce skills in speaking, but translating skills of students taught by these methods are inferior to those of students with traditional training.

An Example of the Psychologist's Concern in Education

My point in going into such detail about a new method of teaching foreign languages is not to stress a technological aid to education but to emphasize what can be done about teaching if a determined effort is made. To introduce the aural-oral method, language departments had to overthrow a tradition of centuries. The new method had to meet the criticism of the traditional teachers. Regardless of which method of teaching eventually prevails, the situation faced by language departments points up features of education that psychologists (human engineers or not) continually emphasize.

1. Education Must Have a Goal. For the first time language teachers are in position to say what this goal is. We do not have to agree that speaking the language like a native is desirable. There may be other goals of greater value. If there are, they should be stated along with the criteria to be followed in evaluation.

2. Education Takes Time. Without its all-day sessions, the Army program would require about 30 college semesters or 15 years. Language departments have recognized this time factor to some extent and have managed to convince administrators that the old three-hours-a-week program is completely unrealistic for their purposes. Many colleges now have five-hours of class per week plus one or more hours in the laboratory. Obviously, more can be covered in more time. This, in turn, means some kind of educational curtailment in other departments. The average college student commonly takes only a year or two of foreign language. Advocates of the aural-oral method must take into account the goals of the students (passing reading examinations in graduate school is a common goal). They must be able to show that their method will meet some goal. In some instances the method is modified to introduce practice in reading, and tests are frequently in writing (because of large classes); in other instances, the students are simply urged to take more courses or read on their own to meet other goals.

3. Education Calls for Equipment. Teachers must be specialized for their functions. Where native speakers cannot be obtained, the teachers themselves must be products of the method, or they will not be able to use it with competence and confidence. Besides the teachers, technical aids can be used to provide the required practice and familiarity.

4. Education is an Individual Matter. Here the aural-oral method faces a difficult challenge in normal classrooms. The teacher cannot work with many people in any one session. The Army class of eight is an almost impossible ideal for public education. The laboratory, too, with classes of 30 cannot be effectively supervised and administered by one teacher or laboratory assistant. His job is to listen to the students in their efforts to speak like natives. Unless a "native" listens and tells them they are right or wrong, there is little virtue to the practice. The student must then be his own judge if his only guide is a tape. If his own voice is recorded and reproduced electronically, it will not even sound like his own voice to him. Students are more easily satisfied with their efforts than are native-speaker instructors. The laboratory technique in language instruction does not do the same job of reinforcement as does the teaching machine. This weakness will perhaps be remedied. For the present it helps teachers underscore the importance of individualizing instruction.

5. Education Must be Based on an Adequate Appreciation of Stimulus-response Variables. The aural-oral method is based on a questionable assumption: just because children learn their language usage by listening and talking is no reason for basing a method of instruction for adults on children's practice; findings on college students cannot be the basis for methods of teaching children. While the assumption eventually may be justified, at present it is nothing more than an assumption. There might be other approaches that would outstrip the advantages of the present method. There probably is "a better way." How well would the Army's students prosper if they spent three months in a foreign country, segregated from English-speaking people, as compared with the six-month training program in this country? What would be the effect of a preliminary grounding in linguistics that would provide a broad view of language structure? How much practice is actually necessary in the use of some one sentence? How many times must a word be used to become a part of a vocabulary? These are questions that now are answered by extraneous pressures and not by competent inquiry through research.

6. Education Must be Programmed. The language teachers using the aural-oral method argue that first one listens, then one talks, later one reads, and finally one writes. This may be the normal pattern for a native language. Is this, indeed, the best method for mastering a foreign language in all respects? Only research can answer such a question, and that research is not yet done. Whatever the answer, the aural-oral method is an attempt at programming in at least a rough way. The details of the program, however, are just as important as the whole program. What are the first words one should learn in German? Should they be *guten Morgen?*

TECHNOLOGY AND PROGRAMMING

The difficult problem of programming must be solved for every subject that is to be taught. So far, as Chapter 10 made clear, whole subjects in their traditional packages are very difficult to program. Smaller lessons are much easier. Perhaps when enough small lessons are programmed, teachers can start learning how to program series of such lessons.

Out of all the attempts to introduce technology to education comes one lesson for which there has been no real psychological explanation. The technologists find that in order to use their equipment and their tools they must first learn the subject. No programmer can work in the abstract. He usually finds it easier to teach programming to a subject-matter expert than to learn the subject matter, but to the extent that he is successful in programming, or in teaching, he finds that he is learning the material. He is discovering what all teachers discover fairly early in their careers, namely, that they only learned their subject when they started to teach it. This observation provides one last practical suggestion:

The best way to teach someone is to let him do the teaching.

As soon as a student has acquired a smattering of a subject he might be given an opportunity, under supervision, to teach someone else. This suggestion, perhaps, can summarize our effort: *Teachers do not teach, they learn.* In the process they initiate the actions that help the students teach themselves.

Chapter Twelve

Practical Applications of Psychology to Learning: A Summary

It is sometimes remarked in public-speaking circles that the good speaker first tells his audience what he is going to tell them, then he tells them, and finally he tells them what he has told them. The same advice might well apply to books. The Preface to this volume indicated what was going to be said. The individual chapters have stated the case. Now it is time to describe what has been said, and to this end I set down for final review a theory of instruction along with some derivations or implications of this theory. Frequently, when teachers present two or three sides of an issue, insecure students ask: "But what do you think?", implying either great confidence in the teacher's judgment or hoping to discover what to offer as an answer to some prospective examination question. I feel an obligation to meet this request and will tell you what I think.

A THEORY OF INSTRUCTION

Any theory of learning contains within itself an implicit theory of instruction and vice versa. Anyone who teaches is applying a learning theory of some kind whether he knows it or not. Therefore we can presume that, just as there are or have been many theories of learning, there should be an equal number of theories of instruction. That this is not actually the case is not too puzzling; the learning theorists have not commonly been interested in education or teaching as such and have taught their own theories of learning in instructional patterns that were based on their own educational histories, rather than on what their own theories should have taught them. Thus, theorists from the time of Pavlov and Thorndike on have lectured away at their students just as they had been lectured at by their own teachers. Occasionally, psychologists who are not primarily learning theorists evolve theories of instruction without specifying a formal learning theory on which the theory of instruction is based. Such theories are likely to be broad, general, and somewhat personal. It will not be easy to trace their derivation to testable principles about learning. Such theories may be correct and helpful to some teachers in some situations but lack the potential for self-corrective testing.

Bruner's Theory

Jerome Bruner (1966), for example, has proposed a theory of instruction without specific reference to a theory or theories of learning. The theory described by Bruner is presumably based on his broad background in psychology and on his own experiences in teaching children in a number of experimental efforts. The theory appears to rely on the reinforcement views of Thorndike, the programming technology of Skinner, and on Bruner's own conceptualization of knowledge and motivation. A brief overview of the theory is in order.

Bruner distinguishes between a theory of learning and a theory of instruction by noting that a learning theory is descriptive—it tells how learning takes or took place. A theory of instruction, he says, is *prescriptive;* it tells how to improve learning and how to discover the best ways in which something can be learned.

In Bruner's view, "A theory of instruction has four major features." His four features are:

1. A motivational feature. The theory must spell out what experiences develop predispositions for learning. (These may apply to learning generally or to learning specific contents or skills.)

2. A structural feature. This feature calls for a theoretical organization of a body of knowledge in some relatively optimal form so that the subject matter can be manipulated and, presumably, grasped by individuals at various levels of ability.

3. A sequence feature. A pattern or program of the arrangement of a given content must be developed for most effective appreciation of the structure.

4. A reinforcement feature. Rewards and punishments must be specified and programmed with the basic intent to switch from immediate and extrinsic rewards to delayed and intrinsic rewards as soon as it is feasible to do so.

Bruner does not attempt to offer proof of his theory of instruction; instead, he presents what he specifically calls illustrations of the four principles. The teacher examining these illustrations may be somewhat distressed to note that they are based on efforts by six high level professionals to teach four children some fairly difficult mathematical concepts. Bruner admits the student-teacher ratio is by no means routine but justifies the operation as an experimental search for principles. Whether the principles could then be applied by the average teacher in the standard classroom is not demonstrated.

It is not my purpose here to criticize Bruner's theory of instruction. As a general orientation toward teaching it is entirely satisfactory. It asks teachers to know their own subjects well, actually very well (the structure principle); to teach it systematically (the sequence principle); to consider and develop the students' interests (the motivation principle); and to make sure that the educational experience is a satisfying one (the reinforcement principle). To the extent that teachers are able to meet these features, we can applaud them. Where the theory suffers is in its failure to meet the crying need of teachers to know what they are doing and why they are doing it; in short, the theory tells you to teach well without telling you how to do so in specific detail. Whether anyone can do better remains to be seen.

The Present Theory

In this chapter I shall attempt to develop a theory of instruction that is based on those principles that have been found to be concrete and specific with respect to the learning process as it has been described in this text. The theory will be incomplete because, like Bruner's, it will include only four principles. These may be and probably are not enough, but they seem to be safe; and I would rather proceed slowly and carefully until a convincing amount of data justifies additional principles. Actually, only the first two principles are learning principles and may be all that a teacher can control. Should it turn out that two principles are all we can offer with security, so much the better. In general, the most effective theories (or, at least, the ideal theories) consist of the smallest number of principles or assumptions. One warning to the teacher: All theories are approximations, subject to correction and modification as new discoveries emerge.

Preamble to a Theory of Instruction

Learning is a continuous process, inseparable from living, so long as the organism is responsive to stimulation. The stimulation must be effective (see Principles II and III below) in that it must persist sufficiently to arouse a sensory and/or motor response.

The learning process itself consists of the formation of associations between neural events (consequence of stimulation). Such associations can consist of only a pair, i.e., a succession of only two stimulation-produced events, or of longer chains (e.g., memorizing a speech or long poem). The exact physiological nature of the "association" that is formed between neural events need not concern us so long as there is a functional relationship formed so that one neural event is followed by another. We can only speculate about neural activity as far as learning is concerned. For practical teaching purposes it is sufficient to know that, when a stimulus is presented that initiates one neural event, another neural event, previously active at the same time, is aroused without benefit of external stimulation. This is a simple statement of Pavlovian conditioning without reference to motor phenomena of any kind, although motor events may frequently be involved and initiate stimulation feedback stimuli. Such stimuli may then activate neural events in their own right and initiate new activities (neural or motoric).

It should be noted that single events are also learned in the sense that certain stimulations occur without any obvious or intended correlates or associates. Thus, if an airplane passes overhead and one merely "notices" this, he might be able to reply to a question later if someone should ask: "Did an airplane go by in the last hour?" Actually, there would always be other activities around any living organism—a certain environment, other unimportant or seemingly irrelevant stimulation that hardly merits mention. If one replies to a question of, "What was that?" just after hearing some thunder by saying, "Thunder," there has been learning, even though only one event of consequence has occurred. Learning is always measured by recall or performance after the passage of time. When a person is looking at something, we normally speak of perception. If we ask that person later what he saw, we are testing learning. Normally, however, we reserve the label "learning" for events somewhat more distant in time and also for the recall of more than one event of a pair. We do not usually say that someone learned that "it thundered", even though he must have learned it. Such learning, like all other, takes place automatically. Things are learned whether we *try* to learn or not. This is the key issue. Learning is conditioning in the original Pavlov sense of the term, i.e., it takes place under *certain conditions*. If the conditions are appropriate, learning will occur. If they are not appropriate, learning cannot occur. Our desires are beside the point. When a teacher says, "He does not want to learn," the teacher may be making a correct statement, but it is also an irrelevant one. What the teacher has failed to do, or is unable to do, is to set up the conditions under which learning can take place. One of these is probably another teacher.

From what has just been said we can deduce that a teacher is a conditioner and must know the principles of conditioning or the conditions under which learning takes place, so that these can be appropriately manipulated. One caveat is important. Not all potential learners are at the same stage of preparation (I avoid the word "readiness") for a given kind of learning. A lion fresh from the jungle is not an apt pupil for jumping through flaming hoops. It can be taught, but it will take time and a lot of effort. A question of efficiency rises. If we assert that all children who are physically normal can learn anything, we may be correct, but we cannot assert that all will learn equally and at the same rate. Their prior backgrounds must be seriously considered. If they are not equal in background, they are not going to be equally effective learners of all things. One must take the costs of equating backgrounds into account. In some cases it might take ten teachers to teach one student what one teacher can teach ten others in the same time. This is an economic and social-cultural problem of no small account, which cannot be solved by learning theorists.

With the above as a preamble we can proceed to a statement of the postulates or principles of a theory of teaching.

Principles and Corollaries of the Theory

Principle I. *Attention.* During a learning period the learner must be active or responsive to the material involved. This activity is not necessarily overt or grossly motoric. The learner must, in short, do something, but this something can consist of looking at, listening to, reciting, or naming what is being presented. In some cases the learner may respond in terms of imagining or imaging (allowing residual vestiges of past stimulations to occur) as responses to the stimulation. In many instances there will be an emotional response involved. This principle incorporates the ancient wisdom of all teachers who recognize that students who are not "paying attention" do not learn what is being taught.

Corollary 1. *An organism will learn anything that arouses attention whether it wants to or not.* This is the rock on which the television industry builds its economic empire. By constantly repeating jingles (the audience cannot close its ears) the television advertiser teaches the consuming public that a certain toothpaste "gives your mouth sex appeal", whether the public wants to know this or not. This corollary is of primary importance, and its substance is largely ignored by both teachers and theorists.

Perhaps it bears restatement: We learn a great deal that we do not care to, need to, or want to know. Learning is an automatic result of the operation of certain conditions. Perhaps another way of underscoring this point is that wanting to learn is of no importance whatsoever as far as learning is concerned. Wanting to learn may help in attention arousal, but even here it might hurt rather than help if the wanting interferes with attention.

Principle II. *All learning takes time.* The time involved is the period when some activity related to the to-be-learned material is taking place. The time necessary to learn different things varies with the nature of the material and the background of the learner. Some people learn some things faster than others because of differences in the materials or the experiences required as background.

The time involved can be made up of separate units that cumulate or can be used in one extended period. If it takes ten seconds to learn something, it might be possible to learn it in two five-second periods or five two-second periods. There is probably some optimum time for each learner for each kind of material. Some periods are probably inefficient because they are too short. If they are too long there may be over-learning, interference, or a waste of time in a real sense.

Corollary 1. *Only so much can be learned in any given time.* If more is taught or presented than can be learned there will be a failure of total learning. If fifteen items are presented in the time it takes to learn ten, then only ten or fewer will be learned.

Corollary 2. *You can only learn one thing at a time.* If you spend your youth in a pool hall or on a golf course, you may become pretty adept at sinking balls into receptacles. You will learn very little geometry or French while engaged in these other pursuits. It is quite likely that most of us are learning something most of the time we are awake. Some of us learn things other people admire (e.g., brain surgery) while others learn to make sausages or drive seven-shift tractors. Some of us, who cannot do much more with a sausage than eat it, look down on the sausage maker, while he looks up to us if we are brain surgeons. Yet there is no stronger foundation for a democratic society than the recognition that we have all learned different things in our time and that our varying skills are testimony only to how we spent or misspent our time, rather than of inherent differences in intelligence. The inhabitant of the most wretched and deprived neighborhood knows (has learned) a great deal about that neighborhood, its ways, customs, and limitations; the most astute professor of sociology could well be an ignoramus as far as such intimate knowledge is concerned. We would do well to recognize the talent of a truck driver or ditch digger and at the same time to realize why he might have a difficult time with calculus.

Principle III. *The internal regulator or model.* Many learning theorists have been preoccupied with rewards, satisfactions, drive reduction, or reinforcement. This persistent appreciation that learning occurs well or best (or only) when the learner is rewarded in some way must be recognized. From ancient times, we have been told that we can catch more flies with sugar. Apparently there has been widespread recognition of the fact that rewards are in some way related to learning. The pervasiveness of this belief cannot be denied, but its correspondence with reality can and must be. It should have been equally clear to observers that people have learned many things under punishment or threats thereof. To counter the flies and sugar aphorism we have "spare the rod and spoil the child." As we have seen (p. 118), Mowrer rests his case against the reward-reinforcement theory on the fact that subjects can learn to be afraid when no reward is forthcoming.

Guthrie attacked the reward theory on the basis of its irrelevance and practical impossibility. He saw that learned behavior occurred *before* the rewards and could not be effected or affected by it. He also saw what was more important: that rewards somehow protected learning by preventing an organism busy with its reward from engaging in other behavior that might be learned to the stimuli that were (still) impinging upon it.

Mowrer has little use for Guthrie's views, but in his own work he inadvertently made use of Guthrie's real contribution. While Guthrie did not say so specifically, he implied that a reward, in effect, serves as a signal that the lesson is over. This is his great contribution to our appreciation of teaching and learning. Mowrer, responding to Guthrie or not, finds that, to make his system work, he also needs some kind of signal device or operation to indicate that the learned behavior is adequate, or that the lesson is finished. He postulates a not too specifically described mechanism to serve this purpose.

You will recall that Mowrer uses the analogy of a thermostat or automatic pilot in an airplane to illustrate his behavior-controlling mechanism. For any learning situation, then, Mowrer postulates some internal process or activity (call it an "image" of the appropriate behavior), which could result in homeostatic balance. Such an image of the performance serves as an index or model of what is to be done or achieved. When the behavior has matched the model, the exercise is over, and the learner can turn to the next event or assignment.

Mowrer's proposal may underlie old primary school practices in spelling wherein a teacher would instruct a pupil to imagine a word somewhere out in space and spell it by reading off the components of the image. The student would spell what he saw in his image and cease activity with the last letter. If the image were a good one, the spelling would be correct. Obviously, a poor image would result in misspelling.

The possibility that such a thermostat-like device or mechanism regulates and terminates behavior has many satisfying features. It explains the great mystery of why "knowledge of results" appears to be an important condition of learning (see Principle IV), and it may also account for the role of rewards in learning in general as well as serve as an explanation of any imitative behavior or learning through watching or observation.

According to the present speculation, some kind of past experience (something learned in its own right) is initiated by some current stimulation and serves as a standard or model to guide behavior. As the learner says, writes, or otherwise creates stimuli that bring into being patterns of stimulation approximating the model, the learner continues to respond until the match is as close as he can produce. Frequently, as in trying to draw a map or a picture, the attempt is a failure. Perhaps the internal model itself is inadequate. Presumably many people have the finger and manual dexterity of Michaelangelo, but their activities do not produce a Pietà. Perhaps they could not visualize the Pietà that guided Michaelangelo.

When a given model is matched, the behavior ceases. The learner *knows* or thinks that he has performed correctly. A student of Heifetz should be properly crestfallen upon completing a selection in the Master's presence. The Master presumably knows what it should have sounded like. If the student knew that as well as the Master, he, too, might become one.

The principle of the model may not be necessary for initial experience or early learning when the models themselves are being formed, but the models may play increasingly significant roles with more advanced learning.

An easy illustration for the model concept is the process of learning how to read. If a word is not in the spoken vocabulary of the reader, he does not respond effectively to the printed code or symbols. Learning a foreign language is more difficult if the foreign words have no English equivalents. No imagery is aroused to serve as models or to inform the learner that he is correct. This is especially so with idioms; the wrong imagery is aroused.

Picture a child reading an English word like PLINTH. It is likely that even sounding it out correctly will bring about no reaction—no imagery, no model. A little later he will not remember reading the word or be unable to recall it.

Principle IV. *Knowledge of results as a response control.* Behavior is continuous with life. Within the continuity of behavior, however, there are constant shifts, starts, and stops. To all appearances behavior is a series of sequences that appear to have a beginning and an end. It is of fundamental importance to appreciate that the end of one apparent sequence always starts the subsequent. There are no real gaps in behavior and no blank minds. The behavior of the moment continues until an appropriate adjustment is made to the stimuli of the moment. The teacher asks for the product of 6 x 6, and the student replies, "36." The observer might perceive a stimulus and a response, but neither student nor teacher has stopped behaving. Only a sequence has terminated, and the observer may not be interested in what follows.

Why does the student stop when he says "36"? He knows that this is the answer expected and that no further action is required. Saying "36" has matched the model that was activated by the stimulus question. It is this model matching that controls the behavior. Suppose the question is asked of someone who does not know English. No model is activated and no specific behavior ensues. Now the teacher can write out the numerals and multiplication sign. If the foreigner is experienced with Arabic numerals and operations, a model is activated. The teacher calls for 8 x 9, and the student responds with "74" or some other wrong answer. If the behavior matches the model the behavior subsides. The student is satisfied. Wrong answers are no different from correct answers. They match the models that the student has acquired or demonstrate that no model has been acquired. Knowledge of results does not mean knowledge of being correct. It amounts to matching models. If the model is correct, so will the answer be. Sometimes the model is vague and inadequate. The student spells a word and it "doesn't look right." The model can not be matched precisely, and the student squirms or tries another operation.

The important consideration in teaching is to provide or insure proper models. Skinner has emphasized the importance of being right as learning proceeds. There is no virtue in mistakes, and mistakes arise because improper models are developed through haste or inattention. The teacher should make every effort to insure the development of proper models by directing attention to significant features of any new experience. If there is any danger of confusion or faulty generalization (and teachers get to know the common errors), special training should be provided for the troublesome items. Psychology students, for example, never seem to learn that "stimulus" is singular and "stimuli" plural. It is necessary to take the time to spell this out and to provide some appropriate practice. Similarly the word "data" is commonly treated as a singular word. This is not of great importance, but if a teacher wants the students to say "data are," then special training is required.

"Knowledge of results" or KR is the human learner's equivalent of a reward for an animal. It has no immediate or crucial role in fixing a learned response. Food for the rat is a signal that no further attention need be paid to other stimuli. For the human learner matching a model plays the same role. In neither case is there any other function for a reward.

With these four principles we have a theory of instruction that comes as close to providing rules for teaching as any learning theory can. If the theory is incorrect, it will have to be corrected by research and experience. If it has some virtues, it might lead to more effective teaching by the practitioner of the theory.

The application of the theory can now be set out in simple steps:

1. A teacher has to know what he wants the learner to do. The blind cannot lead the blind.

2. A learner must "know" what is expected of him. The first step in learning is to develop models. The tin-eared student cannot sing.

3. The teacher must direct or control the attention of the student by one means or another. (There is no difference between sugar and hickory switches except in terms of human relations.) If the student is already happily prepared to attend, the problem vanishes.

4. The teacher must provide time for the learning experience. There is a need for time to generate the model and for time to match it.

While the four points are almost self-evident and simple to state, their implementation is obviously not easy, and the task of the teacher is to find the ways and means for putting the principles to work. The difficulties in the way of using effective techniques are of such a wide variety and number that the teacher who practices the theory faithfully can still find the job impossible. This does not make the theory less correct. It merely demonstrates that complex interactions of contradictory goals can lead to trouble. The theory of a gasoline engine is not refuted by filling the gas tank with water and sugar and showing that the engine will not run. In today's classrooms the multi-purposes of the school may very well be the sugar in the gas-tank and interfere with instruction.

Implications of the Theory

The nature of a theory was briefly mentioned (p. 40) where its function was described as that of summarizing an assortment of data or observations into as few integrated principles as possible. One of the benefits of such a summary is that one can dwell on the principles, their generality, and their implications, and sometimes arrive at deductions that are inherent or implied by the principles but have not been perceived or considered before. In reviewing the theory described above we can begin to ask an almost endless set of questions related to the educational functions. As examples of this operation I have chosen for somewhat extended discussion three unrelated questions of serious importance. I shall then offer, without detailed comment, a list of what appear to me practical implications of the theory for teachers. The support for these suggestions has been presented throughout the text, and the relationship to the theory may seem rather tenuous or distant. The interested reader can enjoy himself working out these relationships for himself.

The three questions I will try to answer, or at least comment on, are: 1. What makes a good teacher? 2. What is the function or purpose of examinations? and, 3. How large should classes be?

THREE BASIC CONSIDERATIONS ABOUT TEACHING

In the general comments that follow, the reader is advised that the suggestions and conclusions are admittedly "idealistic." To put some of them into practice might be extremely expensive and would call for what some might regard as radical upheavals. My excuse for these conclusions is that someone should be idealistic.

What Makes a Good Teacher?

I will assume that anyone offering his services as a teacher is a competent subject-matter expert. If this cannot be assumed, we can go no further. But competence in subject matter is not enough. There are two additional psychological prerequisites. I will state these two prerequisites in the form of propositions.

1. The first proposition deals with the nature or personality of the teacher. Not all people in the profession belong in teaching. *Only those who like to teach can really be classified as teachers*—who teach not be-

cause teaching is clean and respectable work or steady work or secure work, but because these individuals *love their subject.* The teacher, ideally, should be more interested in his subject than in himself. The mathematics teacher must love mathematics. If he does not, he should get out of the field. No teacher should be asked to teach a subject he does not like to teach. As a corollary to this principle, we might add that the practice of the one-room schoolhouse or even most modern primary grades of having one teacher for a number of subjects is a poor one. No teacher can have that much love. Students can be quickly infected with a distaste for a subject if the teacher shows distaste, displeasure, or in any way suggests that he himself is anything less than enthusiastic about his subject. In brief, teachers should be privileged to teach only one course at a time. Further, the present practice of teaching successive classes one after the other is inefficient and confusing. The teacher needs time to get set for each new group of students, to review the achievements in the last meeting, and anticipate the needs for the next. A ten-minute break between classes offers only some physical relief. The teaching machine advocates recommend that teachers spend *most* of their time preparing and revising lessons. While this is economically and socially impractical at present, a teacher should have time to review what has been achieved in the class that just ended, what was left undone, what difficulties arose, and what can be done about these problems. Beyond that the teacher must have time to consider what can be accomplished in the class to come.

While these last comments may appear unrelated to personality questions, they bear directly on the issue of the teacher's poise, equanimity, and awareness of the student's needs. A teacher, like an administrator, should anticipate student problems and be prepared to act prior to the emergence of difficulties rather than re-act.

2. It is not enough to love the subject. **It is also necessary to instill that love or interest in the students.** Teaching is a skilled craft and the teacher must enjoy his craft along with the subject matter. He must like to teach. If he does not, perhaps he belongs in research and not in the classroom. A teacher can indeed be enamored of his field but be indifferent to students; in short, he can, from the student's viewpoint, be dull, boring, cold. Such teachers will not create the basic requirement underlying learning: the drive—anxiety—curiosity—attention function that generates the learning process. There are obviously no good measures of such aptitudes among teachers. Popularity polls do not provide suitable measures. It is not the teacher who should be popular—there is no need for every teacher to be a lovable Mr. Chips—it is the subject matter that

should be popular. Students should feel some regret when a course of study is finished. Perhaps we can never hope to find students objecting to vacations, but we might look forward to something less than unbridled enthusiasm at dismissal bells. There is a danger, of course, that a false kind of enjoyment of courses can be developed by making subjects "easy," by changing the content requirements or lowering standards. The educational trick is to raise the standards and the enthusiasm at the same time. The teacher must be fully aware of his function as an emotion-conditioner, and he must use all the tricks of the trade. Much the same view has been expressed by Carl Rogers, the psychotherapist of "client-centered" fame.

In a lecture at Harvard, Carl Rogers (1967) applied his views on therapy to teaching and indicated, as might be surmised, that the emphasis in teaching is a misguided one. Rogers does not approve of teaching as such. Just as in therapy the client cures himself, so in education the student must do the learning himself—he is not to be taught. The teacher should function as does a therapist in facilitating the attainment of a student's goals. These goals are personal changes and learning, but more in the sense of knowing how to change and how to learn to meet the continuously changing world of the future, in which the student must adapt and learn. The knowledge we impart today will be superseded by tomorrow's new information and technology.

The teacher must behave as a member of a community of learners and help release the curiosity of the students, "to open everything to questioning and exploration." To accomplish these aims the teacher, like the therapist, must possess not some special pedagogical skills but rather "certain attitudinal qualities" that function "in the personal relationship between the facilitator and the learner."

The attitudes Rogers espouses are: genuineness or realness (no hypocrisy), not role playing. A sound set of values or attitudes includes "prizing, acceptance, and trust," which are best translated as "accepting any other individual as a separate person, having worth in his own right." A final attitude is that of empathic understanding. This is more difficult to specify, but it covers an awareness of the way the educational process seems to the student. The teacher then does not judge or evaluate, but feels with the student and shares the student's understanding whether there be bewilderment, frustration, or dismay.

The attitude of empathic understanding is perhaps most frequently absent among teachers. It calls for putting yourself into the student's position. He does not know what you know, and for him some things are difficult that you now think easy. The teacher may have had trouble with these matters himself at one time. Now he is impatient with the lack of progress on the part of the student. There would be no harm to the teacher if he reflected over his own education and kept his own learning history in mind.

The prescription Rogers presents is not so different from that proposed in this text to characterize the effective teacher. The teacher is a model to be copied by the students, and the model must be one that can be admired and identified with. Skinner, it will be recalled, presumably hopes to attain the same ends by his emphasis on positive treatment and the avoidance of aversive measures.

The difficulties with Rogers's orientation are not with Rogers but with the typical school classroom situation with its externally imposed requirements and structure. The teacher can normally take few liberties with the curriculum, and the curriculum does not specify curiosity as one of its objectives. The emphasis on specific attainments of skills and information and the continual demands for evaluation, plus the emphasis on order and discipline imposed from above, force the once idealistic teaching candidate into the role of teacher as we now commonly recognize it. A once noble profession has been so surrounded by external restrictions that those who now are in practice are forced into ignoble, and by that token ineffective, roles.

The implication of these first two propositions is not that teachers are "born" and cannot be made. If this were the case there would be no need for the list of suggestions. Some teachers already on the job may be too resistant to change to adopt many or any of these suggestions, but others might. I can only hope.

The Function of Examinations

In the matter of examinations, I can start with the suggestion that every student should be informed of the specific (detailed) objectives of every course of instruction. Where this can be done by supplying a detailed syllabus, such a syllabus should be provided. It is common practice for teachers to follow a syllabus. Students, equally often, do not even know the teacher has one. Teachers frequently create the impression that they are the only ones who are entitled to know what is coming or what will be covered in a course. I would suggest that students are equally entitled to such information. Not only should they have available detailed information about what is to be studied, but they should know precisely what is expected of them. They should, in short, have detailed information about the nature of examination questions that will be asked and what are regarded as adequate answers.

Some of my acquaintances at the college instructor level are horrified at suggestions such as those just mentioned. They prefer to follow a procedure that I think of as the "educational mystique." In this procedure, the instructor is in full charge, he is the only one who knows what the course is all about. He decides when and how often he will give or "spring" quizzes and what answers are acceptable. His final examinations are anticipated with varying degrees of terror and are passed or failed with varying amounts of cheating, perspiration, and good or bad luck depending upon the student's skill at forecasting the instructor's fancies about suitable questions.

In contrast to this "educational mystique" I recommend the following action with regard to tests, quizzes, or examinations:

1. Examinations should be formally scheduled at specific times. There is no useful function to "surprise quizzes." They can hardly be justified as "motivational," because the motivation involved is questionable. Students should not be frightened into studying. On the contrary, students should come to expect tests at regular intervals as routine exercises that are part of the educational experience. The all-night cram session with black coffee and drugs should have no place in an educational enterprise. Examinations should not be anticipated as traumatic, fearful occasions but as opportunities to display competence. To achieve such a state of mind in the student, it may be necessary to introduce many changes in educational practice from the first grade onward. Daily quizzes should be the routine practice in order to insure the student's readiness for the next stages of a course.

2. Examinations should be based on material covered in a course and should not call for personally devised extrapolations of the course material that some individual teacher decides are important. If such extrapolations are desired, they should be made part of the course or should become the subject matter of another course. Too often a course examination becomes an intelligence test. If a teacher is interested in intelligence scores, then there are probably better tests available than an individual teacher can devise.

3. Students should be informed about the specific questions to be asked and the specific correct answers that are acceptable. If some teachers find this suggestion too shocking, they might accept the practice commonly followed in certain states for testing potential drivers. The candidates are

provided with booklets that list the questions to be answered and the appropriate answers. At the examination, a selection of such questions is presented to the candidate, and he can be required to answer all or some percentage correctly. The important point here is that there is no mystery about the content of the examination. Teachers can similarly provide students with a pool of questions from which the examination will be made up. Some teachers reject such a suggestion with the comment: "Why they'll just memorize the answers." Such a comment implies that there is something wrong with memorizing answers. The subject of memorizing in contrast to understanding has been discussed previously (see pp. 220–221) and need not detain us further. Another common objection is that: "If they know what will be asked, they won't learn anything else." I would reply to such teachers that if they want the students to learn more they can add more questions to the pool.

4. Some subjects are difficult to reduce to a pool of questions with straightforward answers. It is easy enough to determine whether a Boy Scout can tie nine knots correctly or whether he can send and receive Morse code. To decide whether a college freshman can write an "acceptable composition" is not easy. In fact, a number of colleges have arrived at the decision that it is impossible to teach Freshman English and have given up this traditional and hallowed requirement. In courses in the arts and humanities it might be possible to "examine" in some ways other than the question-and-answer procedure. Term papers or actual productions might serve as substitutes. In the grading or evaluation of such productions, there should be greater uses of outside examiners or independent juries. The practice of allowing teachers to evaluate their own products has always been a poor one. Equally undesirable is the use of paper-graders who are not actual experts in the subject field. We might find a solution in arrangements whereby each teacher grades another teacher's students. Every effort should be made to encourage objectivity and anonymity of both student and examiner to avoid the pervasive subjectivity that beclouds grades at all levels of education.

5. The matter of grading has already been mentioned (pp. 95, 242). Here, I would merely remind the teacher that the entire examination process would be vastly improved if the usual grading system were abolished and a simple pass or fail basis were followed. The concept of a sliding scale means that either the examination has not been carefully prepared to represent what is desired of the student or that no real teaching has been done. To determine a passing score by the performance of

the average student is to surrender education to statistics and chance variations. There should be a fixed standard of performance for any given level of teaching. A student who does not meet this level should be allowed to try again after making efforts to remedy his weaknesses. Obviously, such a practice calls for ungraded schools, a long-felt need in education but one which would call for many and expensive changes. I can cheerfully encourage moves in such a direction while recognizing that, actually, little will be done in a hurry. What can be done, however, is to recognize that passing students from grade to grade when they do not actually meet the standards for work at the higher levels results only in a progressively mounting handicap for the student who finds himself called upon for tasks more difficult than those he failed to accomplish satisfactorily earlier.

How Large Should Classes Be?

I will leave the matter of examinations and evaluations to the reader and turn to another problem, that of class size. Here, I can be briefer. At present, the question of how large a class should be has no answer as far as any objective measures might indicate differences relative to smallness or largeness. The answer will probably not come from further research along the lines of current methods and measures. The only alternative is a logical one. The teacher can ask: What is the purpose of a given class assemblage? If it is only to *see* something once or *hear* something once, a class can be as large as possible, the restriction being that each person present can see and hear. If the class is assembled for some other purpose, then the class size should be fitted to that purpose. In general, educators accepting current educational aims and goals might adopt the position that a class must be small enough for the instructor to be able to react to each individual member as often as necessary to meet the goals in the time allotted. Not only should the teacher be able to affect the student; the student, too, should affect the teacher. The teacher should at least come to know the student by *name* and should have some awareness of the achievement status of the student. In practical terms, a class of twenty, or at most thirty, students seems more than large enough.[1] The experience of teach-

1 See W. J. McKeachie (1962), who has reviewed numerous studies of class size and found no definitive conclusions about large vs. small classes. The number of variables and the differences in criteria in judging effectiveness make the problem extremely complex. The class size should be a function of the purpose of the gathering. To the extent that the purpose is not being achieved, the class is too large or too small.

ers over decades seems to point to such a class-size figure as a framework within which they feel they can work. Such experience should not be tossed off lightly. Our problem is to educate people, not process them through an objective examination.

SUGGESTIONS FOR THE TEACHER

I turn now to the listing of specific suggestions for teachers. These suggestions do not follow the order of the chapters of the text, and page references are supplied wherein support for the suggestions is to be found. The reader, as was said at the outset of this chapter, should in each instance ask himself if he can supply this support and, if not, he should refer to the indicated pages. In a sense, these suggestions comprise a syllabus. They represent what the teacher should learn in this "course." The book might just as well have started with this list. The passing score, remember, is 100.

GOALS, STANDARDS, AND CRITERIA

1. Goals and criteria of success in courses must be written out and supplied to all students. These can be in the form of a syllabus with all questions to be answered included. If you want a student to know more, he must take another course or the additional material must be added to the syllabus. The student should always know what is expected of him (p. 290).

2. Examinations should be scheduled. If a student is not ready for a test, he should not take it except for practice. Examinations must be reliable and standardized (hopefully nationwide). The examinee should know what questions are likely to be asked. The examination should not be a trial-by-ordeal (p. 291).

THE ROLE OF THE TEACHER

3. The role of a teacher is that of a conditioner of emotional reactions. The object of teaching is to condition favorable reactions to the subject matter (p. 280).

4. Learning is something that happens to students. If teachers want the credit for good learners, they must accept the blame for bad ones (p. 68).

INDIVIDUAL DIFFERENCES

5. Individual differences must be regarded as such. Every student and teacher is entitled to respect. He behaves as he has been programmed to

do either by nature or by training. Recognition of *temperamental* differences is especially important. Not everyone can learn all skills or responses equally. Everyone can be encouraged to develop his forte (p. 254).

6. The concept of "optimal stimulation" may require different learning arrangements for different people (p. 165).

MOTIVATION

7. Attention and "curiosity" can be developed through a controlled arousal of moderate anxiety (p. 174).

8. Interest and attention come from success. Nothing succeeds like success (p. 176).

9. Attention is a learned response. Students must be reinforced for attentive behavior (p. 167).

ANALYSIS OF THE LEARNING SITUATION

10. Every learning task must be analyzed into specific components that must be learned separately, by drill, if necessary. Drill is the required technique for drill tasks (p. 155).

11. Analyze "acts" into the component "movements" and teach these movements. Do not attempt to teach abstraction (p. 103).

12. In some situations, the first thing to be learned is the last thing to be done. Some sequences must be taught "backward" (p. 77).

13. Analyze response sequences into component steps and "shape" the behavior accordingly (p. 32).

14. Learning requires prior emotional conditioning to cues that can be used as secondary reinforcers (p. 123).

15. Teachers must take note of the possibilities of positive and negative or useful and harmful generalization and determine the degree of discrimination required (p. 45).

16. The teaching-machine concept is more a logical than a psychological one, the mechanical trimmings appear to be unimportant (p. 251).

17. The real virtue of teaching machines is the concept of programming —the notion of logical developments of materials. This is not a new idea, but it is a very valuable one. It points up the need for giving teachers time to determine the order in which materials are to be presented (p. 252).

18. The gadgets and devices used in teaching machines are useful only for controlling attention, prevention of cheating, getting reactions from illiterates, and for recording performances for purposes of improvement of the programs (p. 236).

19. Television productions are only small screen motion pictures. They have no practical instructional virtues over motion picture productions. Use them where they are useful (p. 264).

REINFORCEMENT AND EXTINCTION

20. Knowledge of results is an effective secondary reinforcer for humans. The learner should never be kept in ignorance of the stage of progress. Homework without answers is a test, not a learning exercise (p. 76).

21. Some undesirable behavior can be eliminated by negative practice (p. 203).

22. Learners are not to be punished in order to *weaken* response patterns or get rid of habits. Punishment can be used to *inhibit* such responses and to control the initiation of appropriate responses (p. 125).

23. Teaching, in some situations, involves waiting for a response to emerge. Such emergence can be facilitated by shaping. When a response emerges, it is desirable, if not necessary, to reward it (p. 97).

24. Any rewards, to be effective, must be immediate. The reward value might really be motivational or "arousing" in its operation (p. 126).

25. The "spread of effect" must be controlled within desirable limits (p. 59).

26. Undesirable behavior should not be reinforced. This includes undesirable aspects of what is, in general, an otherwise acceptable performance (p. 93).

27. Negative significates are learned as easily, if not more so, than positive (p. 112).

28. For punishment to be effective it must be immediate to allow conditioning of inhibitory reactions to feedback stimuli. Similarly, rewards are ineffective if they are delayed beyond the effective operation of feedback stimuli (p. 121).

29. Punishment and reward are only unconditioned stimuli for emotional reactions of a negative or positive nature. They do not work in a vacuum. The emotional reaction must occur if they are to be effective (p. 119).

CONTROL OF THE LEARNING PROCESS

30. Avoid the development of "superstitions" by controlling the contingencies of reinforcement in relation to precise discriminated stimuli (p. 95).

31. For breadth of skill, practice should include experience at different points on a continuum of stimuli (p. 53).

32. The *Habit-family Hierarchy* calls for the extinction of higher orders of response in teaching (p. 83).

33. Seeing someone else being reinforced is effective in teaching, if the viewer has the appropriate needs and the necessary prior conditioning to the stimuli involved (p. 131).

34. Learning can occur when the learner merely looks and listens (p. 136).

35. Not all learning requires overt action. Such action is necessary for physical skills but not for learning from lectures or demonstrations (p. 135).

36. Do not allow learners to leave a learning session with an error as the last response (p. 108).

37. The development of *Reactive Inhibition* is to be avoided in teaching. Spacing of lessons is important for this reason (p. 76).

38. Each lesson should begin with a warm-up of easy, related material (p. 214).

39. Negative or interfering emotional reactions as well as interfering response patterns must be eliminated as a first step in teaching (p. 86).

40. A learner must be ready to learn. The desired response must be available (p. 58).

41. Take account of the possibility of latent learning and consider a change in incentives to make the latent learning manifest (p. 113).

42. Because knowledge and performance may differ, look for other variables when performance fails. Consider such other variables in preparation for a future performance (p. 111).

RETENTION AND TRANSFER

43. Time has nothing directly to do with forgetting. It merely allows for interpolated learning experiences. Students should not be expected to retain if there are no defenses introduced against interference (p. 193).

44. Interference from new learning can be reduced by overlearning original material (p. 196).

45. Old learning is never completely lost. Relearning efficiency is the virtue of education. Students should be given practice in and demonstrations of relearning effectiveness (p. 192).

46. Not all new learning interferes with old. Some kinds (same responses to similar stimuli) help retention. Entirely different materials do not interfere with old or help new learning. Teachers should take care to

spell out and specifically teach the similarities and differences between old and new stimuli and responses (p. 195).

47. When a learner is having difficulty with some assignment, it can be assumed that prior learning is interfering, that the stimuli and responses involved are similar to other stimuli to which similar responses are associated. Difficulty in recall of old learning suggests, similarly, a lack of discriminated interpolated learning (p. 197).

48. Teachers can expect identical elements to transfer positively. Such elements must be identified specifically. When transfer is expected and there is no transfer, we must assume that there are unrecognized differences in the situation (p. 212).

49. To secure persistent behavior, develop partial reinforcement schedules (p. 96).

50. Retention depends upon attention, not intention. The student should be encouraged to work as if each chance to study or practice is his one and only opportunity (p. 28).

51. Retention depends on the proper stimulation. Teachers should avoid "trick" questions. Students should be specifically trained to recognize different forms of the "same question" (p. 198).

52. Responses should be practiced in the same situations as those in which they will be called for (p. 199).

INSIGHT AND UNDERSTANDING

53. Insight can occur only if the learner has had prior and appropriate emotional conditioning to the stimuli that constitute an answer (p. 223).

54. "Late" learning can occur in one trial if the components of the response have been acquired earlier. Do not teach a higher level of operation in the absence of lower level equipment or background (p. 147).

55. Early learning can be approached from the point of view of "continuity." Reinforce every correct response even though there seems to be no change in behavior (p. 73).

56. Where possible, train the learner to use mediators (p. 155).

57. The teacher must take the *Habit-family Hierarchy* into account if he is to prepare students for potential "insight" (p. 81).

TEACHING AND LEARNING

58. Teachers learn most about their subjects when they are faced with the responsibility of teaching. Perhaps all students should also be teachers. While the blind must not be permitted to lead the blind, at least some assignments might involve the teaching of one student by another (p. 273).

59. Learning takes time. The time factor is significant both for the short term (each lesson) and the long term (curriculum). Only so much can be learned at a time. If something is added to a curriculum, something else must be dropped or the total time must be increased (p. 26).

These 59 suggestions represent what I currently regard as meaningful for teachers. Obviously, all of them cannot be applied by every teacher in whatever institution. Some of them probably will turn out to be really ineffectual, even meaningless. Each suggestion, however, appears to have the support of some kind of research by psychologists. None is a practical "rule of thumb" handed down from one teacher to another—not that such suggestions are without merit; there have been excellent teachers long before there were psychologists—for in this book we have been concerned with finding "the better way" for those who are not currently using it.

My suggestions are meant to be tentative, subject to revision, omission, and addition. Perhaps other students of the learning and teaching process will be provoked to improve my list. If anything resembling serious attention to the problems of teachers emerges, my effort will have been useful.

Chapter Thirteen

An Illustrative
Appendix:
The Psychology
of
Reading

Throughout the text illustrations of the theoretical principles in application were introduced from a variety of teaching situations and subject matters. At no time was there any extended discussion of any one subject as the effort was a general one directed, presumably, at all teachers.

It seems desirable at this time to consider a specific academic subject at somewhat greater length to illustrate the kinds of questions a teacher should ask about any subject and to examine the problems any subject involves for the prospective teacher. I have chosen the subject of reading because of its interest for me as a psychologist, but the same approach would be taken if geography, arithmetic, chemistry, or any other subject had been selected.

The first point to appreciate is that each of these subjects has been taught before, some of them for centuries, and some intelligent comments have been made about these subjects before you were born. It will pay to attend to at least some history of teaching in any area that concerns you.

Second, as made clear in the first chapter and throughout the text, the approach to be followed is the one I have labeled the human engineering procedure. This procedure, you will recall, emphasized the definition or job analysis of the problem, an examination of the goals to be attained, the criteria by which the goals are measured, and a determination of the variables that must be manipulated and controlled. It might be well to restate for a last time the human engineer's contention that there is a "better way" to teach anything, and to recognize again, for the last time that whatever is developed by way of improvement may not be the last word or even economically or socially justifiable at a given time. I cannot promise to solve the problems of teaching reading or even to explore all of the facets of the subject; that would involve at least another book without any great promise of success. My purpose here is to illustrate a general approach applied to a specific problem. Hopefully it might help a future teacher with some other subject.

Some History of the Problem

The history of the teaching of reading goes back to before the time of Comenius and his picture dictionaries. The "phonic" versus "look and say" method was the subject of debate in American Colonial times and need not detain us here. By 1908, even with primitive instruments for recording eye-movements, most of what is relevant to know about reading from that kind of analysis had been discovered. In 1908 Edmund Burke Huey wrote what should now be revered as a classical work on the subject of the "psychology and pedagogy of reading." Fortunately for modern students, this book has recently been reprinted and is again available. This charming, and still most relevant, work should finally receive the attention it has deserved all through these years of controversy about the reading process and how reading should be taught.

Huey conveys a great appreciation of, almost astonishment at, the fact of reading. Reading is man's supreme achievement, perhaps the most marvelous invention of the human mind and so complex a process that its comprehension would amount to an understanding of how the mind works. Herein lies the special appeal of the reading problem for the psychologist. If we could penetrate the mystery of reading we would know the answers to some of the most persisting problems of psychology; the problem of thinking might be resolved.

Ulrich Neisser (1967), in his prize-winning book *Cognitive Psychology,* makes the same point when he says (p. 136): "Reading is externally guided thinking. Perhaps we should not be surprised that it is so poorly understood; we may not understand it until we understand thought itself."

Neisser bases this remark on the fact that, when we read for "meaning", the reading is far too rapid to be based on any kind of individual letter or even word perception. Further, and helpfully, Neisser proposes an analogy that we shall explore more fully later. He says (p. 135): "There is a somewhat plausible analogy between reading sentences without attending to specific words and recognizing words without attending to specific letters." A sentence that has been read results in a cognitive structure, a "silent stream of thought." Later in his book Neisser (p. 251) again emphasizes the sentence as the unit of comprehension: "It is evident that sentences are understood as wholes, by grasping their underlying structure," and a little later (p. 252), "We deal with sentences we hear (substitute *read*)* by reformulating them for ourselves . . ."

* my parenthesis and italics

Huey's concern over the problem or nature of reading has not been seriously appreciated by most writers on reading. Some of these writers have never sensed the significance of the problem. They tend to take reading for granted, a routine skill to be learned in the first grade, and concern themselves with the practical problems of instruction in reading or in remedying reading defects and failures. Some want to teach children to read at earlier and earlier ages so that they will soon be leaving their cribs with some alleged reading skill as part of their equipment for facing life's problems. Just as an anticipatory note let me observe that Huey advocated the age of ten or so as a perhaps suitable time at which reading instruction might be initiated.

Before we get too deeply involved in the psychology of reading I think it wise to get some historical and sociological perspective. Reading is an ancient art known to the Babylonians and Egyptians long before Biblical times. It was a secret and privileged practice known to and controlled by the priests and passed on to a restricted few down through the Middle Ages. Only small segments of the population were initiated into the mysteries of reading, and the written, then printed, word became holy. The book became the Book and was venerated. Some writers, like Robert Briffault in *The Decline and Fall of the British Empire,* accuse the ruling classes of the Middle Ages of allowing the development of printing and publication so that they could better control the masses with what we now have come to recognize as a mass medium—the printed word. The charge may have been and may even still be true for some literate countries, but nevertheless, we still have a world situation wherein most people cannot read at all. Seriously acceptable data are not available, but it is stated by Eisenberg (1966) that "fully half the world's adults are wholly illiterate," and a third of those who do read cannot meet American fourth grade standards.

In American schools it is variously estimated (Parks & Linden, 1968) that at least ten percent of the children are serious reading problem cases, and that thirty percent of the children are a year or two retarded in their reading. Most failures occur in the first grade and are occasioned by inability to read. Many thousands, if not millions, of American adults are virtually completely illiterate. They cannot read want-ads or take the correct bus to seek employment. Some job-hunters take taxis on job searches because they have no other way of reaching a rumored employer. For those of us who do read adequately the automatic nature of the skill and habits involved makes the inability to read seem some kind of irritating abnormality, a perversion of personality, or some unhappy neurological quirk, and we look for the quick and easy remedy, the panacea that will make everyone read pages at a glance. We ask why Johnny can't read instead of being amazed that Susie does! We fall for fads and fashions in reading techniques and promote a strange variety of nostrums.

I do not mean to get too far afield, but it is necessary to place the reading problem in a setting. It is not an issue that faces only first grade children. It is a local, national, and world problem, and it is not a simple problem. Reading is a multi-faceted skill and is even at this time an undefined operation. We hardly dare ask ourselves: What is reading?

The Definition of Reading

A long time ago, I read a book by an early science-fiction writer—Edgar Rice Burroughs. The book was *Tarzan of the Apes.* You are familiar with the hero of the jungles and need no introduction to him—but if you just "saw the movie" and did not read the book as carefully as I did, you might not know about a fascinating detail of Tarzan's life. Although his mother tongue was an ape language (in his infancy he had been adopted by a tribe of large apes), he taught himself to read with the help of English children's books he found in his dead parents' cabin. He studied the pictures and accompanying letters in the books and hit upon the idea that the little scribbles of black print were substitutes for the pictures. Slowly he mastered the mysteries of print and learned to read without ever having heard a spoken English word. While science fiction is not the best source of information on most subjects, Burrough's account of Tarzan's self-education might throw some light on the current educational problem of reading. How does one go about learning this skill? Did Tarzan, who could not speak English, actually read English?

Consider a possible analogue of some American's sudden transportation to some Pacific Island abandoned by Japanese who might have left behind a suitable library, from children's picture books to illustrated dictionaries and encyclopedias. Could any American learn to read Japanese without benefit of translation or the hearing of Japanese speech? The possibility is not foreclosed, especially if some volume like a currently popular picture-language textbook happened to be available. The modern Robinson Crusoe might pick up some elementary Japanese without ever hearing or saying a Japanese word. What, for example, can be learned from the following lesson in Russian? (Fig. 8.)

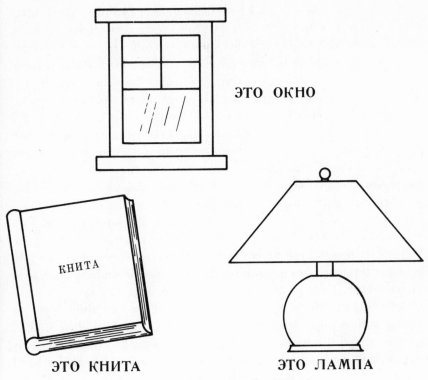

ЭТО ОКНО

ЭТО КНИТА   ЭТО ЛАМПА

FIGURE 8. *Three Russian Words*

Adapted from *Look and Learn Russian* by Aron Pressman (New York: Dell Publishing Co., 1962).

Did you deduce that ЭТО means "this is" or "here is"?

The above excursions into fantasy are designed to bring us face to face with some of the variables in reading. What does reading really consist of? Attempts to define reading have not been completely satisfactory, and a recent try by Wiener and Cromer (1967) to conceptualize reading illustrates the complexity of the problem. Before we consider their analysis of the problems of reading, we should consider some extrapolations from the fantasies I have just described into the world of reality. The extrapolations I want to emphasize are these: First, it is clearly possible, and has been done often enough for children born deaf, to learn to read by using a spelling-out-with-fingers method. (See Goldiamond & Dyrud, 1966.) Such children do have a difficult time of it, and the mastery of reading is a major achievement for them, but the needs for vocalizing cannot be met by these readers. From my work with deaf children I know how difficult it is for them to respond to letters of the alphabet. In contrast, they learn to respond quite well to pictures that mean something to them. My experience with these children makes me even more amazed than I was formerly that anyone ever learned to read. It is truly a marvelous skill. But, at the same time, I have become somewhat convinced that speaking and hearing, while of enormous importance, are not essential to reading. I shall keep making this point but do not wish to be misunderstood. Certain kinds of reading activities are dependent upon the voice, and I am now trying to isolate what is absolutely essential. The emphasis on phonetics and pronunciation then, while important for some aspects of reading, must be evaluated somewhat separately from the essence of reading.

It is also possible for the blind to read, as we all appreciate, although their reading must be done through the sense of touch, not sight. Again, this removes from the essence of reading any necessary concerns about eyes and eye-movements. Again, I am concerned lest you misunderstand. Vision is obviously vital for responses to printed pages.

The late great Helen Keller learned to read without either sight or hearing, and we might learn a good deal about our problem if we studied the educational history of this remarkable woman. Everyone knows the story of how she suddenly realized that a certain stroking of her hand meant "water." With this one scrap of experience or learning her life was transformed.

If we return briefly to our fantasy and recall the foreign language books, we can pursue the problem of essence a little more clearly. When a jungle native comes upon a "spoor" on the trail, he becomes excited. The businessman "on safari" does not comprehend. The native points out the spoor, and still the tourist-turned-hunter does not understand. He cannot read jungle language. He is a jungle illiterate. The native is a qualified reader and knows that a lion or leopard is not far away. What's more, he knows that it is a lion and not a leopard in this case.

Herein we may have the essence of reading. A sign, natural or otherwise, stands for something else to a particular observer. To the uninitiated it may not only fail to stand for something, it may not even be perceived. When I referred to a sign "standing for something", I only intended to indicate that a reaction of some kind takes place in the prepared or trained observer that is different from the reaction, if any, in the untrained observer. We can refer later to the nature of this reaction. For the moment we might anticipate the possible answer and remark that the sign reminds him of something else that is not now present.

If you recall the concept of Pavlovian conditioning, you may already have arrived at reasonably appropriate conclusions. A response to a spoor is a conditioned response. So is any other kind of reading. But the conditioning in reading may be of great complexity and involves the conditioning of meanings.

We can return now to the analysis of the reading operation. Happily we will not have to cover too much of history because of the recent analysis by Wiener and Cromer. They start out by dismissing various earlier definitions of reading as incomplete and inadequate. We can follow their lead for a while and note that they recognize that earlier definitions emphasize various factors such as:

a) discrimination, identification, and comprehension
b) acquisition versus the final product of accomplished reading
c) absolute versus relative criteria for good reading
d) the relation of language skills to reading skills

Eleanor J. Gibson (1965) for example, in her description of reading, emphasizes three phases: "learning to differentiate graphic symbols; learning to decode letters to sounds; and using progressively higher-order units of structure."

Wiener and Cromer object to this definition because it emphasizes only acquisition. This objection is not nearly correct because Gibson is very much concerned with the problem of transfer to new reading materials after original training. She concentrates on the discrimination of letters and decoding them into speech sounds. Gibson's experimental attack may prove of great value for certain phases of the reading hierarchy. Wiener and Cromer are somewhat more justified in their criticism of Gibson's failure to emphasize comprehension.

Geschwind (1962), on the other hand, is criticized for emphasizing only comprehension when he defines reading as: "The word *read* is used in the narrow sense of 'ability to comprehend language presented visually' and not at all in the sense of 'ability to read aloud'." Whether the ability to read aloud is relevant and/or important is a matter we will look into later in greater detail.

A definition by Bond and Tinker (1957) appears to cover the field but is also found wanting because it ignores the acquisition process: "reading involves . . . the recognition of printed or written symbols which serve as stimuli for the recall of meanings built up through the reader's past experience." This definition is much in the style of Huey and will be explored more fully.

Other definitions, according to Wiener and Cromer, confuse different stages of reading and language development; the relative measures of reading skill and the emphasis on meaning or comprehension may confuse reading difficulty with language difficulty.

Wiener and Cromer offer their own definition of reading as a two-step process "involving first identification and then comprehension." Each of these processes is a function of separate variables, thus: *Identification* requires a basic process of attention from which discrimination can evolve. Discrimination requires various kinds of sensory acuities or capacities and is itself a function of various cues. Identification can be aided by language familiarity, especially with word sequences; certain word expectancies provide cues for naming words that follow already familiar words. The new words need not even be seen. Identification is also aided by similarity to already learned words, e.g., hat and mat, and by various phonetic rules about long and short vowels, etc. Such rules need not be known in the sense of having been learned specifically. Gibson (1963) has shown that even at the end of the first grade, children are able to perceive and read, i.e., spell out words that are pronounceable, even though they have never seen these letter combinations before. They can see and "read" "BIM", for example, or "NAR" but do not get IBM or NRA as easily. By the third grade, children are quite good at reading pronounceable nonsense words like GLURK but cannot handle CKURGL as well.

The *comprehension* facet of reading depends, according to Wiener and Cromer, on prior or accompanying language competence. Translation of visual cues into auditory form brings meaning to life if the auditory response itself has meaning. A so-called poor reader may have problems of failure to arouse meanings, even though there is nothing poor about his identification skills. Different environmental backgrounds and dialects may prevent comprehension though identification is adequate. All of us can read James Joyce, but only a few will comprehend much of *Finnegan's Wake,* or even *Ulysses.*

Wiener and Cromer emphasize that comprehension can help identification—the chemist reads chemistry better than a psychologist and vice versa. Both speed and comprehension are aided by more extensive experience.

With sufficient background, identification becomes a secondary skill, and only discrimination is required without stopping for auditory translation. The reader proceeds to experience meanings, and such an activity is the presumed essence of the experience of reading.

The one caveat I would insert at this time is the exclusive dependence on auditory translation that seems to concern Wiener and Cromer. They overlook the reading skills of the deaf and the by now innumerable demonstrations that readings may be too rapid for auditory translations, vocalizations, or even discriminations in their sense of the term.

This brief review of the attempt by Wiener and Cromer to conceptualize reading is important for us because it does emphasize at least two stages in what I would like to describe as a reading hierarchy. These two stages are identification and comprehension. Each of these stages, however, can be broken down into additional steps. I cannot pretend to be able to enumerate each of the steps that deserve identification and analysis, but I want to repeat, and will continue to assert, that reading is not a single or unitary process.

Not only are there different phases or stages of reading, but there are also different purposes for reading, and each phase should be identified with its purpose, with specialized training programs developed, so that process and purpose can meet effectively. Recently Helen Smith (1967) outlined eight different purposes for reading when reading has already developed to some reasonably secure level. She described reading for: 1) general impressions, 2) detail, 3) main idea, 4) sequences [order of events and ideas], 5) directions, 6) comparisons, 7) cause and effect, and 8) generalizations and conclusions. In her own study Smith discovered that good readers were more flexible in their adjustments when the purposes of reading varied as to general comprehension versus reading for details. Her own theoretical remarks suggest that in any analysis of the reading problem we must take account of the reasons for reading and develop appropriate techniques for varied purposes.

Frandsen (1961), an educational psychologist, appears to have appreciated the need to break reading down into stages or kinds of reading. He lists six such phases that may provide a suitable plan for a more effective program of reading pedagogy. His six stages begin with: A pre-reading stage, wherein a child follows a story and can recount an experience. In a second stage he recognizes some sight words, perhaps his name. In a third stage he identifies new words by phonics, form, or context. After that he begins to develop word hierarchies and reads groups of words. In a fifth stage he begins to acquire different techniques for different purposes, such as skimming, general comprehension, outlining, evaluation, and, importantly, rejection. In a final stage he begins to make inferential use of context. It is this final stage that interests me, but I would like to underscore this appreciation of phases, stages, and types of activities with varying purposes, all of which are classed under the rubric of reading. Reading is clearly not an activity. It is a class term or label for a multitude of processes.

This brief summary of different orientations of writers toward reading should suggest that people have little in common in their reactions to the word "reading." Reading, like any other complex skill, consists of many stages, purposes, phases, and attributes. A child can take tennis lessons from a professional and can tell his friends that he played tennis that morning. The relationship between his activities and the game of tennis as played by professionals is clearly nonexistent. Some of you might think you play a fair game of ping pong. On the day you see a professional play you will consider giving up the game.

I have tried to suggest that the word "reading", like most words, has no *specific* meaning. The fact that we use the word so loosely as to cover the halting efforts of the first-grader and the rapid scanning of the professional researcher suggests that we have not really paid attention to the process. Everyone is familiar with the commonly cited statements about Eskimos having 17 different words for snow and South Sea Islanders having a similarly large assortment of terms for coconuts. The fact that we have but one word for reading is revealing. When we succeed in an adequate analysis of reading, we may have an equally large terminology for the various stages or kinds of reading.

The Goals of Reading

With the above as background let me turn to the next feature of our human engineering approach to the teaching of reading: that of the goals to be attained. As with all learning tasks we should start at the end, the goal, the objective, before we design a program for teaching anything, including reading. The objective of reading probably cannot be specified in any single statement. The listing of Helen Smith's purposes is surely incomplete and subjective. Furthermore, they are not limited to various stages or phases of reading. There is probably a large number of objectives that appeal or apply to a society as a whole and many more that will be suitable for some segments of society or some individuals, but not for all. It may repay us to explore some general objectives. A sampling might make the necessary point.

One objective could be that of reciting lines on the stage or on the political stump, lines written by someone else. To read a speech like the late Winston Churchill did is a special skill—if not, more properly, a great art.

To read Shakespeare or other poets for the delight of an audience or for one's own pleasure calls for a love of words and their sounds; the reading must vary in pace and intensity. It calls for pregnant pauses and histrionic flights. When the late John Barrymore whispered, "The play's the thing", he was scarcely audible, yet a thousand people heard him clearly. But is this reading? Could we not learn to recite poetry and orations by listening to others recite, as medieval minstrels did, or as our teenagers learn seemingly unintelligible songs from recordings? Is the written word in these instances any more than a reminder, like musical scores for the reasonably trained musician? Reading poetry or reading aloud for fun, your own or that of others, is one kind of reading and calls for special training.

In any event, the objective of being able to vocalize the writings of others does not appear to be the sole objective of reading and for many of us not even an important one, although it appears to be the logical outcome of the pedagogical methods now most popular in the schools. Divorced from the skills of the actor or poet, such reading amounts to word calling or word naming. I would rate this as a necessary and useful skill but a secondary goal.

Without examining other possible goals, let me turn at once to the goal that I believe could receive most universal endorsement. The goal of reading, I believe, is to make sense out of written communications, whether these be in the form of books, letters, or breakfast cereal box literature. In the case of the last mentioned, it may be that the medium itself is the message, but for the former we can assume that the medium and the message are distinct. To make sense out of written material, the material must contain sense, and sense, generally speaking, comes in sentences. A sentence says something about something. A subject and a predicate with some possible modifiers and assorted parts of speech describe some event, circumstance, or thought. The reason for writing about it is that it is not here and now, and perhaps never was. The reader, suitably trained, reacts to the sentence and, if he can read, reports the meaning of the communication. This is the goal of reading; and our main purpose in teaching people to read is to enable them to get meanings out of written messages.

If we accept this as our purpose, we can proceed to work backwards from the goal to develop the program of reading instruction, step by step, asking ourselves what step is needed just prior to the goal, the step before that, then the next preceding step, and so on backward to the first.

It is not my immediate purpose to trace this backward sequence for you now, and you might well surmise that I could not do so even if I had such a grandiose ambition. Instead, I will examine more closely the goal of attaining meanings from writing, after suggesting some propositions that are clearly not related to the goal.

The Variables in Reading

First we can recognize that vocalizing is not required for reading for sense or meaning. Most competent readers do not move their lips while reading, nor do they implicitly enunciate the words internally, trying them out for sounds. It is true, and recent research supports the early claims of John B. Watson, that we do some verbalizing while thinking and even while reading, but we do not do so in terms of all of the words we read nor, for that matter, the totality of any word itself. The deaf do not vocalize their reading, nor do the blind in reading Braille. The practical Braille reader does not even feel all of the elevated pips in a word but goes on to the next and reads, like the seeing person, a phrase or sentence at a time. The practiced Morse code receiver does not write down individual letters or even listen to them as such, but he catches fairly long sequences before writing down a part of the message. While he is writing, the rest of the message is coming in and is caught, in a sense, at its conclusion, not in transit.

Whatever else we do know about reading, we have known for almost a hundred years that trained adult readers do not read single words and certainly not single letters. We do not read by phonics and we do not "look and say." We read phrases and, if they are short enough, sentences. All the concern over the size and shape of letters and the frightful terrors of English spelling are quite beside the point, even though of great importance for other goals, such as correct spelling or pronunciation. Incidentally, mention should be made of Gibson's (1963) conviction that there are many uniformities of spelling from sounds and that the English language is not quite as horrible as Bernard Shaw believed.

We must constantly remind ourselves that there is more than enough evidence that, as we go about our reading, we do not even see much that is there as well as that we see things that are not there. Nearly every elementary psychology textbook contains a paragraph with some deliberate misprints, which the writer then calls to the freshman's attention. Similarly it is clear that much of the material on a page is not noticed. The printer fits his words to his fixed lines, and we do not bother to catch the end of a word that was divided by a printer as he reached the end of a line. Misprints and other typographical errors are not for the reader, they are proof-readers' problems. If you notice such errors in type, you are probably wasting your time as a reader and show your inappropriate schooling, unless you are a proof-reader.

If we can assume then that vocalizing, overt or otherwise, of some punctilious sort is not of the essence of adult reading, we can more meaningfully evaluate such activity as far as training people to read is concerned. Again, I assert that a knowledge of the alphabet, proper spelling, correct pronunciation, and effective public speaking are admirable skills and should receive attention, but not at the expense of reading for sense. They should be practiced in their own right and at appropriate places in the curriculum. Where they belong is the heart of the human engineering problems that we have not yet solved.

Perhaps we should belabor the point a bit more. To read for sense does not require a knowledge of the alphabet, or any rules of pronunciation about long and short vowels or i before e, or any concern over our non-phonetic English language. Most of us have had our own experiences with words we did not pronounce accurately even though we knew their meanings. As a child I used to think that the word "weapon" was pronounced "weepon"—no one in my neighborhood had ever heard such a word, let alone used it. I had plenty of precedent for reading *ea* as *ee*. There are such words as r*ea*d, pl*ea*se, cr*ea*ture, b*ea*d. I must have generalized from these instead of br*ea*d, pl*ea*sure, or even the past tense of r*ea*d. A high school friend of mine referred to his unhappy "ske-do'lee", and I had a little difficulty in our conversation until I deduced that he was referring to his schedule, which, as you know, the English prefer to pronounce, "shed-yool."

The argument that I have advanced so far is that reading for sense does not consist of any precise and specific attention to the micro-structure of the written (or for that matter, heard) stimulation. Perhaps one last point will complete the case. We do not listen to individual words in a conversation because the individual words make no sense by themselves. Only a sentence makes sense. If I say: "Are you coming to————" and do not finish the question (and you do know it's a question), all I have done is to frustrate you. If I add the word *theatre* or *ballgame* or *dinner,* the whole set of words assumes a unity of meaning. Anyone who reads syllable by syllable is not reading. He is syllabalizing. If he reads word by word, he is name calling. Perhaps here we have two of the words we might use in describing the different aspects of reading mentioned earlier. With more effort and more interest in reading we may approach the Eskimo's interest in snow.

In my approach to the problem of reading I have chosen to turn the emphasis away from the tremendous concentration on eye-movements and visual mechanisms and the concomitant concern about the structure of letters and words onto the, to me, more significant feature of word and sentence meaning. And again I agree that concerns about the perceptual factors are of enormous importance for some phases of reading. I want to focus on reading for meaning. We must keep reminding ourselves that this, too, is only one kind (or phase) of reading.

Criteria

As we have seen, reading is not a simple process or skill. The term *reading* is a name for a number of complex skills, some of which are related to one another and some not. The story of the two soldiers (one Polish who understood Russian and the other American who could pronounce words written in the Cyrillic alphabet but who knew no Russian) might help us understand this point: When the soldiers found a message written in Russian, the American "read" it to the Pole who then told the American what the message contained. Who did the reading?

To consider the process of assessing reading skills, we must determine the various activities that go on under the label of "reading" and assess each skill. The present procedures of testing for speed and comprehension are of little or no value. The speed measure is even dangerous to employ if it amounts to accepting someone's statement that he has finished after he has been handed a test. He might not even have looked at it! This would insure a high score and suggest something. Many so-called speed readers riffle through a text and announce they have read the material. Such reading may impress naive spectators or even testers, but timing such operations is little less than ludicrous. What counts, of course, is what the reader "got" out of the exercise. Here we do not know what to measure without knowing what the reader tried to get out of his assignment. Fearing a test upon completion, he might have tried to memorize the text; finding that that would take too long and make him look like a slow reader, he might have resorted to other efforts: memorized facts and figures, looked for tricky details, or made broad generalizations. The material itself could be familiar to some, strange to others. The problem here is not unlike that faced by Ebbinghaus in 1880. Ebbinghaus resorted to nonsense syllables to solve his problem. Reading testers might do worse. A better solution might be to let the reader see the questions first and then let him read the material. This procedure might make the speed measure a little more interesting, and the comprehension measure could have some virtue. The use of unfamiliar material is, of course, a must. The complicating factor here is prior experience, which is difficult, if not impossible, to equate. Some consideration should be given to how much reading the examinees have done and of what kind. The use of third or fourth grade levels is somewhat meaningless because not all schools have the same curricula. If we knew how much of a graded amount of reading a person has done, we might be able to measure something like a reading I.Q. or reading potential index. The present system of grade level measures has no predictive value and serves little but local or political purposes.

A great number of tests is necessary for each feature or component of reading including, at the lower levels, such items as alphabet recognition in its various scripts and types, phonetic skills, sight words, pronunciation, spelling, and grammar (familiarity with language structure). At higher levels we might wish to test vocabulary, word derivations, synonyms, etc. At still higher levels we could test for comprehension of timed and self-paced passages with and without knowledge of the questions. At still higher levels we could evaluate appreciation of style, etc. At every level some kind of cut-off points would have to be established to define acceptability. At the present time we know nothing about readers with a fourth grade ability. What if no one in the fourth grade can read?

Reading for Meaning

Earlier in the text (pp. 227–228) I discussed teaching for meaning. In that discussion the views of Noble, Osgood, Mowrer, and Paivio were presented. The reader might review that section in connection with the present concern over reading.

According to the description of meaning presented earlier, a meaning is whatever response pattern (emotional and/or imaged) you undergo when a stimulus affects you. In an original experience with some other person, say someone named Joe, you react with sensory and emotional responses. If you hear the name "JOE" applied in the context of these responses, you will be conditioned, to speak loosely, in such a fashion that a subsequent hearing of the name "JOE" will arouse some of the emotional and sensory reactions that occurred originally. This pattern of revived reactions in the absence of the original stimulus is a meaning, in this case, the meaning of "JOE."

If it is readily accepted that sounds like "Joe" can arouse meanings, it is no great theoretical leap to assume that a visual substitute stimulus like the letters J-O-E, seen in the context of a sound like "Joe", will also come to arouse the same or similar emotional and imaged reaction.

The recent work of Paivio (1969) (see p. 225 in this text) on the significance of imagery in learning lends a large measure of support to this view. It will be recalled that Paivio demonstrated that his imagery ratings proved superior to Noble's m ratings as far as learning is concerned.

We now have the basis for an appreciation of the nature of reading for meaning. Visual stimuli that have accompanied meaning reactions (emotional and sensory responses) in the past now arouse at least fractional components of these original reactions. It should be pointed out at once that, for normally hearing (and seeing) people, auditory cues are usually the original, unconditioned stimuli for meaning in reading situations. Somebody else says a word, and we look at it as we hear it. A picture that arouses an unconditioned emotional response and later serves as a base for an imaginal response could serve just as well and does so for deaf children or for children who learn to read by themselves. A good, realistic color photograph in life-size could be regarded as an unconditioned stimulus. I recall my own children, as infants, trying to pick up peas from an advertisement in a magazine. In this connection a picture is considered an unconditioned stimulus by virtue of the principle of generalization. A picture of an apple, for example, is assumed to arouse the reaction that an actual apple would lead to.

The argument thus far is that reading for sense is a matter of arousing feelings and images. This is by no means a new approach. Edmund Huey stated precisely this view in 1908. He was not very secure about it, however, because in his day psychologists like Stout, James, and Tichener were dubious about the role of imagery in reading. It did not appear to these introspectors that imagery could carry the burden. They argued about the problems of images of words like the, and, but, of the prepositions and adjectives, and could not agree that reading could depend on imagery alone. There were too many relational expressions in reading, and they gave up the effort to tie reading to imagery. They were correct to a degree. There probably can be little effective imagery in some expression like "There was a very large and moving," but I would argue that there is also little if any meaning to such a collection of words. It is precisely here that Huey gave up too soon. He saw no way of "imaging" a word like "under" or "upon" and forsook the problem. But recent research in which I have been engaged seems to provide a way out of the difficulty.

For the past several years I have been trying to get at the nature and significance of imagery in learning (Bugelski, 1968a, 1968b, 1970). I have already described the procedures I have been following (the one-bun technique) by which subjects are able to remember many pairs of words.

The point to be appreciated is that there is now no problem about imaging the word "in." It cannot be imaged by itself, anymore than the word "green," but it is not at all difficult to imagine a green tablecloth, or for that matter, a purple cow. I am arguing that the relationships that puzzled the early psychologists are easily imaged if the objects involved in the relationships are brought together. The word "running" cannot be imaged by itself. Something has to be running, a boy or a cat or a brook. When subject and predicate are taken together, in short, when there is a sentence, meaning emerges, and it emerges as a matter of tapping prior experience in terms of imagery and feeling.

In my experiments, subjects are required to imagine two items, e.g., a gate and a fountain pen. Such randomly chosen items are unusual and quite unique. In developing these associations, however, the subjects do not escape their pasts. The gate involved is a specific one—a white picket fence type or an iron rail gate—one they have seen before. The fountain pen again is a specific pen—their own, black or blue, open or capped, writing on the gate or doing something else.

Such creative imagery takes too long to meet normal reading speed requirements—but I make the random associations unique and strange by my selection of the components. If I should ask the subjects to associate a slice of ham with the bun, or a stocking with a shoe, a leaf with a tree and so on, there would be no problem of learning whatsoever. There would be perfect recall, possibly without any practice. It would amount to a free association experience. In normal reading the associations called for are largely routine. A flower is in a vase, a pen in hand, a dog under a table, etc. Such imagery calls for little time, and the reader moves along briskly. If the material is difficult, if new associations are called for, the reading slows down too. What we call reading for meaning I have pictured as a succession of images, not as individual, bare, fleeting glimpses of objects against some screen but as integrated patterns of varied objects experienced in space and time, in color, in motion, in juxtaposition or relation to other objects, which are characterized by ownership, direction, size. Such images are presumably accompanied by flows of feeling and varying emotional states.

The confluence of the theorizing of Huey and current imagery research appears to provide a foundation for a more detailed development of a theory for reading for meaning. The argument that Huey essayed no

longer appears as untenable as even he believed, and his intuitive conclusion that reading was a matter of appreciating meanings, which in turn
could be generated only by sentences, appeals to me as eminently sound.

The Teaching of Reading

We can now turn to the question of pedagogy, the teaching of reading.
You will recall Huey's remark that training in reading should not begin
formally before the age of 10. He was not all that rigid, of course, and
felt that 8 or 9 might be alright if a child was ready for it. The readiness,
however, consisted of having sufficient background and experience to read
sentences (in turn this means having acquired the appropriate vocabulary
and grammar associated with speaking in sentences).

Huey pours scorn upon the typical primers with the "See, see, see Spot
run" kind of sentences on the grounds that nobody, certainly no child,
talks that way. He has little or no use for alphabetical, phonetic, or whole
word approaches as teaching procedures. He might have made the point
(although he does not) that such procedures are the only ones that can
work with six-year-olds confined to classes at an age when they want
nothing to do with sitting quietly in formal classrooms. Huey does make
the point that the poor methods we use appear to work well enough to
justify their continued use, but they establish bad habits and are extremely wasteful of time that could be put to better use teaching arts and
crafts, music, and morals. He recalls, with some feelings of warmth, the
education of the Greeks, which consisted largely of athletics, music, and
poetry. We have illustrations from other fields, e.g., typing, that sixth-
graders can learn as much typing in one year as children who began typing in the fifth grade, and who have typed for two years by the time of
the comparison. It is probable that the same kinds of results would be
found if the subjects were learning to read.

I should not leave you with the impression that Huey has no regard
for alphabets and phonics or other features of reading pedagogy. He
merely regards them as outside the subject. Of course children should
learn the alphabet—they will need it to use a dictionary, and they can
learn it by ear, by singing it, and they can learn the appropriate visual
identification in games or with flash cards. And, of course, they will learn
some sight words. Every three-year old watching television today can
read a great many detergent, deodorant, and mouth-wash names; they also
learn a lot about time, and can read TV programs in the newspaper at
astonishingly early ages. Huey would not discourage instructing children

in sight words that represent their names, street names, food product labels, etc. These come naturally and provide a working base for phonics. It is simply that such materials should not be confused with reading matter. Reading matter consists of sentences in paragraphs that serially tell a story or give a sequential account of something.

The approach described by Huey suggests pretty much that reading is not something we should teach in school. It should be learned, and he says so, as our basic language is, in the home, in an atmosphere of books, magazines, newspapers, and reasonably grammatical conversation with a varying and consequently rich vocabulary. When these factors are absent, reading will be retarded. There is a kind of social evidence for Huey's arguments if our stereotype of the slum home is at all realistic. If slum parents do not tell stories, never read them to children, and if they speak in slang or in a dialect, or do not speak at all to the child, it is unlikely that such a child will become an efficient and avid reader. If other skills are not practiced, and if such other skills underlie real reading, again we will have reading problems.

There is virtually no controlled research to support this theory; but some very recent efforts in the St. Louis schools, where stories with enriched vocabularies were read to school children three times weekly over the school PA system, appear to have resulted in significant improvements in both reading and I.Q. measures. (See *Time Magazine,* August 10, 1970, pp. 55–56.) This is the kind of research that must be developed before we are likely to make much progress in reading pedagogy.

The ideas expressed in this chapter are not as novel as they might appear. Not much in the psychology of teaching is. It always pays to go back to history. The same general view we found in Huey's 1908 work was expressed by Comenius in the seventeenth century. In 1964 George Gallop arrived at similar conclusions, apparently quite independently. In *The Miracle Ahead,* the psychologist and polling expert Gallop, argues for a drastic curriculum revision with reading placed rather late in the educational scheme. He advocates first teaching children to reason and debate, to draw conclusions logically on the basis of evidence and fact, to memorize effectively, and perceive quickly. He wants to develop a kind of creative intelligence, which would enable a child to learn to read almost without effort when the need arose. On this note he harmonizes again with Huey, who stresses the motivational feature that is missing in our usual reading routines. The child may have no need to read, the need may be in the teacher. More progress might be made if the child were so trained as to have a strong need to read. This may explain why many children teach themselves to read via comic books; what apparently happens in these cases is that the children get "hooked" on the comic books. The wise parent reads them to the child only often enough to whet the appetite, and the child takes it from there.

It might be soul-satisfying, and easy for Gallop and others, to criticize schools and their curricula and to advocate attractive and perhaps revolutionary change. The chances are probably zero, however, that any school system would really embark on a program that delayed reading instruction beyond the first grade. We must work in a real and somewhat demanding world and consider the restrictions that prevail. I cannot encourage any really serious innovations in current procedures of teaching reading if teachers cannot control the situation in the face of certain criticism. What is needed is the fostering of more and more research on the various phases of reading. Work like that of Gibson is promising. Slowly we are coming to realize that some children will learn to read no matter how we teach them. Children trained by phonetics inevitably come to recognize "sight" words, and look-and-say learners also pick up phonic tricks. We cannot afford to be either revolutionary or archaic but must continue to evaluate each new approach on the basis of evidence and in the light of our goals. Nor can we afford to ignore the great technological advances now represented in our homes and schools by television and computers. Someday, we may seriously have to raise the question if reading is a skill of any importance at all. Marshall McLuhan (1964) has already asked this question.

At this time I would like to hark back to my earlier remarks wherein I quoted Neisser and Huey to the effect that, if we could understand reading, we might *ipso facto* understand thinking and vice versa. In the early years of Behaviorism, John B. Watson characterized thinking as inner speech, a matter of talking to one's self. The doctrine that talking and thinking are identical was not novel with Watson, but he gave the view tremendous impact and status. In the process of reducing thought to inner speech, Watson vigorously denounced any suggestions that imagery played any role in thought.

While mulling over Watson's views, it occurred to me that the inner speech theory could only be tested by demonstrating that speechless organisms (animals, deaf mutes, appropriately paralyzed people) could not think. I believe that all of these do think and there is evidence for all.

To prove that some organism cannot think is a bit of a problem. It is difficult to prove that anything is not true. An easier prospect might be to demonstrate that one does think. Such speculation led me to begin a study of deaf mute children, under the age of four, to see how they behaved in what might be considered a thinking situation. I (Bugelski, 1970) provided these children with sets of pictures (five animals and five objects). Two pictures would be shown at a time: one animal, e.g., a horse, and one object, a ball, and after five pairs were shown, the animal pictures would be shown one at a time, and the child would be asked to point out which object went with which animal. Getting such instructions over to deaf-mute children is no easy task, but it can be done. The children were able to learn to select the appropriate response cards after an average of 17.7 trials. Another group of matched deaf children now were shown a somewhat different set of stimulus pictures. Instead of showing only a horse and then a ball, the stimulus card showed a horse standing on a ball, while the response card showed only the ball. The children were shown five such pictures with an animal interacting with an object (a pig held a knife in its mouth, a dog had a scissors balanced on its nose, a chicken carried a flag, and a mouse sat in a cup). The number of trials necessary to learn dropped to 8.6. A control group of hearing children performed in the same way, though slightly better. With the hearing children it was possible to suggest the same events portrayed in the pictures with a sentence like: "A chicken is carrying a flag." Some children only heard sentences like this, others were also shown a picture of a chicken and then one of a flag. Still others saw the "interaction" pictures. The children who heard the sentences learned as well as those who only saw the "integrated" pictures and, consequently, we are left with some ambiguous possible conclusions: the children spoke to themselves, and the inner speech carried the burden of learning, or the children imaged the chicken carrying the flag, and this imagery provided the basis for learning, or both kinds of processes were practiced. Children who saw only separate pictures of a chicken and of a flag did poorly. This was equally true of deaf and hearing children.

The fact that deaf children can learn with both isolated or "unit" picture pairs and do better with "integrated" stimulus cards suggests that the correct conclusion is the second of the three I just listed. An integrated picture is easily learned because it is, in effect, a sentence. If I show you a picture of a cat and one of an umbrella and ask you to remember that a cat "goes with" an umbrella, you will not be likely to remember as well as if I showed you a picture of a cat carrying an umbrella.

Note that I use a sentence to describe the latter picture. There is a subject, predicate, and object, as well as a couple of articles, (*the* and *an*). If we are concerned with the important points, we must note the cat and the umbrella. The sentence structure and composition is unimportant.

The same picture could be described in a thousand words. We could say, "the umbrella is over the cat," "the cat is under the umbrella." We could add adverbs and adjectives at our pleasure without contributing to what is conveyed or aroused in us by the picture. The picture, I argue, is a sentence, and the sentence consists of an image of two or more interacting sources of stimulation. In conditioning terms, when two stimuli interact, one becomes able to arouse the response to the other. Similarly, if one image is intimately related to another through any source of arousal, the two will subsequently become integrated in such a way that one can initiate the other, and the joint imagery will, in effect, create a sentence, whether spoken or not.

To incorporate what I have just described into the topic of our concern, I will now argue that in reading we are exciting within ourselves a succession of rapid, fleeting images, some of which we name, and others with which we do not bother. In most cases, I will contend, the words are irrelevant and, to a large extent, formalities we have come to expect and respect. The formalities help keep the language patterns uniform and standard, although they do keep changing with the years. The word "book" was originally "beech" because the bark of the beech was used for writing. The word "an" usually introduces a word beginning with a vowel, and "is" must have a singular subject, and so on. Such language formalities are irrelevant to the reading process. The same reader reactions can be developed in different languages by longer or shorter literary messages. In Polish, for example, one need not say: "The cat is carrying an umbrella" in response to the picture. All you need to say is: "Kot nosi parasol." There is a saving of three words and no loss of meaning. In Latin we say "via" to communicate, "by way of" or "vox populi, vox Dei," to say as much as "The voice of the people is the voice of God." Four words for ten.

I come now to a tentative conclusion, which will need a major experimental effort to support it; namely that thinking and reading, if not identical processes, at least share the same kind of underlying presumed neural activity. They both consist of generating series of images wherein one image is incorporated with or integrated with another. Some writers like to say that readers (or thinkers) impose a structure upon the stimulation. I do not pretend to know what this means, although I have a feeling that they are saying the same thing. Perhaps we have here a kind of evidence for my point. Language does not communicate. It merely arouses private and highly personal imagery and feelings. The problem of communication is not one of finding the right words but one of finding words that mean the same thing, that is, words that give rise to the same imagery and feeling in all persons involved (Mowrer, 1960b).

How this can help us in understanding reading for practical or pedagogical purposes, I am not prepared to say. My interest in reading is incidental to my interest in thinking, and what I have described is a picture of reading as thinking, controlled or guided through printed stimuli. The linguistic features of language, I have argued, are conventional but necessary evils. Reading and thinking go on in sentences where images form both subject and predicate. Without subject and predicate (which includes an object, where necessary) no thinking can go on.

The analysis of the nature of reading presented in this chapter has not produced a recipe for teaching this skill. That was not my intention. The discussion was meant to provide an extended illustration of the psychological principles involved in teaching any skill or subject, with an emphasis on the fact that most subjects have been taught for centuries with varying degrees of success. I emphasize the need to define the area and problem, determine the goals and criteria by which they are measured, and locate the variables that need to be controlled. Because "reading" turns out to be such a broad and comprehensive operation, I could not provide a detailed description of all the pertinent variables or even issues.

Because of the almost overwhelming criticism that our society is generating over the subject of how reading (and just about everything else) is taught in our schools, I cannot refrain from a final comment of support for our teachers. Our society has created an educational system which has imposed on teachers the burden not only of teaching our children academic subjects but also of rearing them in virtually every aspect of their lives. Functions that were formerly controlled in the home have been sloughed off onto teachers without providing them with the corresponding parental control and one-to-one feasibilities. In this text I have tried to show why it is easy for a psychologist to teach a rat or dog a simple trick. To teach 30 children all their parents want them to know, and at the same time create highly intelligent desirable citizens, would be a rather different level of challenge for a psychologist. Although the clock of history cannot be reversed, it is obviously past the time when teachers must begin to reject the additional burdens imposed upon them and to return some of these to the parents. One of the best places to start would be the reading problem, which, as I have tried to show, is a matter of building a vocabulary and an experience with sentences. This is probably a crucial family variable and can be established in the schools only at great cost.

Teachers cannot serve as parental surrogates; they should see their function for what it is, that of models of academic activities whose knowledge and skills in their disciplines bring them gratification. Considering the student-teacher ratios in most modern schools, even this is asking for more than can be delivered to the satisfaction of all concerned. Society must be willing to pay the price, in a not-so-far-fetched sense, for the pollution it has developed in the schools; just as it now has come to realize that it must pay for the air it breathes.

Bibliography

(Numbers in brackets represent the pages of this book on which the works listed below are cited.)

Alter, M., and Silverman, R. E., 1962. The response in programed instruction. *J. Programed Instr.*, I, pp. 55–78 [243].

Amsel, A., 1958. The role of frustrative nonreward in nonreward and noncontinuous reward situations, *Psychological Bull.*, 55, pp. 102–119 [185].

Bandura, A., and Walters, R., 1963. *Social learning and personality development.* New York: Holt, Rinehart, and Winston [133].

Barlow, J. A., 1961. The teacher and the teaching machine. AID, I [243].

Baskin, S. *See* Churchill and Baskin (1958).

Battig, W. F., and Brackett, H. R., 1961. Comparison of anticipation and recall methods in paired-associate learning. *Psychological Reports*, 9, pp. 59–65 [186].

Beach, L. R. *See* Parsons, Ketcham, and Beach (1958).

Bessant, D. E. *See* Dodwell and Bessant (1960).

Bills, A. G. and Stauffacher, J. C., 1937. The influence of voluntarily induced tension on rational problem solving. *J. Psychology*, 4, pp. 261–271 [162].

Bilodeau, E. A., Bilodeau, I. McD., and Schumsky, D. A., 1959. Some effects of introducing and withdrawing knowledge of results early and late in practice. *J. Experimental Psychology*, 58, pp. 142–144 [65, 245].

Blodgett, H. C., 1929. The effect of the introduction of reward upon the maze performance of rats. *University of California Publications in Psychology*, 4, pp. 113–134 [112].

Blumenthal, J. C., 1960. *English 2600.* New York: Harcourt, Brace and Company [236].

Bodner, F. *See* Hogben and Bodner (1944).

Bond, G. and Tinker, M., 1957. *Reading difficulties: then diagnosis and correction.* New York: Appleton-Century-Crofts [309].

Bower, G., Lesgold, A., and Tieman, D., 1969. Grouping operations in free recall. *Journal of Verbal Learning and Verbal Behavior*, 8, pp. 481–493 [225].

Brackett, H. R. *See* Battig and Brackett (1961).

Brown, R., 1958. *Words and things.* Glencoe, Ill.: Free Press of Glencoe, Inc. [129, 154].

Bruner, J. S., 1960. *The process of education*. Cambridge, Mass.: Harvard University Press [14, 63].

Bruner, J. S., 1966. *Toward a theory of instruction*. Cambridge, Mass.: The Belknap Press of the Harvard University Press [278].

Bugelski, B. R., 1956. *The psychology of learning*. New York: Henry Holt and Co. [39, 68, 161].

Bugelski, B. R., 1962. Presentation time, total time, and mediation in paired-associate learning. *Journal of Experimental Psychology*, 63, pp. 409–412 [26].

Bugelski, B. R., 1964. *The psychology of learning applied to teaching*. (First edition) Indianapolis: Bobbs-Merrill [IX].

Bugelski, B. R., 1968b. Images as mediators in one-trial paired-associate learning. II: Successive lists. *Journal of Experimental Psychology*, 77, pp. 328–334 [226, 319].

Bugelski, B. R., 1970. Words, things, and images. *American Psychologist*, 25, pp. 1002–1012. 28 [319, 323].

Bugelski, B. R., and Alampay, D., 1961. The role of frequency in developing perceptual sets. *Canadian Journal of Psychology*, 15, pp. 205–211 [179].

Bugelski, B. R., and Cadwallader, Jr., 1956. An experimental test of the "Transfer and retroaction surface." *Journal of Experimental Psychology*, 52, pp. 360–366 [216].

Bugelski, B. R., and Hersen, M., 1966. Conditioning acceptance or rejection of information. *Journal of Experimental Psychology*, 71, pp. 619–623 [94].

Bugelski, B. R., and Hutt, E. M., 1962. A note on increasing the efficiency of Luchin's mental sets. *American Journal of Psychology*, 75, pp. 665–667 [172].

Bugelski, B. R., Kidd, E., and Segmen, J., 1968a. Images as mediators in one-trial paired-associate learning. *Journal of Experimental Psychology*, 76, pp. 69–77 [319].

Cadwallader, J. *See* Bugelski and Cadwallader (1956).

Carpenter, C. R., and Greenhill, L. P., 1963. *Comparative research on methods and media for presenting programmed courses in Mathematics and English*. University Park, Pa.: The University of Pennsylvania Press [243].

Ceraso, J., 1967. The interference theory of forgetting. *Scientific American*, 217, pp. 117–124 [195].

Chapanis, A., Garner, W. R., and Morgan, C. T., 1949. *Applied experimental Psychology*, New York: John Wiley and Sons [6].

Chausow, H. M. *See* Erikson and Chausow.

Churchill, R., and Baskin, S., 1958. *Experiment on independent study* (mimeo.). Yellow Springs, Ohio: Antioch College [20].

Cohen, I., 1962. Programed learning and the Socratic dialogue. *American Psychologist*, 17, pp. 772–775 [250].

Conant, J. B., 1961. Slums and suburbs: a commentary on schools in metropolitan areas. New York: McGraw-Hill [174].

Crespi, L. P., 1944. Amount of reinforcement and level of performance. *Psychological Review*, 51, pp. 341–357 [113].

Crowder, N. A., 1960. Automatic tutoring by intrinsic programing. In Lumsdaine, A. A., and Glaser, R. (eds.), *Teaching machines and programed learning*. Washington, D. C.: National Education Association, pp. 286–298 [253].

Dashiell, J. F., 1927. *Fundamentals of objective psychology.* Boston: Houghton Mifflin [167].

Deterline, W. A., 1962. *An introduction to programed instruction.* New York: Prentice-Hall, Inc. [232].

Dewey, J., 1938. *Experience and education.* New York: The Macmillan Company [19, 36].

Dodwell, P. C., and Bessant, D. E., 1960. Learning without swimming in a water maze. *Journal of Comprehensive Physiological Psychology,* 53, pp. 422–425 [161].

Dollard, J. *See* Miller and Dollard (1941).

Doman, G., Stevens, G. L., and Orem, R. C., 1963. You can teach your baby to read. *Ladies' Home Journal,* May [8].

Dunlap, K., 1932. *Habits: their making and unmaking.* New York: Liveright [203].

Dyrud, J. *See* Goldiamond and Dyrud (1966).

Ebbinghaus, H., 1885. *Memory.* Trans. H. A. Ruger and C. E. Bussenius. New York: Teachers College, Columbia University, 1913 [17].

Eigen, L. D. *See* Markle, Eigen, and Komoski (1961).

Eisenberg, L., 1966. The epidemiology of reading retardation and a program for preventive intervention. In *The disabled reader.* John Money (ed.). Baltimore: The Johns Hopkins Press [305].

Ellson, D. G., 1938. Quantitative studies of the interaction of simple habits. I. Recovery from specific and generalized effects of extinction. *Journal of Experimental Psychology,* 23, pp. 339–358 [72].

Emmons, W. W. *See* Simon and Emmons (1955).

Erikson, C. G., and Chausow, H. M., 1960. Chicago's TV College: *Final Report of a three-year experiment of Chicago City Junior College in offering courses for credit via open-circuit television.* Chicago, Ill.: Chicago City Junior College [265].

Estes, Wm., 1960. Learning. In Chester W. Harris (ed.), *Encyclopedia of educational research.* New York: The Macmillan Company [16].

Estes, W. K., 1944. An experimental study of punishment. *Psychological Monograph,* 47, Whole No. 263, p. 40 [90].

Estes, W. K., Koch, S., MacCorquodale, K., Meehl, P. E., Mueller, C. G. Jr., Schoenfield, W. N., and Verplanck, W. S., 1954. *Modern learning theory.* New York: Appleton-Century-Crofts, Inc. [137].

Evans, J. L., 1960. *Squaring two-digit numbers ending in 5.* Albuquerque, New Mexico: TMI. Grolier [239].

Faw, V., 1949. A psychotherapeutic method of teaching psychology. *American Psychologist,* 4, pp. 104–109 [163].

Flanders, J. P., 1968. A review of research on imitative behavior. *Psychological Bulletin,* 69, 5, pp. 316–337 [133].

Forgus, R. H., 1954. The effect of early perceptual learning on the behavioral organization of rats. *Journal of Comparative and Physiological Psychology.* 47, pp. 331–336 [149].

Forlano, G., 1936. *School learning with various methods of practice and reward.* New York: Teachers College, Columbia University [164].

Fransden, A. M., 1961. *Educational psychology.* New York: McGraw-Hill [311].

Freeman, F. N. *See* Wood and Freeman (1932).

Friendly, A., Jr., 1963. The army's language school. *Saturday Review,* 46, 7, pp. 72–73 [269].

Gagne, R. M., 1962. Military training and principles of learning. *American Psychologist,* 17, pp. 83–91 [34].

Gallop, G., 1964. *The miracle ahead.* New York: Harper & Row [321].

Garner, W. R. *See* Chapanis, Garner, and Morgan (1949).

Gates, A. I., 1917. Recitation as a factor in memorizing. *Archives of Psychology,* 40, pp. 1–104 [164].

Geschwind, N., 1962. The anatomy of acquired disorders of reading disability. In J. Money (ed.), *Progress and research needs in dyslexia.* Baltimore: Johns Hopkins Press [309].

Gibson, E., 1965. Learning to read. *Science,* 148, pp. 1066–1072 [309].

Gibson, E., Osser, H., and Pick, A. D., 1963. A study in the development of grapheme-phoneme correspondences. *Journal of Verbal Learning and Verbal Behavior,* 2, pp. 142–146 [310, 314].

Glazer, R. *See* Lumsdaine and Glazer (1960).

Goldiamond, I. and Dyrud, Jr., 1966. Reading as operant behavior. In *The Disabled Reader.* Jack Money (ed.), Baltimore: The Johns Hopkins Press [307].

Goldstein, L. S., and Gotkin, L. G., 1962. A review of research: Teaching machines vs. programed textbooks as presentation models. *Journal of Programed Instruction,* I, pp. 29–42 [243].

Gotkin, L. G. *See* Goldstein and Gotkin (1962).

Greenhill, L. P. *See* Carpenter and Greenhill (1963).

Greenspoon, J., 1955. The reinforcing effect of two spoken sounds on the frequency of two responses. *American Journal of Psychology,* 68, pp. 409–416 [33].

Guthrie, E. R., 1944. Personality in terms of associated learning. In J. McV. Hunt (ed.), *Personality and the behavior disorders.* New York: Ronald Press [218].

Guthrie, E. R., 1952. *The psychology of learning.* New York: Harper & Brothers, Publishers [103, 204, 253].

Harlow, H., 1949. The formation of learning sets. *Psychological Review,* 56, pp. 51–65 [217].

Harlow, H., and Harlow, M. K., 1962. Social deprivation in monkeys. *Scientific American,* 202, pp. 3–10 [184].

Harlow, M. K. *See* Harlow and Harlow (1962).

Hayes, K. J., 1953. The backward curve: a method for the study of learning. *Psychological Review,* 60, pp. 269–275 [74].

Hebb, D. O., 1938. Studies of the organization of behavior: I. Behavior of the rat in a field orientation. *Journal of Comparative and Physiological Psychology,* 25, pp. 333–352 [169].

Hebb, D. O., 1949. *The organization of behavior.* New York: John Wiley and Sons [141].

Hebb, D. O., 1958. The motivating effects of exteroceptive stimulation. *American Psychologist,* 13, pp. 109–113 [165].

Hebb, D. O., 1966. *A textbook of psychology.* Philadelphia: Saunders [145].

Hernández-Peón, R., Scherrer, H., and Jouvet, M., 1956. Modification of electric activity in cochlear nucleus during "attention" in unanesthetized cats. *Science*, 123, pp. 331–332 [171].

Heron, W. *See* Thompson and Heron (1954).

Hersen, M. *See* Bugelski and Hersen (1966).

Hilgard, E. R., 1956. *Theories of learning*. New York: Appleton-Century-Crofts, Inc. [15, 39, 40].

Hogben, L., and Bodner, F., 1944. The loom of language. New York: W. W. Norton [216].

Holland, J. G., and Skinner, B. F., 1961. *The Analysis of behavior: a program for self-instruction*. New York: McGraw-Hill Books [236, 242].

Huey, E. B., 1908. *The psychology and pedagogy of reading*. New York: The Macmillan Co. (Reprinted 1968 by MIT Press, Cambridge, Mass.) [304].

Hull, C. L., 1930. Knowledge and purpose as habit mechanisms. *Psychological Review*, 37, pp. 511–525 [77].

Hull, C. L., 1943. *Principles of behavior*. New York: Appleton-Century-Crofts, Inc. [45, 72, 118, 182].

Hutt, E. M. *See* Bugelski and Hutt (1962).

Jacobsen, L. *See* Rosenthal and Jacobsen (1967).

Jensen, A. R., 1969. How much can we boost I.Q. and scholastic behavior? *Harvard Educational Review*, 39, No. 1, Winter [150].

Jones, Mary C., 1924. The elimination of children's fears. *Journal of Experimental Psychology*, 7, pp. 382–390 [52, 102].

Jouvet, M. *See* Hernández-Peón, Scherrer, and Jouvet (1956).

Kagan, J. S., 1969. In: Discussion: How much can we boost I.Q. and scholastic achievement. *Harvard Educational Review*, 39, No. 2, Spring [150].

Katona, G., 1940. *Organizing and memorizing: Studies in the psychology of learning and teaching*. New York: Columbia University Press [221].

Keller, F. S., 1953. Stimulus discrimination and Morse Code learning. *Transactions of the New York Academy of Sciences*, Series II, 15, pp. 195–203 [6, 31, 180].

Ketcham, W. A. *See* Parsons, Ketcham, and Beach (1958).

Kidd, E. *See* Bugelski, Kidd, and Segmen (1968a).

Koch, S. *See* Estes *et al.* (1954).

Koerner, J. D., 1963. *The miseducation of American teachers*. New York: Houghton Mifflin Co. [3].

Kohler, W., 1927. *The mentality of apes*. New York: Harcourt, Brace [223].

Komoski, P. K. *See* Markle, Eigen, and Komoski (1961).

Lesgold, A. *See* Bower, Lesgold, and Tieman (1969).

Lester, O. P., 1932. Mental set in relation to retroactive inhibition. *Journal of Experimental Psychology*. 15, 681–699 [200].

Leuba, C., 1940. Images as conditioned sensations. *Journal of Experimental Psychology*, 26, pp. 345–351 [124, 169].

Leuba, C., 1955. Toward some integration of learning theories. *Psychological Reports*, I, pp. 27–33 [165].

Leuba, C., 1963. Using groups in independent study. *Antioch College Reports*, No. 5 (June) [20].

Levinson, B., and Reese, H. W., 1967. Patterns of discrimination learning set in pre-school children, fifth graders, college freshmen, and the aged. *Monographs of the Society for Research in Child Development, 32,* (7, Whole No. 115) [218].

Lewin, K., 1948. *Resolving social conflicts.* New York: Harper & Brothers [163].

Linden, J. D. *See* Parks and Linden (1968).

Luchins, A. S., 1946. Classroom experiments on mental set. *American Journal of Psychology,* 59, 295-298 [172].

Lunsdaine, A. A., and Glazer, R. (eds.), 1960. *Teaching machines and programed learning: A source book.* Washington, D. C.: National Education Association [232].

McCollough, C. and Van Etta, E. L., 1958. Experimental evaluation of teaching programs utilizing a block of independent work. Paper read at Symposium: Experimental studies in learning independently. American Psychological Association, Washington, D. C., September [20].

MacCorquodale, K. *See* Estes *et al.* (1954).

Macfarlane, J. W., 1963. From infancy to adulthood. *Childhood Education,* 39, pp. 336-342 [141].

McGeoch, J., 1942. *The psychology of human learning.* New York: Longmans, Green and Co. [183, 193].

McKeachie, W. J., 1962. Procedures and techniques of teaching: a survey of experimental studies. In N. Sanford (ed.), *The American College.* New York: John Wiley and Sons [293].

McLuhan, M., 1964. *The medium is the message.* New York: Random House [322].

Malinowski, B., 1938. The problem of meaning in primitive languages. In *The meaning of meaning.* (by Ogden and Richards) New York: Harcourt, Brace, & Co. [223].

Markle, S. *See* Meyer, S. (1960a).

Markle, S., Eigen, L. D., and Komoski, P. K., 1961. A programed primer on programing. Vol. I, Frame 80. New York: The Center for Programed Instruction, Inc. [252].

Markle, S., 1963. The lowest common denominator: a persistent problem in programing. *Programed Instruction,* II, No. 3, pp. 4-5 [234, 252, 254].

Mayer, M., 1961. *The schools.* New York: Harper & Brothers [11].

Mechanic, A., 1964. The responses involved in the rote learning of verbal materials. *Journal of Verbal Learning and Verbal Behavior,* 3, pp. 30-36 [161].

Meehl, P. E. *See* Estes *et al.* (1954).

Melton, A. W., 1959. The science of learning and the technology of educational methods. *Harvard Educational Review,* 29, pp. 96-106 [16].

Meyer, S., 1960a. A test of the principles of "activity," "immediate reinforcement," and "guidance," as instrumented by teaching machines. Unpublished doctoral dissertation, University of Buffalo [243].

Miller, J. V. *See* Murphy, Miller, and Mirsky (1955).

Miller, N., and Dollard, J., 1941. *Social learning and imitation.* New Haven: Yale University Press [132].

Mirsky, I. A. *See* Murphy, Miller, and Mirsky (1955).

Moore, O. K. *See* Pinas, M. (1963) [6, 31].

Morgan, C. T. *See* Chapanis, Garner, and Morgan (1949).

Mowrer, O. H., 1960 (a). *Learning theory and behavior.* New York: John Wiley and Sons [117, 182, 245].

Mowrer, O. H., 1960(b). *Learning theory and the symbolic processes.* New York: John Wiley and Sons [117, 223, 224, 325].

Mueller, C. J., Jr. *See* Estes *et al.* (1954).

Murphy, J. V., Miller, R. E., and Mirsky, I. A., 1955. Interanimal conditioning in the monkey. *Journal of Comparative and Physiological Psychology,* 48, pp. 211–214 [52].

Neisser, U., 1967. *Cognitive psychology.* New York: Appleton-Century-Crofts [304].

Noble, C., 1952. An analysis of meaning. *Psychological Review,* 49, pp. 403–418 [224].

Orem, G. L. *See* Doman, Stevens, and Orem 1963).

Osgood, C. E., 1949. The similarity paradox in human learning: a resolution. *Psychological Review,* 56, pp. 132–143 [215].

Osgood, C. E., 1952. The nature and measurement of meaning. *Psychological Bulletin,* 49, pp. 197–237 [224].

Osgood, C. E., Souchi, G. J., and Tannenbaum, P. H., 1957. *The measurement of meaning.* Urbana: The University of Illinois Press [224].

Osser, H. *See* Gibson, Osser, and Pick (1963).

Paivio, A., 1969. Mental imagery in associative learning and memory. *Psychological Review,* 76, pp. 241–263 [318].

Paivio, A., 1970. On the functional significance of imagery. *Psychological Bulletin,* 73, pp. 385–392 [225].

Parks, G. E., and Linden, J. D., 1968. The etiology of reading disabilities: An historical perspective. *Journal of Learning Disabilities,* 1, pp. 318–330 [305].

Parsons, T. S., Ketcham, W. A., and Beach, L. R., 1958. Effects of varying degrees of student interaction and student-teacher contact in college courses. Paper read at American Sociological Society, Seattle, Washington, August [20].

Pavlov, I., 1927. *Conditioned reflexes.* Trans. Anrep. New York: Oxford University Press [41].

Penfield, W., and Rasmussen, T., 1950. *The cerebral cortex of man.* New York: The Macmillan Company [193].

Pick, A. D. *See* Gibson, Osser, and Pick (1963).

Pinas, M., 1963. How three-year-olds teach themselves to read—and love it. *Harpers,* 226, pp. 58–64 [6].

Postman, L., 1962. Rewards and punishments in human learning. In L. Postman (ed.), *Psychology in the making.* New York: Alfred Knopf [59].

Postman, L., and Schwartz, M., 1964. Studies of learning to learn. I. Transfer as a function of method of practice and class of verbal materials. *Journal of Verbal Learning and Verbal Behavior,* 3, pp. 37–49 [218].

Powell, J., 1963. The role of repetition in associative learning of children and adults. Unpublished master's thesis, The University of the State of New York at Buffalo [153].

Pratt, C. C., 1939. *The logic of modern psychology.* New York: The Macmillan Company [222].

Rasmussen, T. *See* Penfield and Rasmussen (1950).

Reese, H. W., 1965. Imagery in paired-associate learning in children. *Journal of Experimental Child Psychology*, 2, pp. 290–296 [225].

Reese, H. W. *See* Levinson and Reese (1967).

Richardson, A., 1969. *Mental imagery*. New York: Springer Publishing Company, Inc. [135].

Riesen, Austin, 1947. The development of visual perception in man and chimpanzee. *Science*, 106, pp. 107–108 [142].

Rock, I., 1957. The role of repetition in associative learning. *American Journal of Psychology*, 70, pp. 183–193 [151].

Roe, A., 1960. Automated teaching methods using linear programs. Automated research project, Dept. of Engineering, University of California at Los Angeles [243].

Roethlisberger, F. J., and Dickson, W. J., 1939. *Management and the worker*. Cambridge, Mass.: Harvard University Press [256].

Rogers, C., 1967. The interpersonal relationship in the facilities of learning. In *Humanizing Education:* The person in the process. Robert R. Leeper, (ed.), Washington, D. C. Association for supervision and curriculum development, pp. 1–18 [289].

Rosenthal, R., and Jacobsen, L., 1967. *Pygmalion in the classroom*. New York: Holt, Rinehart, and Winston [173].

Rosenthal, R., 1970. Another view of Pygmalion. *Contemporary Psychology*, 15, p. 524 [173].

Saltzman, I. J., 1949. Maze learning in the absence of primary reinforcement: A study of secondary reinforcement. *Journal of Comparative and Physiological Psychology*, 42, pp. 161–173 [75].

Scherer, G. A. C., and Wertheimer, M., 1964. *A psycholinguistic experiment in foreign language teaching*. New York: McGraw-Hill Book Co. [271].

Scherrer, H. *See* Hernández-Peón, Scherrer, and Jouvet (1956).

Schmuller, A. M. *See* Thorpe and Schmuller (1954).

Schoenfeld, W. N. *See* Estes, *et al.* (1954).

Schramm, W., 1962. Learning from instructional television. *Review of Educational Research*, 32, pp. 156–167 [265].

Schramm, W., 1962. *Programed Instruction Today and Tomorrow*. New York: Fund for Advancement of Education [232].

Schultz, R. W. *See* Underwood and Schultz (1960).

Schumsky, D. A. *See* Bilodeaus, Bilodeaus, and Schumsky.

Schwartz, M. *See* Postman and Schwartz (1964).

Segmen, J. *See* Bugelski, Kidd, and Segmen (1968a).

Silverman, R. E. *See* Alter and Silverman (1962).

Simon, C. H., and Emmons, W. W., 1955. Learning during sleep? *Psychological Bulletin*, 52, pp. 328–342 [161].

Skinner, B. F. *See* Holland and Skinner (1961).

Skinner, B. F., 1938. *The behavior of organisms*. New York: D. Appleton-Century [87].

Skinner, B. F., 1948 (a). *Walden II*. New York: The Macmillan Company [4, 93, 96, 183].

Skinner, B. F., 1948(b). Superstition in the pigeon. *Journal of Experimental Psychology*, 38, pp. 168–172 [95].

Skinner, B. F., 1951. How to teach animals. *Scientific American*, 185, pp. 26–29 [31].

Skinner, B. F., 1954. The science of learning and the art of teaching. *Harvard Educational Review*, 24, pp. 86–97 [232].

Skinner, B. F., 1955. Freedom and the control of men. *American Scholar*, Winter 1955–56 (special issue) [96].

Skinner, B. F., 1956. A case history in scientific method. *American Psychologist*, II, pp. 221–233 [10, 92].

Skinner, B. F., 1958. Teaching machines. *Science*, 128, pp. 969–977 [35, 232].

Slamecka, N., 1969. A temporal interpretation of some recall phenomena. *Psychological Review*, 76, pp. 492–503 [194].

Smith, H., 1967. The responses of good and poor readers when asked to read for different purposes. *Reading Research Quarterly*, 3, pp. 53–83 [311].

Snow, R. E., 1969. Review of Pygmalion in the Classroom. *Contemporary Psychology*, 14, pp. 197–199 [173].

Snygg, D., 1954. Learning: an aspect of personality development. In *Learning theory, personality theory, and clinical research*. The Kentucky Symposium. New York: John Wiley and Sons [16].

Sokolov, E. N., 1960. Neuronal models and the orienting reflex. In M. A. Brazier (ed.), *The central nervous system and behavior. Transactions of the third conference*. New York: Josiah Macy, Jr. Foundation, pp. 187–276 [48].

Solomon, R. L., 1949. An extension of control group design. *Psychological Bulletin*, 46, pp. 137–150 [256].

Souci, G. J. *See* Osgood, Souci, and Tannenbaum (1957).

Spence, K., 1954. Current interpretations of learning data and some recent developments in stimulus-response theory. In *Learning theory, personality theory, and clinical research*. The Kentucky Symposium. New York: John Wiley and Sons [16].

Spence, K., 1956. *Behavior theory and conditioning*. New Haven: Yale University Press [74].

Spence, K., 1958. A theory of emotionally based drive (D) and its relation to performance in simple learning situations. *American Psychologist*, 13, pp. 131–141 [50].

Stauffacher, J. C. *See* Bills and Stauffacher (1937).

Stern, G. G., 1963. "Measuring noncognitive variables in research on teaching." In *Handbook of Research on Teaching*, N. L. Gage (ed.), Chicago, Ill.: Rand McNally, pp. 398–447 [163].

Stevens, G. L. *See* Doman, Stevens, and Orem (1963).

Stolorow, L., 1961. *Teaching by machine*. Washington, D. C.: U. S. Dept. of Health, Education, and Welfare; Government Printing Office [232].

Switzer, H. F., 1939. Studies in retention. *Journal of Educational Psychology*, 30, pp. 641–656 [164].

Tannenbaum, P. H. *See* Osgood, Souci, and Tannenbaum (1957).

Thompson, W. R., and Heron, W., 1954. The effects of restricting early experience on the problem-solving capacity of dogs. *Canadian Journal of Psychology*, 8, pp. 17–31 [142].

Thorndike, E. L., 1898. Animal intelligence: An experimental study of the associative processes in animals. *Psychological Monographs*, 2, No. 4 [56].

Thorndike, E. L., 1932. *The fundamentals of learning.* New York: Teachers College, Columbia University [58, 125].

Thorndike, E. L., 1946. Expectation. *Psychological Review,* 53, pp. 277–281 [132, 161].

Thorndike, E. L., and Woodworth, R. S., 1901. The influence of improvement in one mental function upon the efficiency of other functions. *Psychological Review,* 8, pp. 247–261 [212].

Thorpe, L. P., and Schmuller, A. M., 1954. *Contemporary theories of learning.* New York: The Ronald Press [39].

Tieman, D. *See* Bower, Lesgold, and Tieman [1969].

Tolman, E. C., 1932. *Purposive behavior in animals and men.* New York: D. Appleton-Century [109].

Tolman, E. C., 1938. Determiners of behavior at a choice point. *Psychological Review,* 45, pp. 1–41 [110, 160].

Tulving, E., 1962. Subjective organization in free recall of "unrelated" words. *Psychological Review,* 69, pp. 344–354 [198].

Underwood, B. J., and Schultz, R. W., 1960. *Meaningfulness and verbal learning.* Chicago: J. B. Lippincott [197].

Van Atta, E. L. *See* McCollough and Van Atta (1958).

Verplanck, W. S. *See* Estes *et al.* (1954).

Viteles, M. S., 1932. *Industrial psychology.* New York: W. W. Norton [8].

Walters, R. *See* Bandura and Walters (1963).

Ward, L. B., 1937. Reminiscence and rote learning. *Psychological Monographs,* 49, No. 220 [218].

Watson, J. B., 1930. *Behaviorism (rev. ed.)* New York: W. W. Norton [4, 101].

Watson, J. B., and Rayner, R., 1920. Conditioned emotional reactions. *Journal of Experimental Psychology,* 3, pp. 1–14 [102].

Wertheimer, M. *See* Scherer and Wertheimer (1964).

Wiener, M. and Cromer, W., 1967. Reading and reading difficulty: a conceptual analysis. *Harvard Educational Review.* 37, 620–643 [307].

Wolfle, D., 1951. Training. In Stevens, S. S. (ed.), *Handbook of Experimental Psychology,* Chapter 34. New York: John Wiley & Sons [53].

Wolpe, J., 1962. The experimental foundations of some new psychotherapeutic methods. In Bachrach, A. J. (ed.), *Experimental foundations of Clinical Psychology.* New York: Basic Books [102].

Wood, B. D., and Freeman, F. N., 1932. *An experimental study of the educational influences of the typewriter in the elementary school classroom.* New York: The Macmillan Company [63].

Woodworth, R. S. *See* Thorndike and Woodworth (1901).

Youtz, R. E. P., 1938. Reinforcement, extinction, and spontaneous recovers in a non-Pavlovian reaction. *Journal of Experimental Psychology,* 22, pp. 305–318 [72].

Zaporozhets, A. V., 1961. The origin and development of the conscious control of movements in man. In N. O'Connor (ed.), *Recent Soviet Psychology.* New York: Macmillan (Pergamon), pp. 273–289 [54].

Zeaman, D., 1949. Response latency as a function of the amount of reinforcement. *Journal of Experimental Psychology,* 39, pp. 466–483 [113].

Index of Subjects